AF712485

SAS/AF®
User's Guide, Version 5 Edition

SAS Institute Inc.
SAS Circle ☐ Box 8000
Cary, NC 27512-8000

The correct bibliographic citation for this manual is as follows: SAS Institute Inc. *SAS/AF® User's Guide, Version 5 Edition*. Cary, NC: SAS Institute Inc., 1985. 223 pp.

SAS/AF® User's Guide, Version 5 Edition

ISBN 0-917382-63-3

89 4 3

Base SAS® software, the foundation of the SAS System, provides data retrieval and management, programming, statistical, and reporting capabilities. Also in the SAS System are SAS/GRAPH,® SAS/FSP,® SAS/ETS,® SAS/IMS-DL/I,® SAS/OR,® SAS/AF,® SAS/REPLAY-CICS,® SAS/DMI,® SAS/QC,® SAS/SHARE,® SAS/IML,® SAS/STAT,™ SAS/DB2,™ SAS/SQL-DS,™ SAS/CPE,™ SAS/ASSIST,™ and SAS/ACCESS™ software. Other products include SYSTEM 2000® Data Management Software, with basic SYSTEM 2000,® QueX,™ Multi-User,™ Screen Writer,™ CREATE,™ and CICS interface software; SAS/RTERM® software; NeoVisuals™ software; and SAS/C® and SAS/CX™compilers. *SAS Communications,® SAS Training,® SAS Views,®* and SASware Ballot® are published by SAS Institute Inc. The Institute is a private company devoted to the support and further development of the software and related services.

Contents

Illustrations

Figures

Screens

Tables

Acknowledgments

Program authorship includes design, programming, debugging, and support.

Developers

BUILD	D. Kumar
CIMPORT	P. Busby
CPORT	P. Busby
DISPLAY	P. Busby

Jim Goodnight, Deva Kumar, and Phil Busby did the major design work for SAS/AF software; Roger Williams wrote the message file subsystem; and Marge Carson supports the full-screen subsystem.

Preface

SAS/AF software, together with base SAS software, is an application facility for creating a user-friendly front end to business or information-processing applications, customized training programs, or help facilities. The software can be combined with other software in the SAS System for a complete information center tool.

The *SAS/AF User's Guide* must be read along with the *SAS User's Guide: Basics,* which is the primary description of the SAS language and the procedures in base SAS software. The *SAS/AF User's Guide* documents a collection of SAS procedures for creating and displaying screens that facilitate user access to the SAS System or customized training programs. SAS/AF procedures are part of the SAS System and behave like other SAS procedures. To begin using the procedures in this manual you need two things:

- You should understand the SAS System (documented in the *SAS User's Guide: Basics*).
- You should have an application or a training need.

The first chapter in this manual, "Introduction to SAS/AF Software," should be read first for a brief summary of the SAS/AF procedures and the types of screens you can create. Next, read the appendix "Operating System Notes." This information will help you use your operating system's capabilities to get your data into and out of the SAS System. Then to get started with your own application, read the next chapter, "A Menu-driven Application," for a complete example of creating a book sales system. Refer to the last chapter in the book for a computer-based training application.

To start learning more about writing SAS programs, go to the *SAS User's Guide: Basics* chapter entitled "Introduction to the SAS Language." If you are using OS batch or TSO, you can also refer to the *SAS Introductory Guide*.

What is the SAS System?

The SAS System is a software system for data analysis. The goal of SAS Institute is to provide data analysts one system to meet all their computing needs. When your computing needs are met, you are free to concentrate on results rather than on the mechanics of getting them. Instead of learning programming languages, several statistical packages, and utility programs, you only need to learn the SAS System.

The SAS System is an all-purpose data analysis system. To base SAS software, you can add tools for graphics, forecasting, data entry, and interfaces to other data bases to provide one total system. SAS software runs on IBM 370/30xx/43xx and compatible machines in batch and interactively under OS and TSO, CMS, VSE, and SSX; on Digital Equipment Corporation VAX™ 11/7xx series under VMS; Data General ECLIPSE® series under AOS/VS; MV series under AOS/VS; Prime Series 50 under PRIMOS® and IBM PC AT/370 and XT/370 under VM/PC. Note: not all products are available for all operating systems.

Base SAS software provides tools for:

- information storage and retrieval
- data modification and programming
- report writing
- statistical analysis
- file handling.

Information storage and retrieval The SAS System reads data values in virtually any form from cards, disk, or tape and then organizes the values into a SAS data set. The data can be combined with other SAS data sets using the file-handling operations described below. The data can be analyzed statistically and can be used to produce reports. SAS data sets are automatically self-documenting since they contain both the data values and their descriptions. The special structure of a SAS data library minimizes maintenance.

Data modification and programming A complete set of SAS statements and functions is available for modifying data. Some program statements perform standard operations such as creating new variables, accumulating totals, and checking for errors; others are powerful programming tools such as DO/END and IF-THEN/ELSE statements. The data-handling features are so valuable that base SAS software is used by many as a data base management system.

Report writing Just as base SAS software reads data in almost any form, it can write data in almost any form. In addition to the preformatted reports that SAS procedures produce, SAS software users can design and produce printed reports in any form, as well as punched cards and output files.

Statistical analysis The statistical analysis procedures in the SAS System are among the finest available. They range from simple descriptive statistics to complex multivariate techniques. Their designs are based on our belief that you should never need to tell the SAS System anything it can figure out by itself. Statistical integrity is thus accompanied by ease of use. Especially noteworthy statistical features are the linear model procedures, of which GLM (**G**eneral **L**inear **M**odels) is the flagship.

File handling Combining values and observations from several data sets is often necessary for data analysis. SAS software has tools for editing, subsetting, concatenating, merging, and updating data sets. Multiple input files can be processed simultaneously, and several reports can be produced in one pass of the data.

Other SAS System Products

With base SAS software and SAS/AF software, you can integrate SAS software products for graphics, data entry, operations research, and interfaces to other data bases to provide one total system:

- SAS/FSP software—interactive, menu-driven facilities for data entry, editing, retrieval of SAS files, letter writing, and spreadsheet analysis
- SAS/GRAPH software—device-intelligent color graphics for business and research applications
- SAS/REPLAY-CICS software—interface that allows users of CICS/OS/VS and CICS/DOS/VS to store, manage, and replay SAS/GRAPH displays
- SAS/OR software—decision support tools for operations research and project management
- SAS/ETS software—expanded tools for business analysis, forecasting, and financial planning

- SAS/IMS-DL/I software—interface for reading, updating, and writing IMS/VS or CICS DL/I data bases
- SAS/IML software—multi-level, interactive programming language whose data elements are matrices.

SAS Institute Documentation

Using this manual Chapter 1 of this manual provides an overview and describes the capabilities of SAS/AF software. Chapter 2 contains a complete example of using SAS/AF software to create a menu-driven business application.

Procedure descriptions follow alphabetically in the next chapters. Each procedure description is self-contained; you need to be familiar with only the most basic features of the SAS System and SAS terminology to use most procedures. The statements and syntax necessary to run each procedure are presented in a uniform format throughout the manual.

Following the procedure descriptions is a chapter that describes a complete computer-based training application.

There are five appendices, including operating system notes; a guide to the SAS Display Manager System for full-screen terminals; a discussion of full-screen editing capabilities with the SAS System; a discussion of the SAS user profile; and a description of the SAS Menu System provided with SAS/AF software.

If you have any problems with this manual, please take time to complete the review page at the end of this book and send it to SAS Institute. We will consider your suggestions for future editions. In the meantime, ask your installation's SAS Software Consultant for help.

SAS release? To find out which release of SAS software you are using, run any SAS job and look at the release number in the notes at the beginning of the SAS log. This user's guide documents Version 5 SAS/AF software.

Other SAS Institute manuals and technical reports Below is a list of other manuals that document Version 5 SAS System software:

SAS User's Guide: Basics, Version 5 Edition
SAS User's Guide: Statistics, Version 5 Edition
SAS/GRAPH User's Guide, Version 5 Edition
SAS/FSP User's Guide, Version 5 Edition
SAS/OR User's Guide, Version 5 Edition
SAS/ETS User's Guide, Version 5 Edition
SAS/IML User's Guide, Version 5 Edition

The SAS Technical Report Series documents work in progress, describes new supplemental procedures and covers a variety of applications areas. Some of the features described in these reports are still in experimental form and are not yet available as SAS procedures.

Write to SAS Institute for a current publications catalog, which describes the manuals as well as technical reports and lists their prices.

SAS Services to Users

Technical support SAS Institute supports users through the Technical Support Department. If you have a problem running a SAS job, you should contact your site's SAS Software Consultant. If the problem cannot be resolved locally, your local support personnel should call the Institute's Technical Support Department at (919) 467-8000 on weekdays between 9:00 a.m. and 5:00 p.m. Eastern Standard Time. A brochure describing the services provided by the Technical Support Department is available from SAS Institute.

Training SAS Institute sponsors a comprehensive training program, including programs of study for novice data processors, statisticians, applications programmers, systems programmers, and local support personnel. *SAS Training,* a semiannual training publication, describes the total training program and each course currently being offered by SAS Institute.

News magazine *SAS Communications* is the quarterly news magazine of SAS Institute. Each issue contains ideas for more effective use of the SAS System, information about research and development underway at SAS Institute, the current training schedule, new publications, and news of the SAS Users Group International (SUGI).

To receive a copy of *SAS Communications* regularly, send your name and complete address to:

SAS Institute Mailing List
SAS Institute Inc.
SAS Circle, Box 8000
Cary, NC 27512-8000

Sample library One of the data sets included on the base SAS software installation tape is called SAS.SAMPLE. This data set contains sample SAS applications to illustrate features of SAS procedures and creative SAS programming techniques that can help you gain an in-depth knowledge of SAS capabilities.

Here are a few examples of programs included:

ANOVA	analyzing a Latin-square split-plot design
ARIMA5	fitting an intervention model to an ozone time series
CENSUS	reading hierarchical files of the U.S. Census Bureau Public Use Sample tapes
HARRIS	reading Harris Poll tapes coded in column-binary format
PDL	fitting a polynomial distributed lag regression model
TEACH	teaching arithmetic to your child.

Check with your SAS Software Consultant to find out how to access the library since it may have been put on disk at your site.

SUGI

The SAS Users Group International (SUGI) is a nonprofit association of professionals who are interested in how others are using the SAS System. Although SAS Institute provides administrative support, SUGI is independent from the Institute. Membership is open to all users at SAS sites, and there is no membership fee.

Annual conferences are structured to allow many avenues of discussion. Users present invited and contributed papers on various topics, for example:

- computer performance evaluation and systems software
- econometrics and time series
- graphics
- information systems
- interactive techniques
- statistics
- tutorials in SAS System software.

Proceedings of the annual conferences are distributed free to SUGI registrants. Extra copies may be purchased from SAS Institute.

SASware Ballot SAS users provide valuable input toward the direction of future SAS development by ranking their priorities on the annual SASware Ballot. The top vote-getters are announced at the SUGI conference. Complete results of the SASware Ballot are also printed in the *SUGI Proceedings*.

Supplemental library SAS users at many installations have written their own SAS procedures for a wide variety of specialized applications. Some of these user-written procedures are available through the SUGI supplemental library and are documented in the *SUGI Supplemental Library User's Guide*. The procedures in the supplemental library are sent to each installation that licenses base SAS software, although only a few procedures are supported by SAS Institute staff.

Licensing the SAS System

The SAS System is licensed to customers in the Western Hemisphere from the Institute's headquarters in Cary, NC. To serve the needs of our international customers, the Institute maintains subsidiaries in the United Kingdom, New Zealand, Australia, Singapore, Germany, and France. In addition, agents in other countries are licensed distributors for the SAS System. For a complete list of offices, write or call:

SAS Institute Inc.
SAS Circle
Box 8000
Cary, NC 27512-8000
(919) 467-8000

Chapter 1

Introduction to SAS/AF® Software

INTRODUCTION
SAS/AF SCREENS

INTRODUCTION

The procedures in SAS/AF software make it easy to create a user-friendly front end to other products in the SAS System that you are currently using in your information center. With SAS/AF software you can also design a customized training program for your users or an on-line query or help facility.

Screens 1.1 and **1.2** show how easy it can be to produce a report.

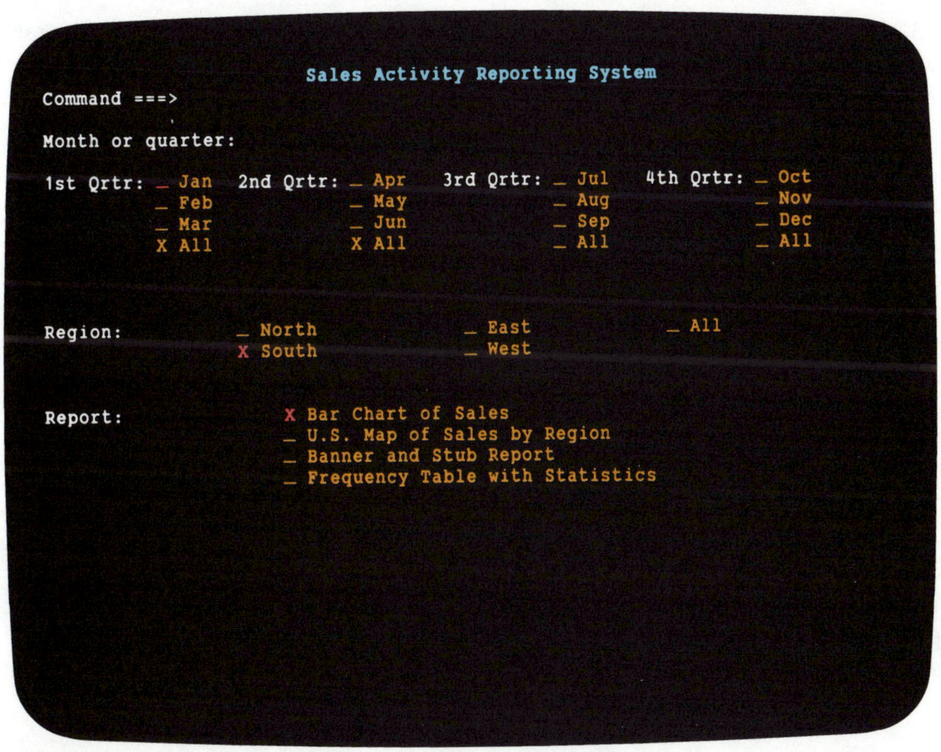

Screen 1.1 Producing a Report Using SAS/AF Software

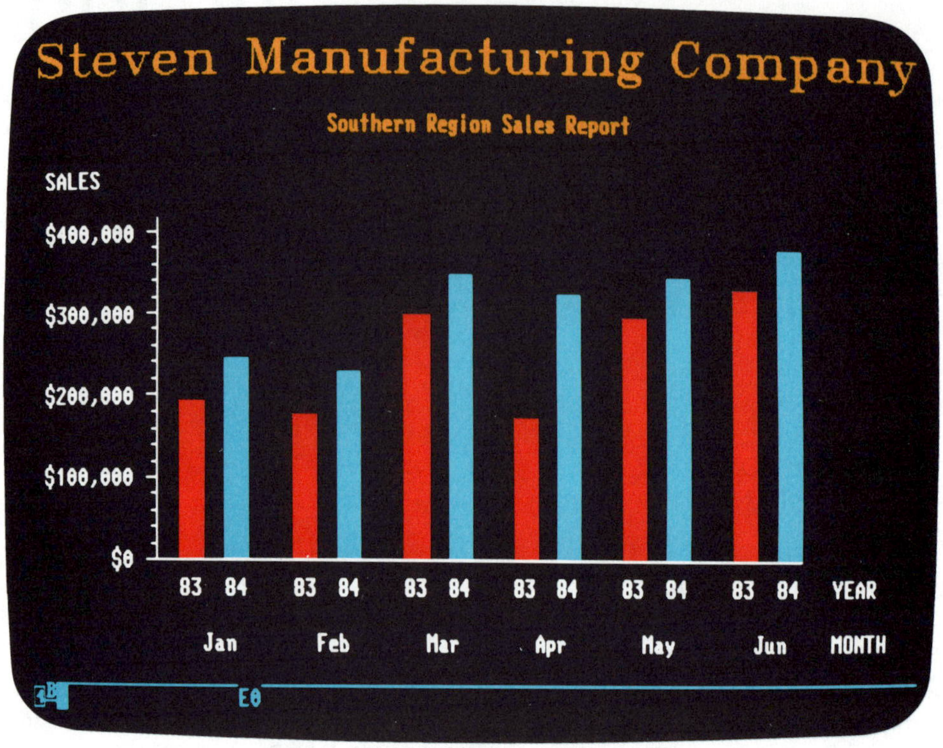

Screen 1.2 A Bar Chart Produced Using SAS/AF Software

Using SAS/AF software to structure user access to the SAS System has several advantages:

- You can use one information system to handle many different activities. You can create the menus to control the system for end users exactly the way you want. Another advantage is that organizing all activities into one system identifies duplication and helps you to eliminate unnecessary steps.
- You have the flexibility of teaching your staff as little or as much as you want about the SAS System, and end users with widely varying degrees of expertise can share the same system. SAS programs can be prepared and submitted from SAS/AF screens by users who know nothing about data processing.
- After your data processing staff writes a production SAS program once, end users supply only the information that changes from one application to another, reducing original programming.
- In addition to saving development time, you can assure that more SAS jobs will run correctly the first time and also save computer time.

SAS/AF software also gives you the flexibility to customize your in-house training programs. You can build training courses of any length, for any audience, on any subject you choose! You can individualize the instruction to meet the needs of any audience—no matter how diverse their backgrounds.

SAS/AF SCREENS

You use SAS/AF procedures to create and display seven types of screens.

Screen	Description
CBT	presents instructional material and questions and answers interactively, for example, as part of computer-based training courses.
FORM	gives specifications for printing to devices for procedures in the SAS/FSP software product.
HELP	displays information you want users to see, for example, an on-line documentation reference or help facility when help is requested.
KEYS	specifies function key definitions to be used by SAS full-screen procedures.
LIST	contains values used to validate user entry fields.
MENU	provides a list of alternatives from which a selection is made.
PROGRAM	contains SAS statements to be submitted to the SAS System with optional fill-in-the-blank fields that can be inserted in the SAS statements before they are submitted.

All activities within SAS/AF software are controlled by one of the following procedures:

Procedure	Description
BUILD	for creating or editing screens
DISPLAY	for displaying CBT, HELP, MENU, or PROGRAM screens
CPORT	for converting a library of screens into a sequential file in transport format for sharing with other operating systems
CIMPORT	for converting a transport format sequential file created by CPORT into a library of screens in local or host-dependent format.

To see how you can use these SAS/AF features together, follow the development of a SAS/AF information system in a book sales department, which is presented in the chapter "A Menu-Driven Application."

Chapter 2

A Menu-Driven Application

INTRODUCTION

The Book Sales Department at ACE Publishing Company needs an automated way to handle book sales. All staff members in the department share the responsibilities and can perform all of the following tasks:

- taking book orders
- invoicing customers
- crediting paid invoices
- printing daily, weekly, and monthly sales reports.

The sales staff should be able to work from a menu to perform any of these tasks, without knowing any data processing or SAS programming.

In this example, ACE Publishing Company has SAS/GRAPH, SAS/FSP, and SAS/AF software. If you have other SAS software at your site, you can easily adapt this example to your own environment.

WHAT YOU WANT

You want to design a system that lets you choose tasks easily from a menu of numbered activities. To select an activity, you enter the number of the activity on the command line or press a key. An example of how the initial menu screen may look is shown in **Screen 2.1**.

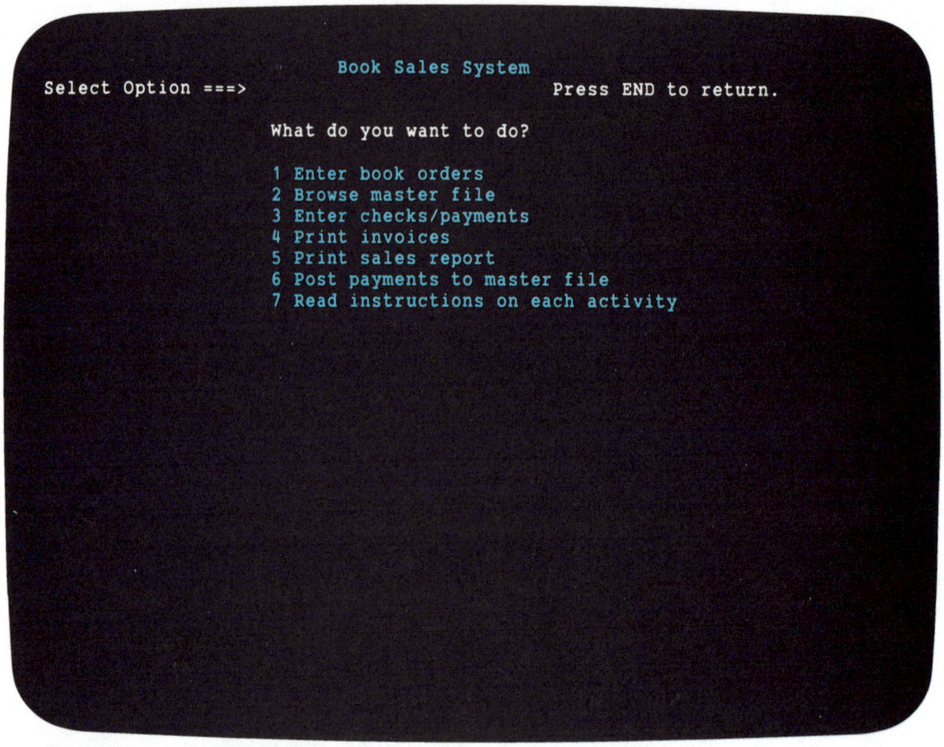

Screen 2.1 Primary MENU Screen

Sometimes when you select a menu item, a SAS program is executed immediately. Other times when you choose an item, another menu appears on the screen with other selections to be made. Each of these new selections can lead to programs, menus, and help screens containing documentation. Sometimes the task to be performed requires that you answer certain questions relating to that activity. You are asked to enter the answers to questions or to fill in information on the screen. The answers you give are then substituted in a program that is submitted to the SAS System and executed automatically when you exit from the screen.

For example, when you select item 1 from the menu shown in **Screen 2.1**, you expect to see a screen for entering book orders. Since SAS/FSP software is installed at ACE Publishing Company, you can display an FSEDIT screen for entering the day's book orders. Enter a 1 on the command line of the primary menu and press ENTER to see the data entry screen shown in **Screen 2.2**.

When you are ready to print the day's invoices, select item 4 from the menu; however, certain questions need to be answered before the invoices can be printed.

Fill in the appropriate blanks in **Screen 2.3** and then press END. A program to print invoices is submitted to the SAS System, and the original menu is displayed. The next morning, you get the invoices ready to mail; see **Figure 2.1** for a sample invoice.

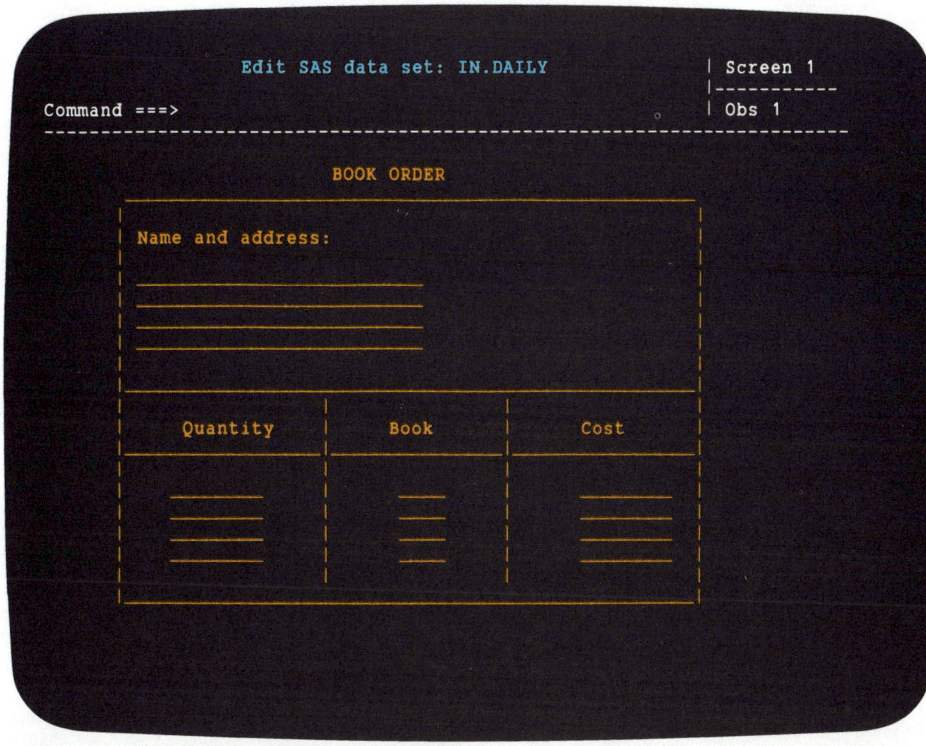

Screen 2.2 FSEDIT Screen for Data Entry

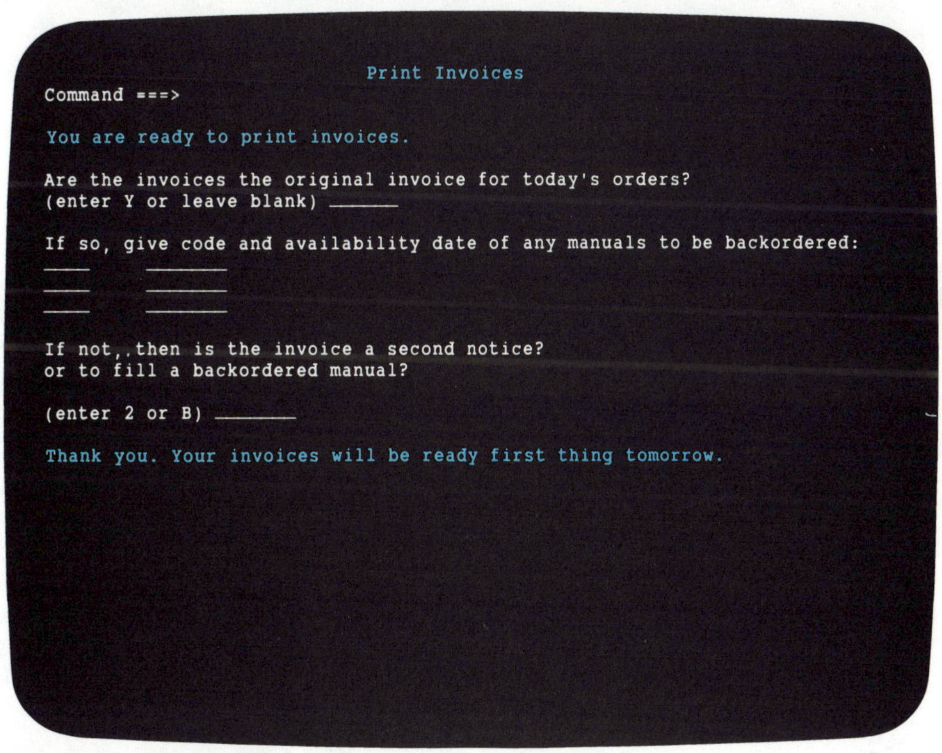

Screen 2.3 Printing Invoices

ACE Publishing Company
1134 N. Peace Street
Macon, GA 40511

INVOICE #90411 OCTOBER 2, 1984

MS. MARY DOE
HIGH SCHOOL LIBRARY
190 SCHOOL STREET
FAIRFIELD, VA 22016

Quantity	Book	Cost	Total
100	User's Guide, 1980 Edition	$0.00	$0.00
25	Introductory Guide	$4.95	$123.75
		AMOUNT DUE	$123.75

BACKORDERED	AVAILABLE
User's Guide, 1980 Edition	26JUN84

When the back ordered manuals listed above are available, we will place your order and you will be invoiced separately.

Figure 2.1 Printed Invoice

GETTING STARTED

In order for the book sales staff to have such an automated system, you must build the screens containing menus and programs in such a way that they remain in the background, transparent to the user. You can use SAS/AF software to do this. The BUILD procedure can be used to set up the background for the book sales application. The DISPLAY procedure shows the user only those parts of the book sales system that are necessary to do the job.

SAS Catalog

Menus, programs, and help facilities that you build with the BUILD procedure are stored in a SAS catalog that can be stored in a SAS data library.[1]

A catalog is a SAS file and is named with a two-level name like a SAS data set, but the second-level name must be seven characters or less. All other rules for naming SAS files apply to naming your SAS catalog.

When you are ready to build the screens for the book sales application, you first access your SAS data library as usual. Then, after you have invoked the SAS System, use the CATALOG= option in the PROC BUILD statement to reference the catalog where you plan to build and store your screens. For example, if your SAS data library has been referenced using libref IN, you can use statements like these to begin building screens:

```
PROC BUILD CATALOG=IN.APPS;
RUN;
```

APPS is the name of the catalog in the SAS data library referenced previously with libref IN.

When you execute the above statements for the first time, a catalog listing with no entries appears on your terminal. As you create screens, their names and some information about them are written in the catalog directory in **Screen 2.4**.

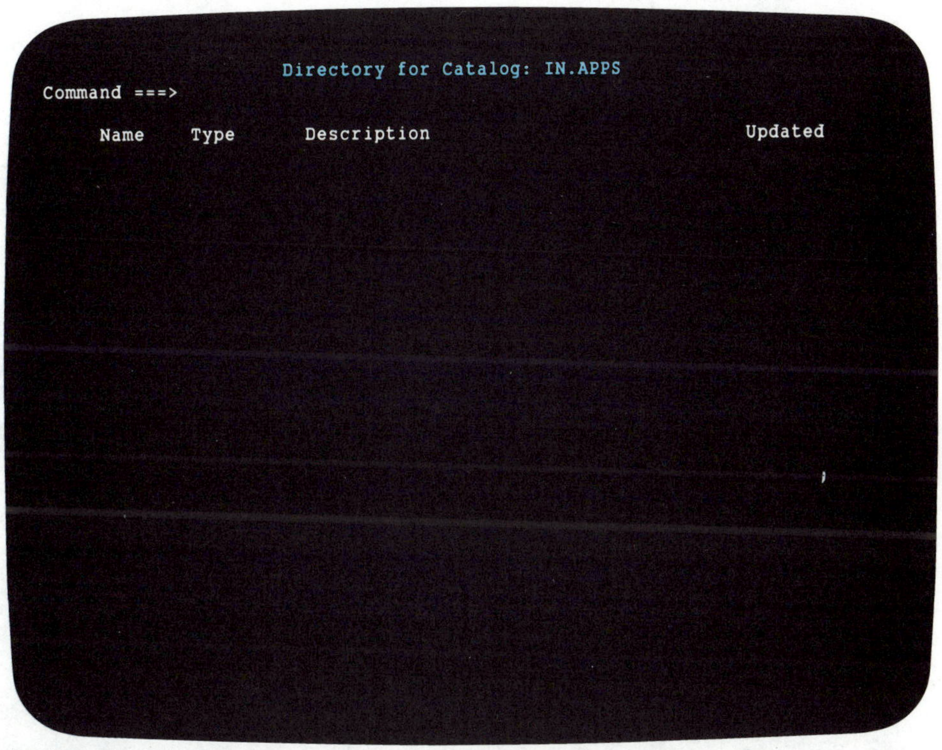

Screen 2.4 Viewing the Catalog Directory for the First Time

Primary Menu

To build a new screen or to edit an old one, enter the EDIT command on the command line along with the name and type of the screen you are building:

```
EDIT name.type
```

where

name names the screen for identification in the catalog. Names for screens follow the same rules as other SAS names: eight characters or less beginning with a letter followed by letters, numbers, or underscores. (Some operating systems let you begin names with an underscore.) Note that two screens in the same catalog can have the same name, as long as the screens are of different types.

type specifies the type of screen. Screens can be any of the following types: CBT, FORM, HELP, KEYS, LIST, MENU, or PROGRAM. (See "The BUILD Procedure" chapter for a complete description of each screen type.)

Usually an application like the book sales system begins with a menu. Items selected from this menu can lead down many paths. In this example, the first menu that a user sees is called the *primary menu* to distinguish it from other menus later in the system.

To build a MENU screen for the book sales example, enter the command

```
EDIT BOOKS.MENU
```

on the command line and press ENTER. A blank MENU screen appears on your terminal, as shown in **Screen 2.5**.

Screen 2.5 A New MENU Screen

You can design the MENU screen in any way. Some people find it easier to enter text using line commands, which requires that screen lines be numbered. Enter the command

```
NUMS ON
```

on the command line and press ENTER. You can use the numbered area to copy, move, delete and add lines, and perform other text editing. Editing commands are described in the "Full-Screen Editing" appendix.

For this example, enter a list of sales activities on the MENU screen shown in **Screen 2.6**. You can enter the menu items anywhere on the screen.

You specify the relationship between the item number and the activity using MENU attributes.

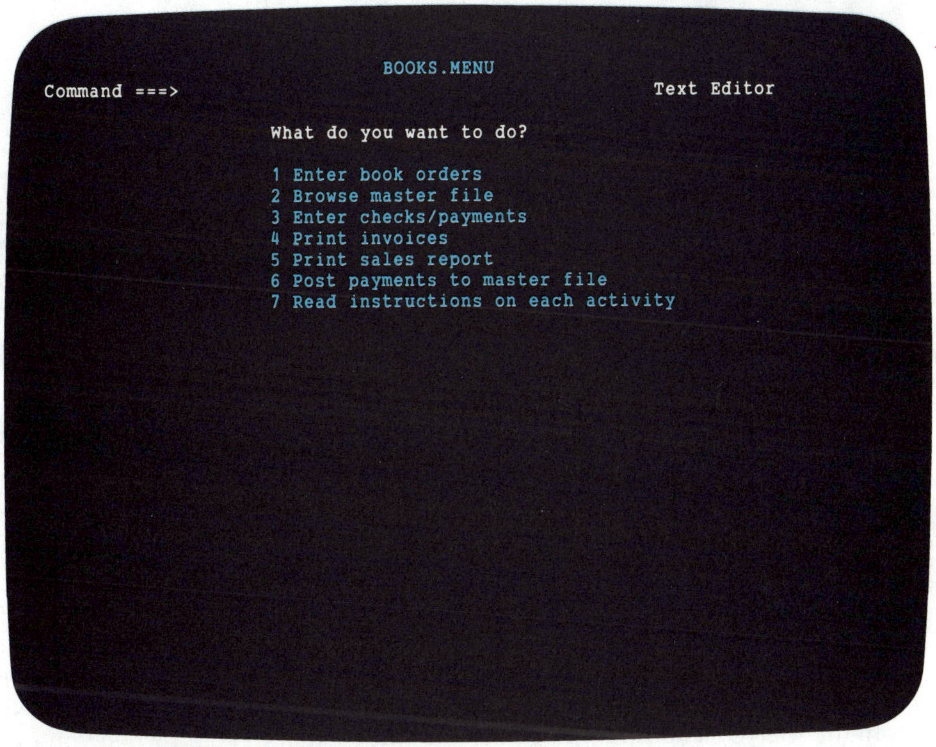

Screen 2.6 Building a MENU Screen

Menu Attributes

To give instructions to the SAS System about what to do (that is, what screen to reference) when an item is selected from this menu, you define subpanels corresponding to each menu item. Subpanels are other screens that you build using PROC BUILD.

On the command line of the MENU screen enter

```
ATTR
```

then move the cursor to a place below the menu, and press ENTER. A screen for specifying up to sixty subpanels is displayed at the cursor location, as shown in **Screen 2.7**.

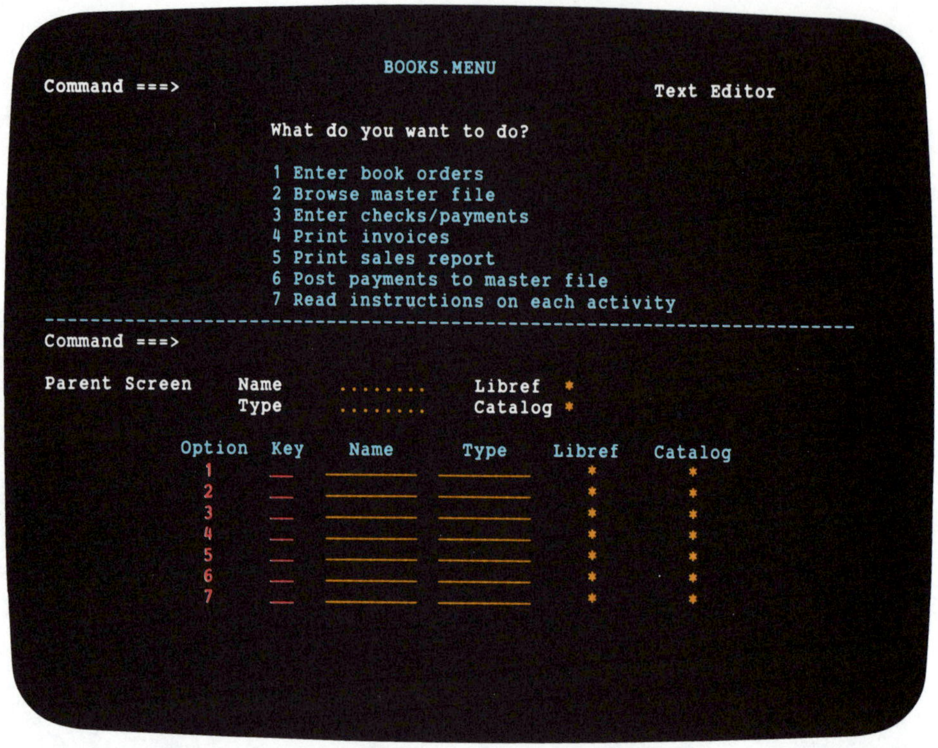

Screen 2.7 Defining Menu Attributes

Parent Screen

On this form, you are asked to define the parent screen for BOOKS.MENU. A screen's parent is the screen that is displayed when you press the END key from that screen. If the parent screen field on the MENU screen's attribute display is left blank, as in **Screen 2.7**, you return to the SAS System when you press END from the MENU. If you want to go back to the operating system when you exit, you can write a program to exit from SAS using a PROGRAM screen with an ENDSAS statement and define that PROGRAM screen as the MENU's parent.

Subpanels

Now you want to describe the screens that are processed as the result of selecting each task in the primary menu. If you want to be able to press a key rather than enter a number to select a task, this form can be used to define those keys. For each menu item in BOOKS.MENU, indicate on the form a key and a screen name and type for the subpanels. Key values must be valid function keys on your terminal, Name must be a SAS name, and Type must be one of the valid screen types: CBT, FORM, HELP, KEYS, LIST, MENU, or PROGRAM.

If any of the screens you name on this form are stored in a SAS catalog different from the one you are using to store the current screen, the Libref and Catalog name should be specified. An asterisk (*) indicates that the screen is in the current catalog.

Screen 2.8 shows the attributes for the primary menu screen, BOOKS.MENU.

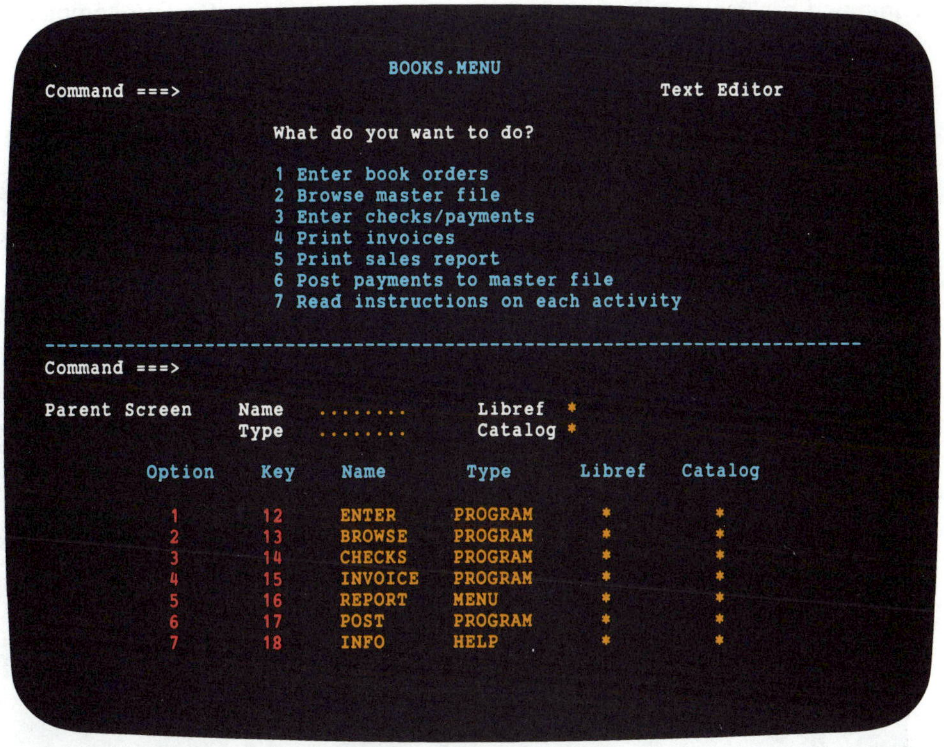

Screen 2.8 Attributes of the MENU Screen

When you give a Key number on the form, you can press that function key rather than entering the item number from PROC DISPLAY. Note that the Key selections listed override normal function key meanings in effect for the menu. Press END to remove the attribute panel from the display.

THE SYSTEM

The system you have defined through subpanels on the primary menu includes several programs, a menu, and documentation about the system. You can build the corresponding screens using PROC BUILD. First, return to the catalog directory shown in **Screen 2.9** by pressing the END key. The primary menu is now stored in the screen catalog. (The blank to the left of the screen name in the directory is the selection field where commands can be entered. See **Selection Field Commands** in "The BUILD Procedure" chapter for more information.)

The HELP Screen

Item 7 on the primary menu in the book sales system is a request for instructions on how to use the system. HELP screens contain text and are typically used to provide documentation or special information about the system. They are easy to build; with the editing capabilities available, you can format the screen any way you want to provide the needed information. **Screen 2.10** is an example.

To build the new screen, enter an EDIT command on the command line of the catalog directory giving the name of the screen you want to build:

```
EDIT INFO.HELP
```

Then enter the necessary information on the blank HELP screen. The NUMS ON command can make editing easier since it gives you access to line commands for manipulating your text.

```
                      Directory for Catalog: IN.APPS
Command ===>

  Name     Type      Description                          Updated

_ BOOKS    MENU      BOOKS.MENU                           04APR84
```

Screen 2.9 The Catalog Directory

```
                                INFO.HELP
Command ===>                                          Text Editor

000010BOOK SALES SYSTEM
000020
000030Below is a detailed description of the book sales process and how
000040to accomplish each task through the primary menu screen.
000050
000060Book Orders
000070-----------
000080
000090Each day, you want to enter the day's book orders.  All mail
000100orders received and and phone orders taken during the day must be
000110added to the day's orders.
000120
000130To enter book orders, press item #1 from the primary menu screen.
000140You can enter and exit from the book orders data entry screen as
000150often as you want during the day.
000160
000170Once the day's orders have been entered, you want to print the
000180day's invoices. Select item #4 from the primary menu to run the
000190job to print invoices. The job should be run each evening before
000200leaving; invoices will be printed overnight and ready to use as
000210packing slips the next day.
000220
000230Checks/Payments
000240---------------
000250Each day, you want to enter all checks and payments for posting to
000260the master file at the end of the day.
```

Screen 2.10 The HELP Screen

The PROGRAM Screen

Several tasks in the book sales system that appear on the primary menu screen require PROGRAM screens. The first three items on the menu

- enter book orders
- browse master file
- enter checks/payments

use simple SAS programs (two simple PROC steps) that display data entry screens or observations in a SAS data set. The three programs corresponding to these items are very similar; they require no answers from the user, and they consist of two simple PROC steps. (These are simple program screens; later examples illustrate more complex program screens that require user responses.)

Background

For example, when you are ready to enter book orders, select item 1 from the master menu. A screen designed using the FSEDIT procedure in SAS/FSP software is displayed.

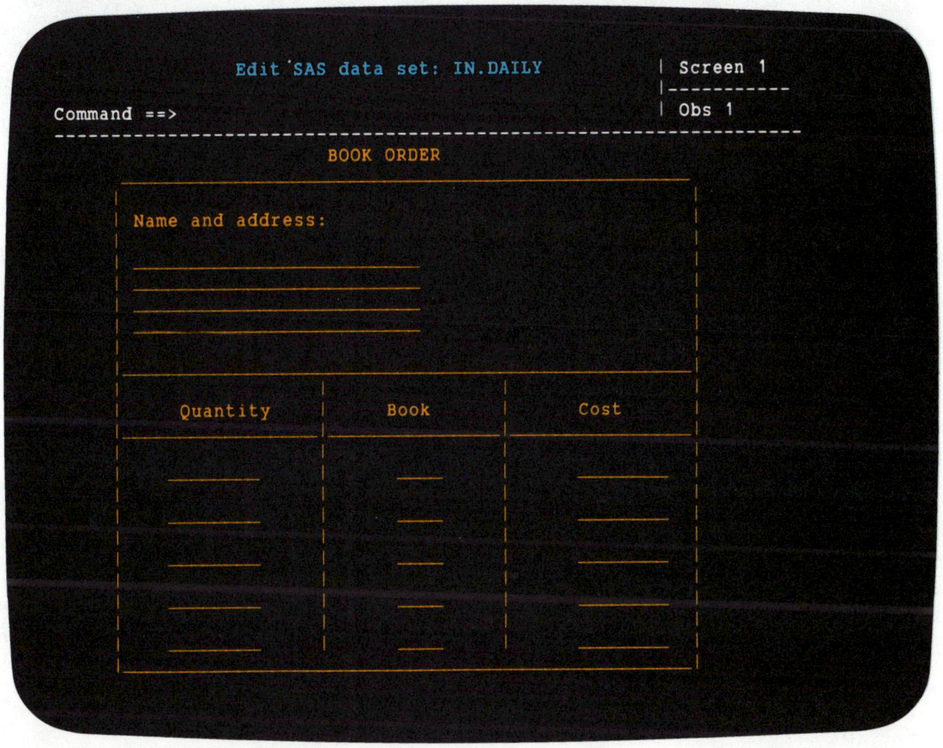

Screen 2.11 FSEDIT Screen for Data Entry

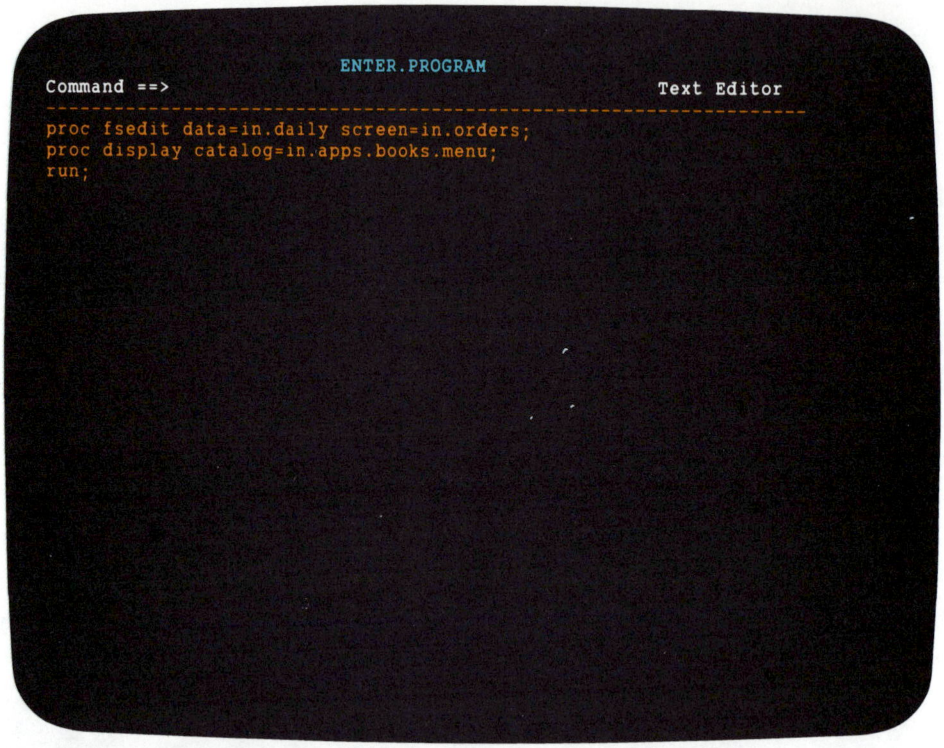

Screen 2.12 A PROGRAM Screen to Display the FSEDIT Screen

To build the PROGRAM screen that produces this FSEDIT screen, enter the EDIT command on the command line of the screen catalog

```
EDIT ENTER.PROGRAM
```

giving the name and type of the screen you want to build.

Screen 2.12 shows a PROGRAM screen that causes **Screen 2.11** to be displayed.

The PROGRAM screen consists of two parts: what you see and what the system sees. The two parts are divided by a dashed line that extends the width of the screen. The first part is optional; it is required only if user responses are needed in order to run the program in the second part. User responses are supplied in user fields denoted with an ampersand on the upper portion of the screen. User fields are discussed later. This PROGRAM screen begins with a dashed line to separate the two parts since the user-entry portion is not needed. Enter

```
FILL -
```

on the command line of the PROGRAM screen, place the cursor in column one of the line where you want the dashed line to appear, and press ENTER. Then you can enter the program statements that are submitted to the SAS System when this screen is referenced.

This program executes the FSEDIT procedure in SAS/FSP software to display the data entry screen for entering the day's book orders. The SAS data library described by libref IN and the SAS data set DAILY already exist; the SCREEN data set has also been defined. (See the *SAS/FSP User's Guide* for more information.) Note that the files needed in the book sales system are not referenced in each program; all files are referenced automatically when the user enters the system.

When you enter book orders for the first time in a given day, SAS data set DAILY contains no observations. Each evening, observations in this data set are added to the master file and then deleted from DAILY. (This is done by the program in the INVOICE.PROGRAM screen later in this chapter.)

By default, after the statements in a PROGRAM screen have been submitted to the SAS System and executed, you are returned to the SAS System. The PROC DISPLAY step in the example above causes the program to return to the primary menu when you press the END key. Remember that you do not define a parent screen for PROGRAM screens. Instead, you tell the program where to return through programming statements.[2]

If you have an existing program that you want to duplicate in a PROGRAM screen, the INCLUDE command can be used to copy the program into your screen, or you may want to include existing programs using the %INCLUDE statement. You can edit these programs while in PROC BUILD using the X command on the command line to communicate directly with the host operating system. The INCLUDE and X commands are described in the "Full-Screen Editing" appendix. The %INCLUDE statement is documented in the *SAS User's Guide: Basics*.

Other Simple PROGRAM Screens

When you want to browse the master file to check on an order or invoice, select item 2 from the menu. The program corresponding to that selection may look like the one shown in **Screen 2.13**.

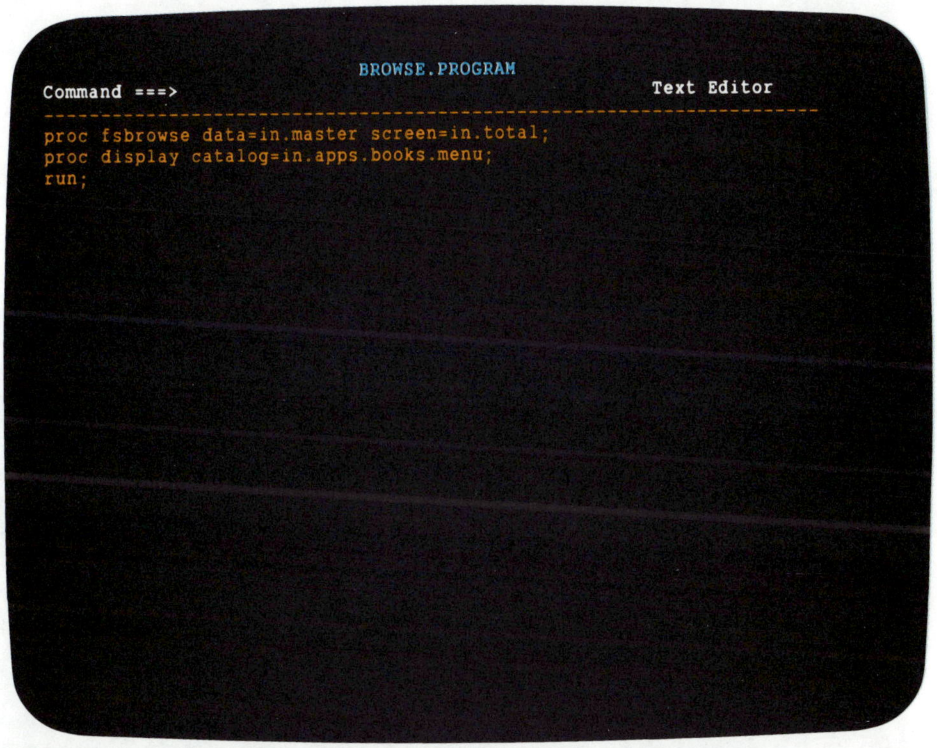

Screen 2.13 A PROGRAM Screen for Browsing a SAS Data Set

The master file for the system is the file containing all book orders, both new and old, and a record of payment for each order. You may want to browse this file in order to answer a question about an order. The master data set is another part of the book sales system that has been previously defined. When the user selects this menu item, the first observation in the master file is displayed on the terminal, as shown in **Screen 2.14**. (For a description of the FSBROWSE procedure, see the *SAS/FSP User's Guide*.)

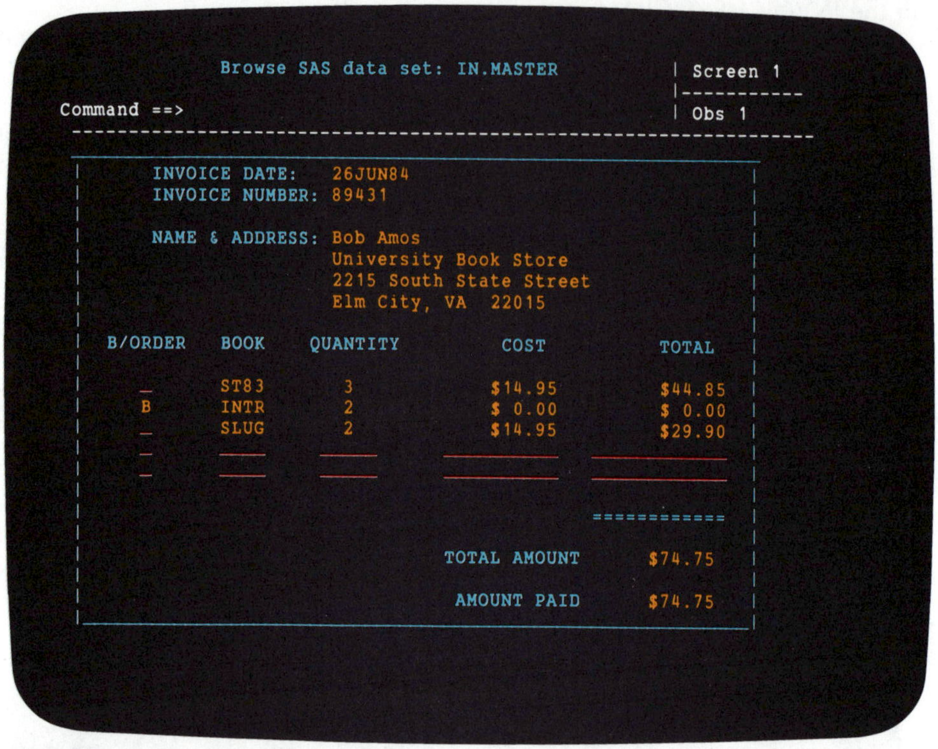

Screen 2.14 Browsing a Master File

To enter checks or payments, menu item 3, the program is similar, as shown in **Screen 2.15**.

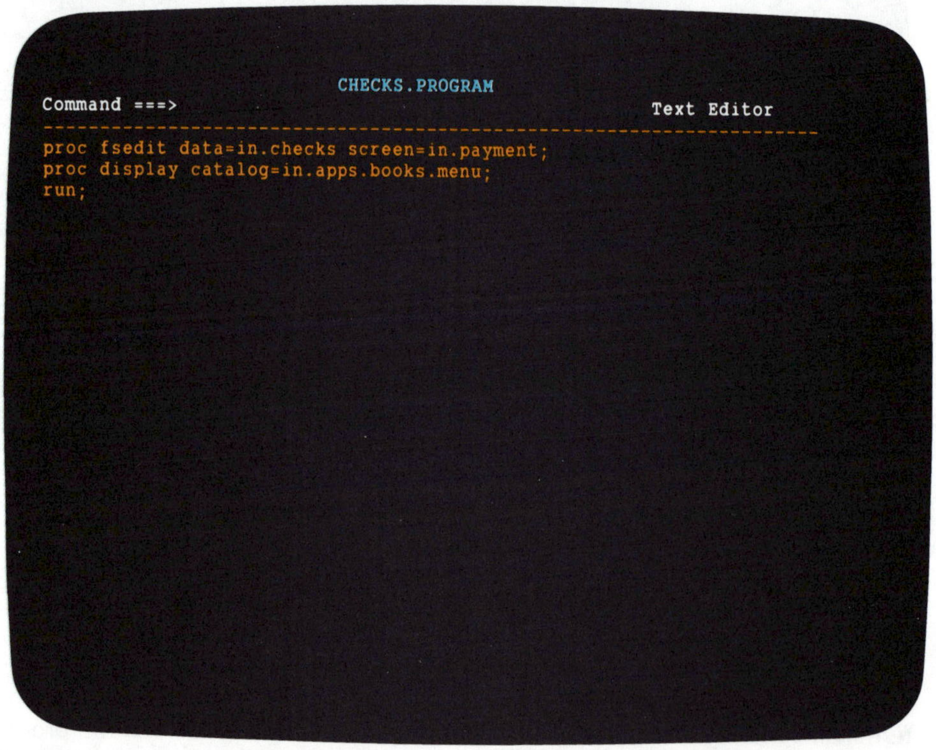

Screen 2.15 A PROGRAM Screen for Entering Checks or Payments

The result of executing the statements in **Screen 2.15** is a screen for entering the day's checks. This file is posted to the master file by a later program.

The catalog directory in **Screen 2.16** now contains entries for all these programs.

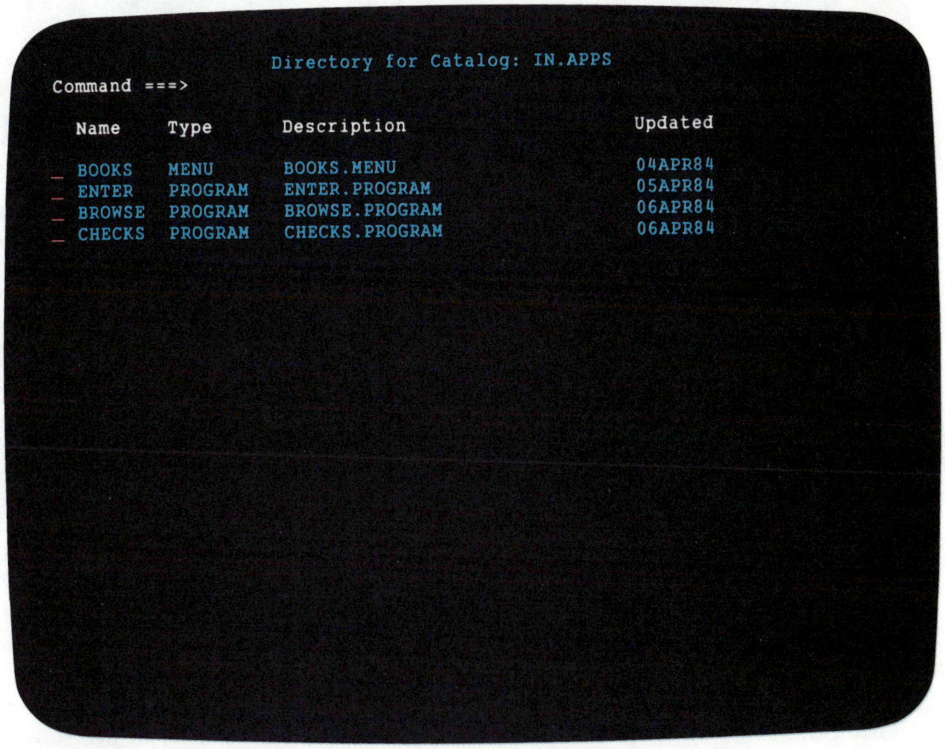

Screen 2.16 The Catalog Directory after Building Several Screens

A PROGRAM Screen with User-Supplied Values

You can also design a PROGRAM screen with blanks that the user fills in; your response generates code in the SAS program below the dashed line. When the book sales system is used, only the portion containing the blanks that need to be filled in appears.

For example, before an invoice can be printed, the system needs to know whether the invoice is the first and, thus, also included in the shipment; whether it is the second notice on an unpaid invoice; or whether a backordered book is being shipped on a previous invoice. You supply the appropriate answers and press the END key to exit from the screen, and the invoices are automatically printed.

To build the PROGRAM screen in **Screen 2.17** to print invoices, enter the command

```
EDIT INVOICE.PROGRAM
```

to view the blank screen. At the top of the screen, enter text and any questions for which you need a user response. Answers given in the user fields (indicated by an &) are automatically inserted in the code entered below the dashed line.

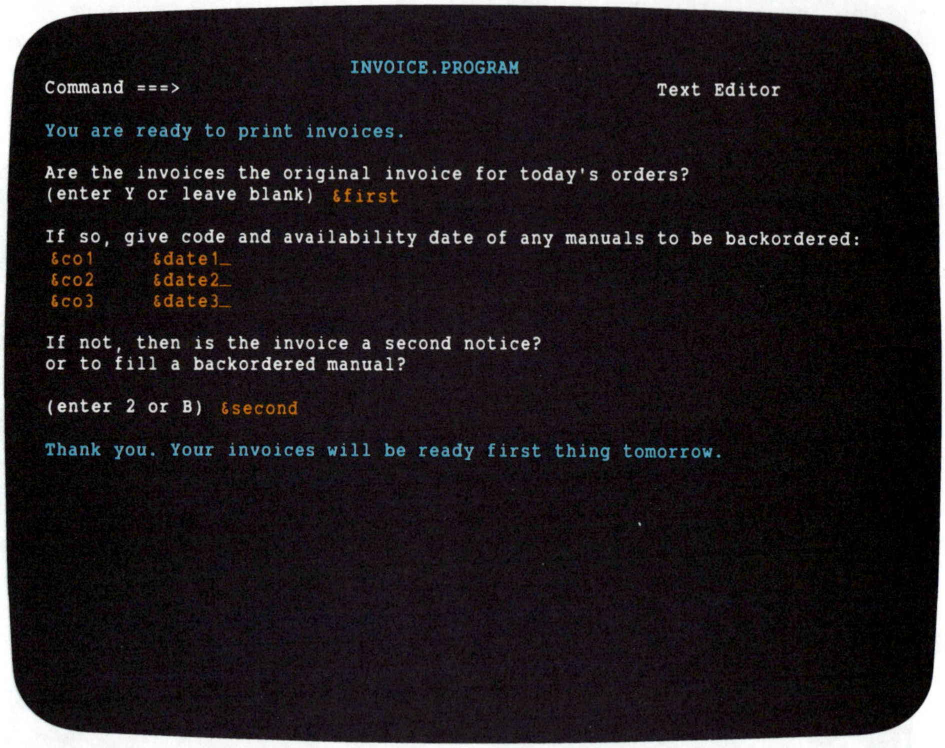

Screen 2.17 A PROGRAM Screen with Blanks to Be Filled In

Using the scroll keys and commands, cover as much or as little of the screen as you need for entering the user portion. When this portion of the screen is displayed later, you may also have to scroll to view all the material.

When you have finished entering the portion of the screen that is shown to the user, enter

```
FILL -
```

and place the cursor in column one where you want the dashed line. After the dashed line, enter the SAS code to be executed. Below is the complete text for screen INVOICE.PROGRAM.

```
------------------------------------------------------------------------
                           INVOICE.PROGRAM
Command ===>                                                Text Editor

You are ready to print invoices.

Are the invoices the original invoice for today's orders?
(enter Y or leave blank) &first

If so, give code and availability date of any manuals to be backordered:
&co1      &date1_
&co2      &date2_
&co3      &date3_

If not, then is the invoice a second notice?
or to fill a backordered manual?
```

(continued on next page)

(continued from previous page)

```
(enter 2 or B) &second

Thank you. Your invoices will be ready first thing tomorrow.

----------------------------------------------------------------------
##first
data today;
  set in.daily;
  invdate=today();        /* today's date */
  number=put(_n_,3.);
  invoice=invdate||left(number); /* generate invoice number  */
  file invoice;
  put #6 @50 invdate worddate20.;
  put #10 @20 name / @20 billad1 / @20 billad2 / @20 billad3 ///;
  put @20 'Quantity' @40 'Book' @60 'Cost' @75 'Total'/ @20 65*'-'/;
  array books (j) $ 4 book1-book5;
  array cost (j) cost1-cost5;
  array quantity (j) qnty1-qnty5;
  array key (j) $ 1 k1-k5;
  array total (j) tot1-tot5;
  do over books;
    /* if order is not in stock, item flagged, cost set to zero */
      if books|=' ' and
      (books=&co1 or books=&co2 or books=&co3) then do;
      key='b'; cost=0;
      end;
    /* total cost per item calculated */
    total=quantity*cost;
  put @21 quantity 5.  @31 books $bkfmt. @60 cost dollar8.2
        @72 total dollar12.2;
    /* total cost for order calculated */
    grtotal+total;
    end;
    put @60 'AMOUNT DUE'  @72 '____________'
        /@72 grtotal dollar12.2;
#co1 put #30 @21 'BACKORDERED'   @60 'AVAILABLE';
     put @21 &co1 $bkfmt. @60 &date1 date7. ;
#co2 put @21 &co2 $bkfmt. @60 &date2 date7. ;
#co3 put @21 &co3 $bkfmt. @60 &date3 date7. ;
     put // @25
     'When the backordered manuals listed above are available, we'/
 @25 'will place your order and you will be invoiced separately.';

##second
  /*program statements needed to print second invoices*/

##
data in.master;              /* add today's invoices to master */
  set in.master today;
data in.daily;              /* delete observation from DAILY */
  set today(obs=0);
proc display catalog=in.apps.books.menu;
run;
```

Screen 2.18 A PROGRAM Screen to Print Invoices

When you have responded to questions on the screen from PROC DISPLAY and pressed the END key to finish, the program below the dashed line is passed to the SAS System for execution.[2] The program produces the day's invoices.[3]

Features of the PROGRAM Screen

User fields When you respond to a question that appears in the top portion of the screen, your answer is used in the program below the dashed line. Responses become values of user fields, denoted on the PROGRAM screen in PROC BUILD by an ampersand (&) followed by a name:

```
&NAME
```

The values you enter are substituted in the program below the dashed line before the program is submitted for execution. Note: the use of ampersand fields is a SAS/AF feature that is separate from the SAS macro facility.

In this example, the first user field, *&first*, is given a value of Y if the invoices are for today's orders. In that case, user fields *&co1-&co3* and *&date1-&date3* may also be given values. If the invoices are not the first, then *&second* should have a value of 2 or B, indicating that the invoices are to contain a second notice or that they are to fill backordered books. There is no limit to the number of user fields that can appear above the dashed line. Attributes of the user fields are defined using an Attribute Definition Screen, described below.

Conditional execution In the program below the line, the command

```
##FIRST
```

tells the system that if the user field *&first* is left blank, then the statements that follow are not to be executed. Commands of the form

```
#VARIABLE
##VARIABLE
##
```

are called *conditional execution indicators*. These allow code to be executed conditionally based on whether or not user values are entered. Conditional execution indicators may be nested one level. The lowest level is specified by a single pound sign (#) preceding the variable name. The indicator is in effect until either another conditional execution indicator of the same or higher level or until the end of the program statements is encountered. Double pound signs (##) not followed by a variable are used to end the effect of all previous indicators.

For example, in the program above there are two levels of conditional execution indicators. If the user field *&first* is blank, then the *##first* indicator prevents the DATA step that follows from being executed. This DATA step prints the day's invoices, indicating backordered books when appropriate. If the DATA step is submitted (*&first* is nonblank), the *#co1* command tells the system to submit the statements that follow for execution if the value of *&co1* is nonblank. Similarly, the *#co2* and *#co3* indicators can prevent the PUT statements that follow from being executed if the corresponding user fields are left blank.

The report-writer DATA step that prints the first invoices is followed in the program by a different report-writer step that prints invoices if *&second* is filled in on the screen.

User-field attributes When you have finished writing the SAS program to be executed, enter the ATTR command to display a screen for defining attributes of user fields mentioned on the PROGRAM screen. You may be able to use default attributes for each user field, or you can fill in other attributes.

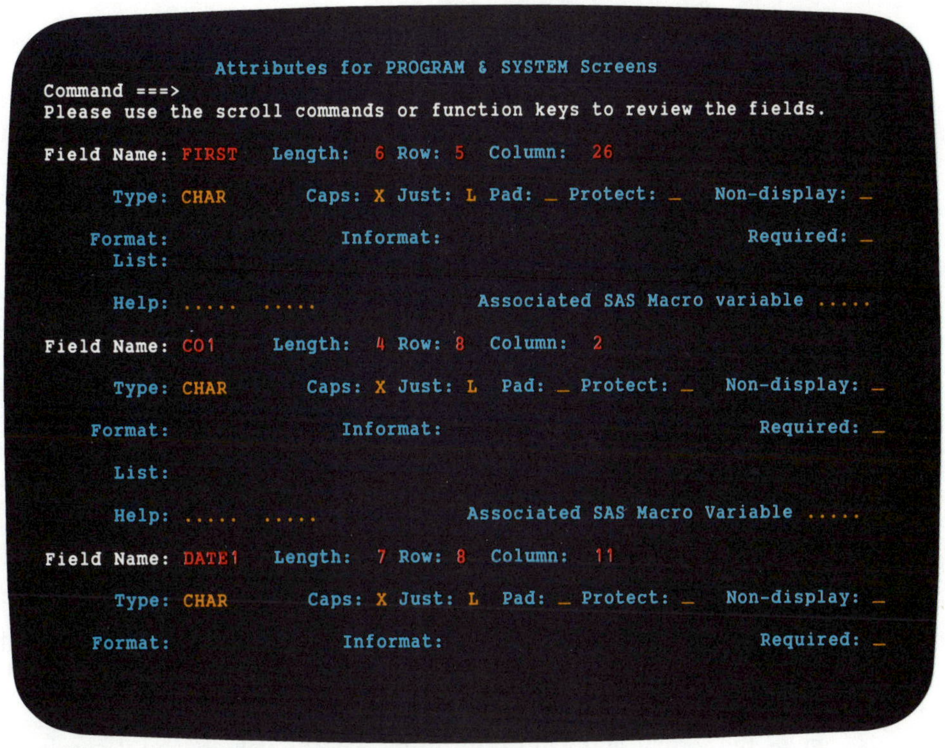

Screen 2.19 Attributes of User Fields

Each user field has the following default attributes:

Length
: is equal to the total length of the name (including the ampersand) plus any underscores concatenated to the name. Thus, user field *&first* has length six since six characters including the ampersand are in its name; *&date1* has length seven since six characters are in the name and the variable name is followed immediately by an underscore (_) when it first appears in the program screen.

Row and Column
: is the row and column location of the first appearance of the user field name on the program screen.

Type
: is set to CHAR by default unless the field is of length one, in which case type is set to ACTION. See "The BUILD Procedure" chapter for a description of all possible user field types.

Caps
: turns on caps by default, indicating that values entered should be set to uppercase.

Just
: refers to the way values of the user field are displayed; set to L for left aligned by default. R is for right aligned and C for centered.

Pad
: indicates the character you want to appear on the screen where values are to be entered. The default pad character is an underscore (_). For example, for the user field *&first*, if you enter a question

mark (?) as the pad character, the user's screen for that question will look like this:

```
--------------------------------------------------------

Are the invoices the original invoice for today's orders?
(enter Y or leave blank) ??????

--------------------------------------------------------
```

A blank pad value means that no character appears on the display screen to indicate where to fill in the value. If the field is associated with a SAS macro variable, the pad character is overwritten by the macro variable's value.

Protect
: is left blank by default and indicates that the field is unprotected and values can be written in. If you enter an X, the field appears on the screen in PROC DISPLAY, but the user cannot enter values in the field.

Non-display
: is left blank by default and indicates that the field appears on the screen from PROC DISPLAY. Enter an X if you want to mask the field from the user's view.

Format
: gives the format you want used to display the values, and it can be a SAS or user-defined format. If the format given is a user-defined format, the format library where the format is stored must be allocated to any jobs that refer to the format for printing.

Informat
: gives the variable's informat, the format used to read values on the program screen.

Required
: is left blank by default; enter X if the user must enter a valid value in the field.

List
: gives either a list of valid values for the user field or the name of a LIST screen when used after an equals sign that contains valid values for the user field. If valid values are specified, any other value that is entered in the user field is flagged as an error. See the LIST screen description, below.

Help
: gives the name of a HELP screen that appears if the user enters the HELP command or presses the HELP key while the cursor is in this field.

Associated SAS macro variable
: gives the name of a SAS macro variable that automatically assumes the value specified.

To define the attributes of each user field in this program correctly, you need to make the following changes to the default values:

- For variables DATE1, DATE2, and DATE3: change Type to numeric (NUM), change Format and Informat to DATE7., and remove CAPS indication.

- For variables CO1, CO2, and CO3: enter an equals sign (=) followed by the name BOOKS.LIST to tell the system the name of a LIST screen for identifying valid values.
- For variable SECOND: add B and 2 as list of valid values.

When you press the END key from this program screen, the attributes specified in the Attribute Definition Screen are saved and stored with the program.

The LIST Screen

In the attribute list, you specified BOOKS.LIST as the name of a LIST screen containing valid values for three user fields, &CO1, &CO2, and &CO3. A LIST screen is accessed only with PROC BUILD; it cannot be viewed with PROC DISPLAY.

Setting up a list of valid values To build the LIST screen, enter

```
EDIT BOOKS.LIST
```

on the command line and press ENTER. The screen shown in **Screen 2.20** is displayed at your terminal.

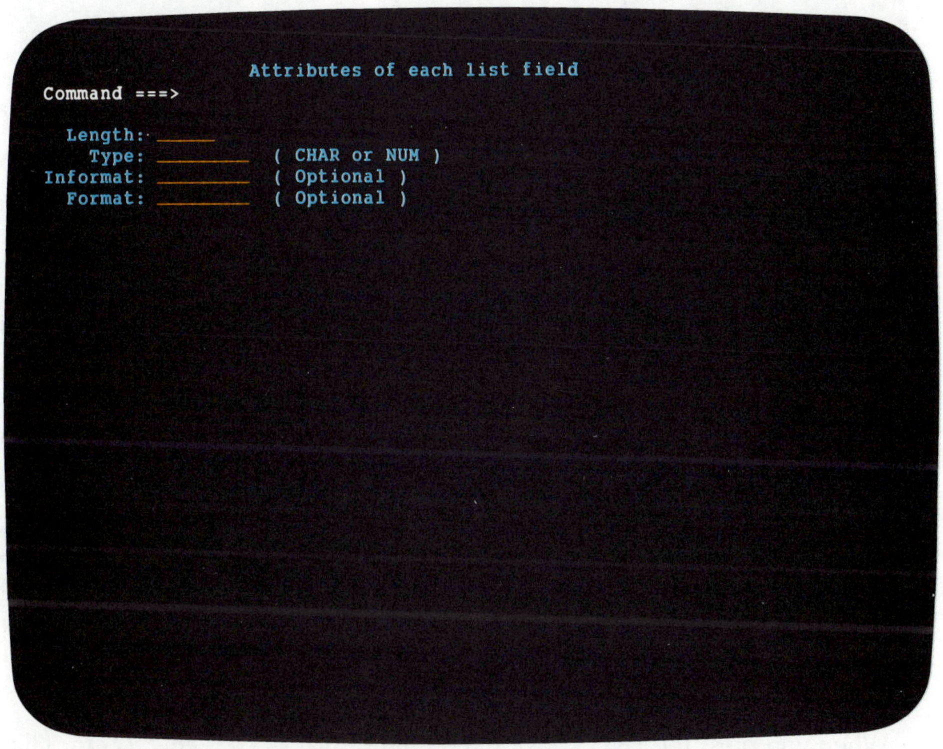

Screen 2.20 Building the LIST Screen

Use this screen to identify the length, type, and, optionally, the informat and format of valid values for the list entries. List entries need not be of the same length as the user field values, in which case the comparison is done for the shorter length. In this example, book titles in the book sales system are coded using a four-character alphanumeric code. The five books available have the following codes:

Title	Code
User's Guide, 1980 Edition	UG80
Supplemental Library User's Guide	SLUG
Graphics Guide, 1982 Edition	GR82
Introductory Guide	INTR
Statistics Guide, 1983 Edition	ST83

A format called $BKFMT. has been created that maps the four-character code to the title in the list above. This format is used to print the book names when any reports are printed. (The *SAS User's Guide: Basics* describes the FORMAT procedure for setting up user-defined formats.)

Fill in the attributes of the user field.

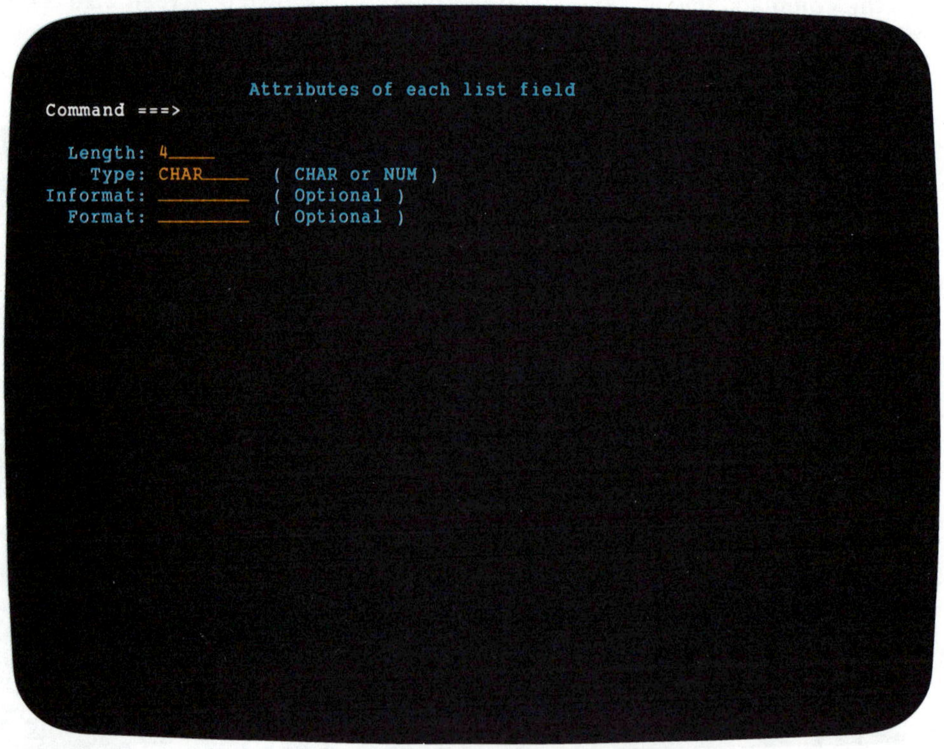

Screen 2.21 Filling in Attributes of the User Field: The LIST Screen

When you press the END key, a screen full of blanks (**Screen 2.22**) for filling in values appears on your terminal. You can scroll forward if you need additional blanks.

Note that the number of blanks for entering each value corresponds to the variable's length attribute.

Now fill in the five valid values as shown in **Screen 2.23**.

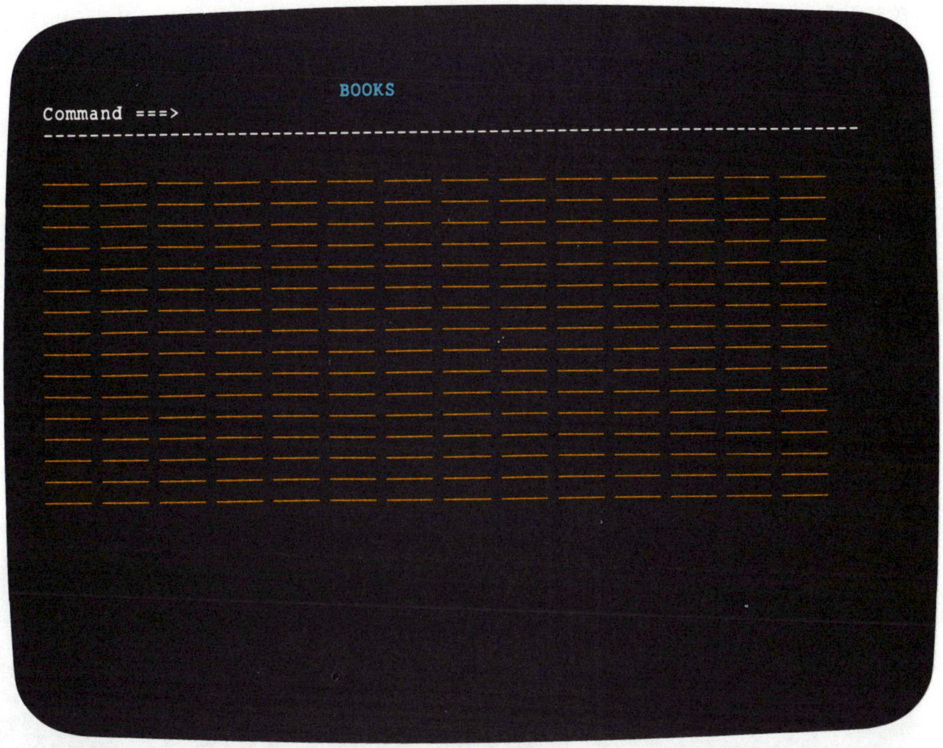

Screen 2.22 A Screen for Entering Valid Values: The LIST Screen

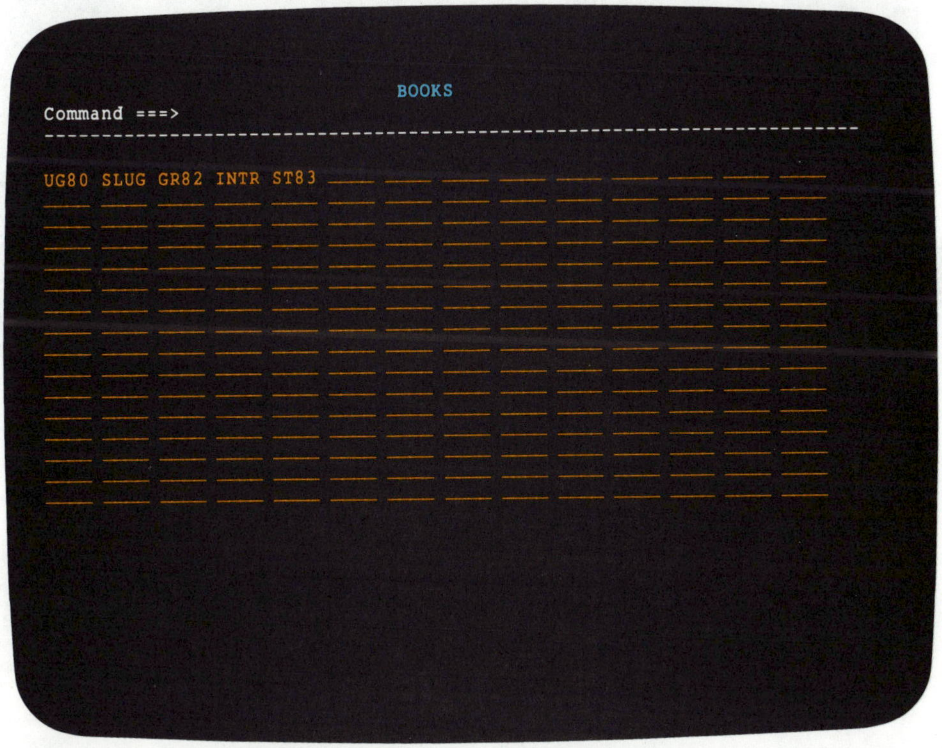

Screen 2.23 Entering Valid Values: The LIST Screen

Valid values can be entered in any order anywhere on the screen. When you press the END key to return to the catalog, PROC BUILD automatically sorts the values in ascending order and for numeric variables removes any duplicates.

In PROC DISPLAY when you fill in the blanks on this screen, only the values given in the LIST screen above are allowed for the user fields CO1-CO3. If another value is entered by mistake, the entry is flagged as an error, and you cannot continue until you enter a correct value.

Accessing Menus from the Primary Menu

If you want a sales report, there are several types of reports from which to choose. Item 5 on the primary menu offers a selection of reports.

You create a new MENU to list the available reports using the EDIT command

```
EDIT REPORT.MENU
```

and then begin entering menu items as before in **Screen 2.24**.

```
                              REPORT.MENU
Command ===>                                                Text Editor

What type of report do you want printed?

 1 List of Today's Orders
 2 Current Warehouse Inventory
 3 Weekly Sales Report
 4 Monthly Sales Report
 5 Monthly Graphical Displays of Book Sales
 6 Year-to-date Sales Report
 7 End-of-year Accounting Report
 8 End-of-year Graphical Displays of Book Sales
 9 List of Outstanding Accounts
```

Screen 2.24 Accessing Menus from the Primary Option Menu

Enter the ATTR command to define the parent and subpanels for the report menu in **Screen 2.25**.

Each subpanel can reference a PROGRAM screen containing a SAS program that uses any of the report-writing features of the SAS System. For example, item number 5 from the report menu is a graphical display of monthly book sales. The item corresponds to the PROGRAM screen shown in **Screen 2.26**.

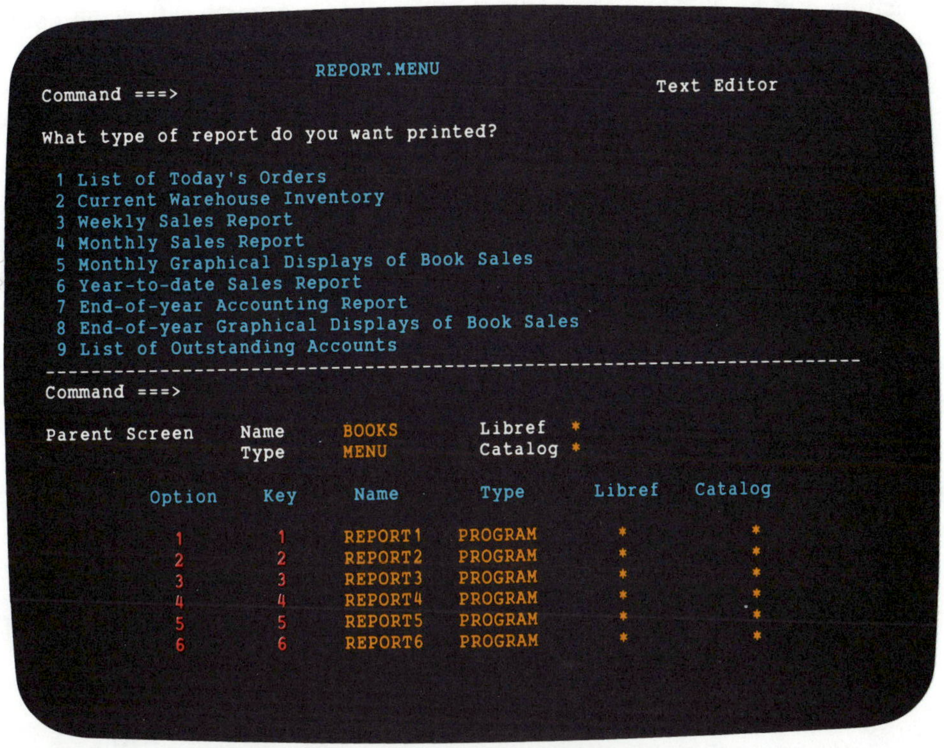

Screen 2.25 Defining the Parent Screen and Subpanels

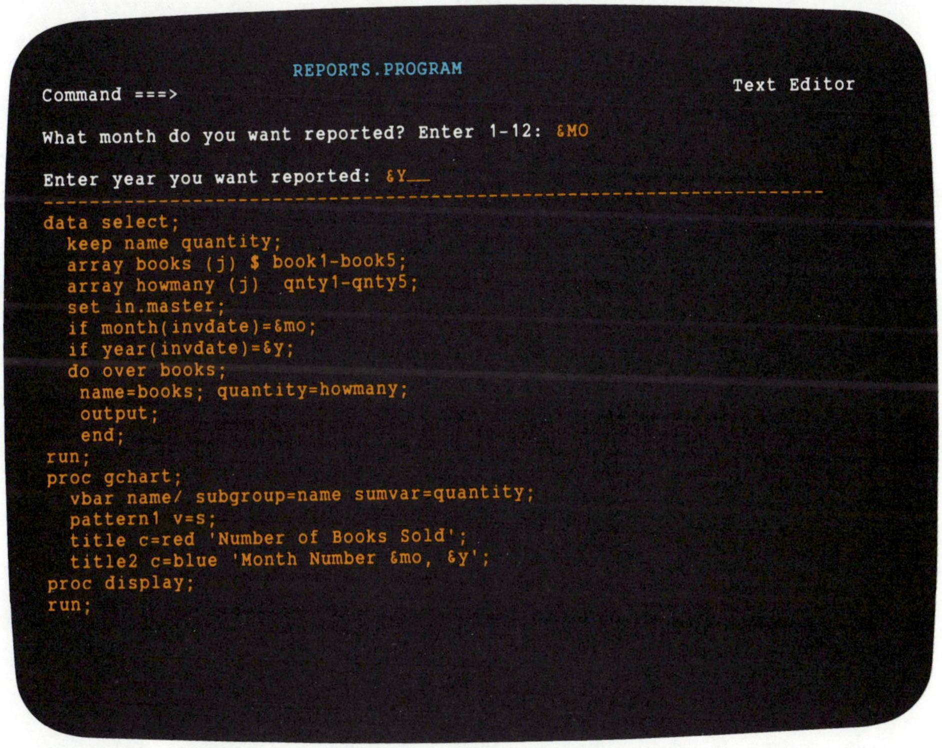

Screen 2.26 A PROGRAM Screen for Writing a Report

The program produces one simple vertical bar chart showing the number of each type of book sold during the month. The same PROGRAM screen could produce several graphs or other reports.

After you select this report and execute the program, you are returned to the primary menu to choose another task by the PROC DISPLAY statement. The statements

```
PROC DISPLAY;
RUN;
```

display the last menu seen, the next CBT frame after a branch, or the previous screen specified on a PROC statement.

Output 2.1 A Vertical Bar Chart of Sales

```
                                 BAR CHART OF SUMS
QUANTITY SUM

         |                                                       *****
         |                                                       *****
  180000 +                                                       *****
         |                   *****                               *****
         |                   *****                               *****
         |                   *****                               *****
  160000 +                   *****                               *****
         |                   *****                               *****
         |                   *****                               *****
         |                   *****                               *****
  140000 +                   *****                               *****
         |                   *****                               *****
         |       *****       *****                               *****
         |       *****       *****                               *****
  120000 +       *****       *****                               *****
         |       *****       *****                               *****
         |       *****       *****                               *****
         |       *****       *****                               *****
  100000 +       *****       *****                               *****
         |       *****       *****                               *****
         |       *****       *****                               *****
         |       *****       *****       *****                   *****
   80000 +       *****       *****       *****                   *****
         |       *****       *****       *****                   *****
         |       *****       *****       *****                   *****
         |       *****       *****       *****                   *****
   60000 +       *****       *****       *****                   *****
         |       *****       *****       *****                   *****
         |       *****       *****       *****                   *****
         |       *****       *****       *****       *****       *****
   40000 +       *****       *****       *****       *****       *****
         |       *****       *****       *****       *****       *****
         |       *****       *****       *****       *****       *****
         |       *****       *****       *****       *****       *****
   20000 +       *****       *****       *****       *****       *****
         |       *****       *****       *****       *****       *****
         |       *****       *****       *****       *****       *****
         |       *****       *****       *****       *****       *****
         ------------------------------------------------------------------

                  GR82        INTR        SLUG        ST83        UG80
```

Finishing the Book Sales System

Item 6 in the book sales system is for posting payments to the appropriate book order in the master file. This PROGRAM screen asks no questions of the user and returns no output. It executes a simple program that merges the payments with the master file. When you select item 6 from the primary menu, the program below is executed, and then you are returned to the primary menu.

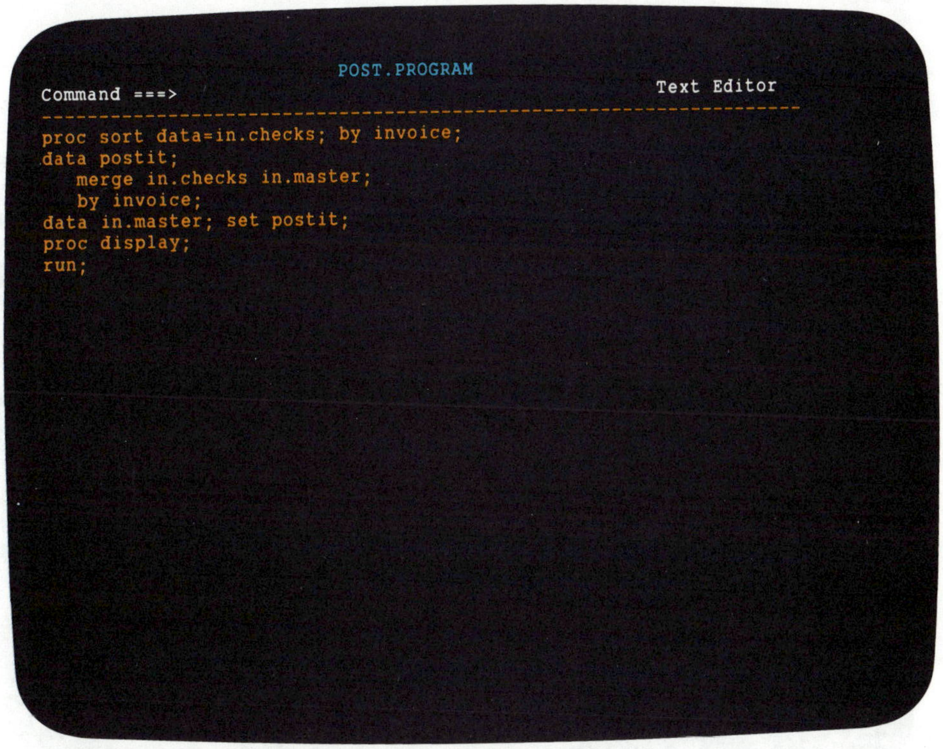

Screen 2.27 A PROGRAM Screen

USING THE BOOK SALES SYSTEM

Up to now in developing the system, you have used PROC BUILD to create screens. The rest of this chapter shows you how to use PROC DISPLAY to view the screens within the system you have designed.

A Run-through

You want access to the menu-driven system to be simple. At ACE Publishing, you log on, then enter a simple command like

```
BOOKS
```

to have the primary book sales system menu displayed on the screen.

Behind the scenes, this command represents a command procedure containing the operating system commands and SAS statements needed to reference all files and data sets, calls the SAS System, and invokes PROC DISPLAY to gain access to the book sales system.

In the PROC DISPLAY statement,

```
PROC DISPLAY CATALOG=IN.APPS.BOOKS.MENU;
```

the CATALOG= option requires a four-level name that defines the SAS catalog and screen to be accessed. When this statement is executed, the primary menu is displayed.

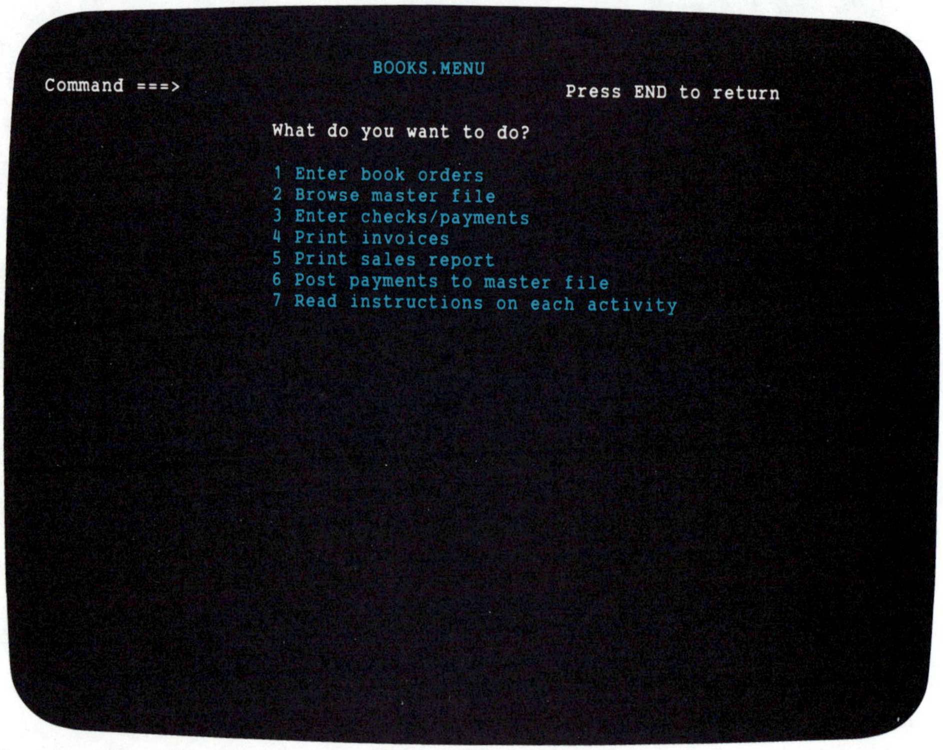

Screen 2.28 The Primary Menu from PROC DISPLAY

Enter Book Orders

To begin, you want to enter the day's book orders. On the command line, enter a 1 and press ENTER. The data entry screen for SAS data set IN.DAILY is then displayed. The screen has been modified to resemble an order form. Enter book order information on the form shown in **Screen 2.29**.

Press the FORWARD key to continue entering orders. See a description of the FSEDIT procedure in the *SAS/FSP User's Guide* for more information.

When you are ready to stop entering orders, exit from the data entry screen by pressing the END key. You are returned to the primary menu.

Now you want to credit outstanding accounts by entering the payments received today. Enter 3 on the command line and press ENTER. A data entry screen for entering payments is displayed. **Screen 2.30** is a sample entry.

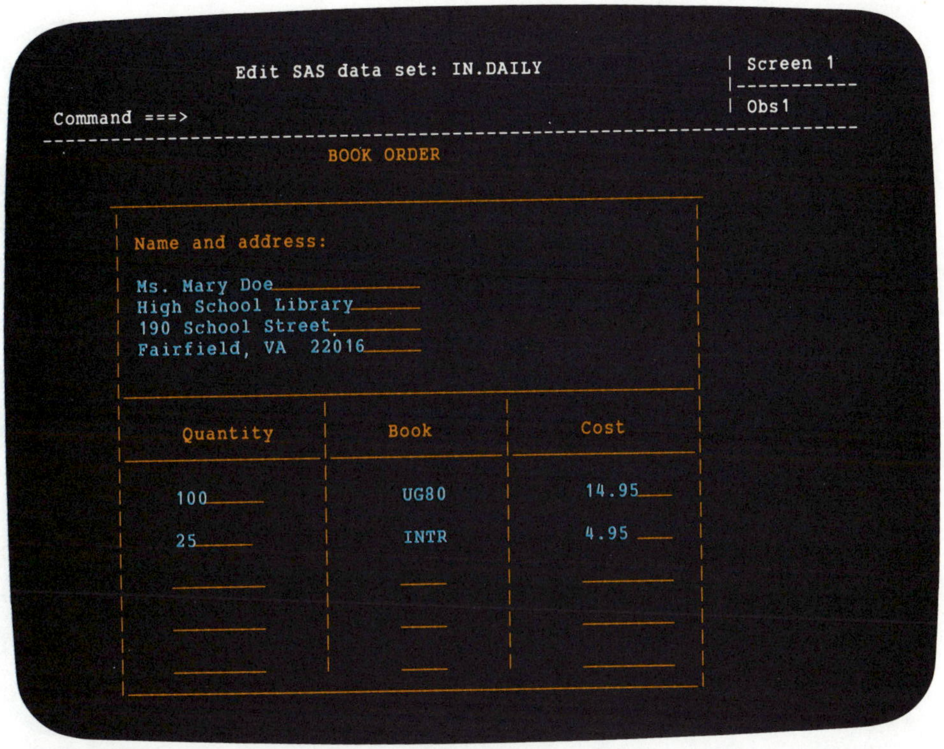

Screen 2.29 FSEDIT Screen for Data Entry

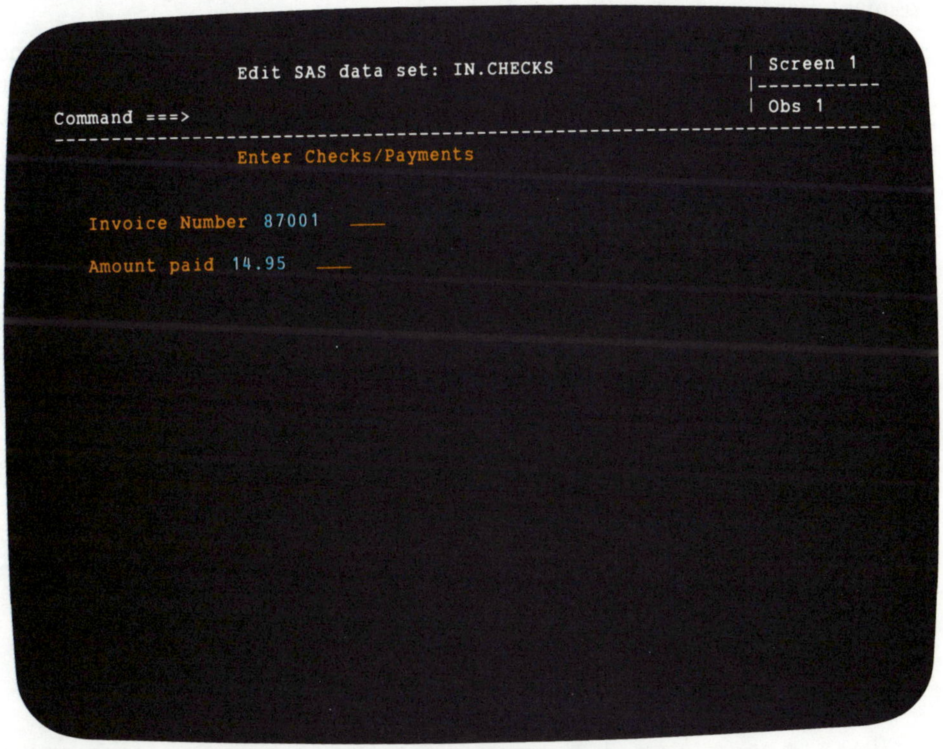

Screen 2.30 A Data Entry Screen for Entering Payments

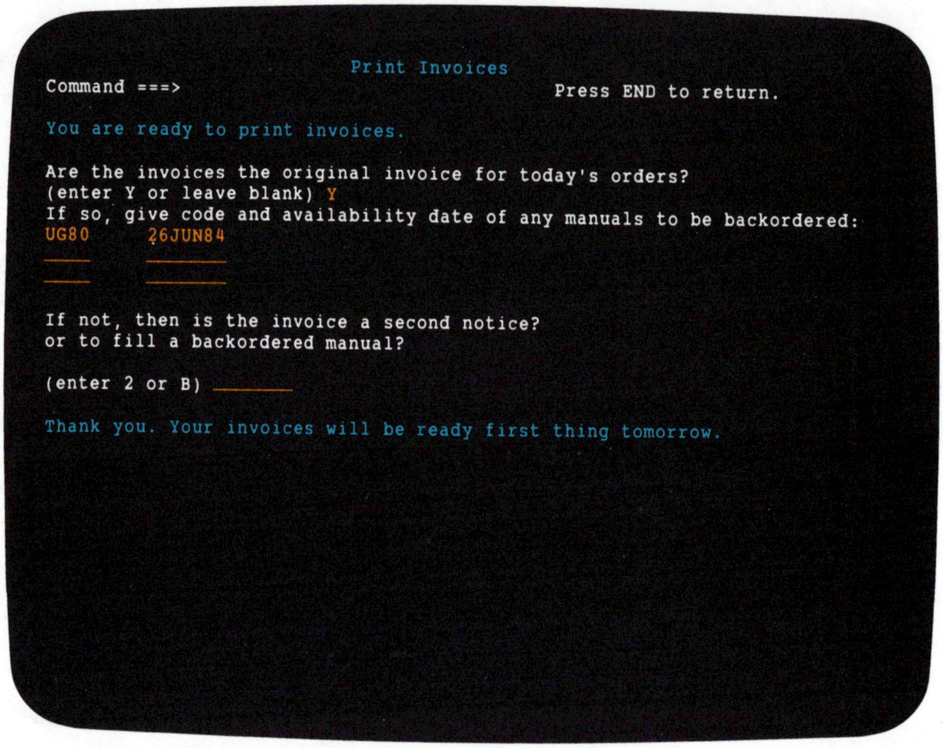

Screen 2.31 Printing Invoices

After today's checks have been recorded, press the END key to return to the primary menu.

To print invoices enter 4 on the command line and press ENTER; then respond to the questions in **Screen 2.31**. For this example, you want to print first invoices, and the *User's Guide* is to be backordered. Just enter a Y in the data entry field for &first and the backorder information.

When you press the END key, the invoice program is submitted to the SAS System; you return to the primary menu.

You may also want to post the day's checks to the master file. The SAS program to do that is submitted when you enter 6 on the command line of the master menu and press ENTER. The primary menu remains displayed.

After you have performed all daily activities or if you want to get out of the system to return later, enter END on the command line or press the END key from the master menu. This returns you to the operating system where you can logoff as usual.

Your invoices are printed and available the next day so that the order can be filled. See **Figure 2.2** for a sample invoice.

ACE Publishing Company
1134 N. Peace Street
Macon, GA 40511

```
INVOICE #90411                                  OCTOBER 2, 1984

MS. MARY DOE
HIGH SCHOOL LIBRARY
190 SCHOOL STREET
FAIRFIELD, VA  22016

Quantity            Book                  Cost            Total
-----------------------------------------------------------------

  100    User's Guide, 1980 Edition       $0.00           $0.00
   25    Introductory Guide               $4.95         $123.75

                                        AMOUNT DUE  __________
                                                        $123.75

BACKORDERED                             AVAILABLE
-----------                             ---------

User's Guide, 1980 Edition              26JUN84

    When the back ordered manuals listed above are available, we
    will place your order and you will be invoiced separately.
```

Figure 2.2 Invoice Printed Using SAS/AF Software

NOTES

1. A SAS catalog is **not** a regular SAS data set. It contains screens, not observations, and has a different format and access method from regular SAS data sets. However, it can be stored in a SAS data library along with regular SAS data sets. A catalog data set can only be processed by procedures in SAS/AF or SAS/FSP software and by base SAS software utility procedures like, CONTENTS and COPY. For more information, see the "SAS Files" chapter in the *SAS User's Guide: Basics*.

2. When you are using SAS/AF software with SAS display manager, it is a good idea to use the command DMS ON on the command line of the program screen under development with PROC BUILD. This makes it possible for display

manager to display any error messages that result when the program is executed from PROC DISPLAY.

3. The SAS program in this example may include features that are unavailable under some operating systems.

Chapter 3

The BUILD Procedure

Operating systems: All

ABSTRACT

You can use the BUILD procedure to create menu-driven, business or information processing applications or computer-based training courses. These applications are composed of screens containing help facilities, menus, subpanels, computer-based training and other educational applications, and application programs.

INTRODUCTION

PROC BUILD is used to create screens that are stored in a SAS data library. Some of the screens are used by SAS procedures; others are displayed using PROC DISPLAY. In the PROC BUILD statement, you indicate the SAS data library and the SAS catalog where you want the screens to be stored; the procedure maintains a directory of screens in the catalog.

You can create seven types of screens with the procedure. Four of the screen types are created using PROC BUILD editing commands and are displayed to the user with PROC DISPLAY:

- CBT screens are instructional material or question and answer screens for computer-based training.
- HELP screens are used to explain or clarify features of other screens.
- MENU screens provide a selection of tasks or activities. Each selection references another screen that contains HELP documentation, a SAS program, instructional material, or another menu.
- PROGRAM screens contain two sections: the top portion of the screen is an optional fill-in-the-blank section used to prompt or execute statements conditionally in the lower portion of the screen—the programming section. The programming section contains SAS statements that are submitted to the SAS System.

Three screen types are defined on pre-formatted, fill-in-the-blank screens and are used by other procedures in the SAS System:

- FORM screens specify paper, device, and destination information to be used when SAS output is routed to a printer.
- KEYS screens specify function key definitions to be used with SAS procedures.
- LIST screens contain valid values for fields in fill-in-the-blank screens, such as PROGRAM screens.

SPECIFICATIONS

The following statements can be used to invoke the BUILD procedure:

PROC BUILD *options;*
  SELECT *screens;*

PROC BUILD Statement

The form of the PROC BUILD statement is

PROC BUILD CATALOG=*SAScatalog options;*

CATALOG= **must** be specified. It gives the name of the SAS catalog where you want to enter and store new screens or edit existing screens.

As with SAS data set names, SAS catalog names are two-level names of the form

libref.catalog

where *libref* refers to the SAS data library where the catalog is stored and *catalog* identifies the specific catalog. The second level name follows the SAS naming rules except that it should not exceed seven characters. If you do not specify a two-level name, your catalog is placed in the WORK storage area and is erased at the end of your SAS session. To store your SAS catalog permanently or to use one that has been previously stored, specify a two-level name. The SAS System then knows where to look for an existing screen data set and where to store a new or edited one.

These options can appear in the PROC BUILD statement:

MERGE=*libref.catalog*
: gives the name of a SAS catalog to be copied to the catalog specified by CATALOG=.

REPLACE
: tells the procedure to replace members in the CATALOG= catalog with those of the same name in the MERGE= catalog. If REPLACE is not specified, like-named members are not replaced.

SELECT Statement

SELECT *screens;*

The two-level names of screens of the form

name.type

to be copied from the MERGE= catalog to the CATALOG= catalog are given by the SELECT statement. If the MERGE= option is specified in the PROC BUILD statement and the SELECT statement does not appear, all screens are copied. (The REPLACE option specifies that like-named members are also copied.)

CATALOG DIRECTORY

When you execute the PROC BUILD statement, the procedure displays a directory containing all screen entries in the catalog. After the command line, the directory lists the name and type of each screen in the catalog, a short description, and the date the screen was last updated. A selection field beside each entry allows you to indicate when you want to edit, browse, or rename one of the screens.

Screen 3.1 shows the format of the PROC BUILD catalog directory with some sample entries where

Name
: is up to eight characters in length including numbers, letters, and any special characters except the period (.) and semicolon (;).

Type
: is one of the screen types CBT, FORM, HELP, KEYS, LIST, MENU, or PROGRAM.

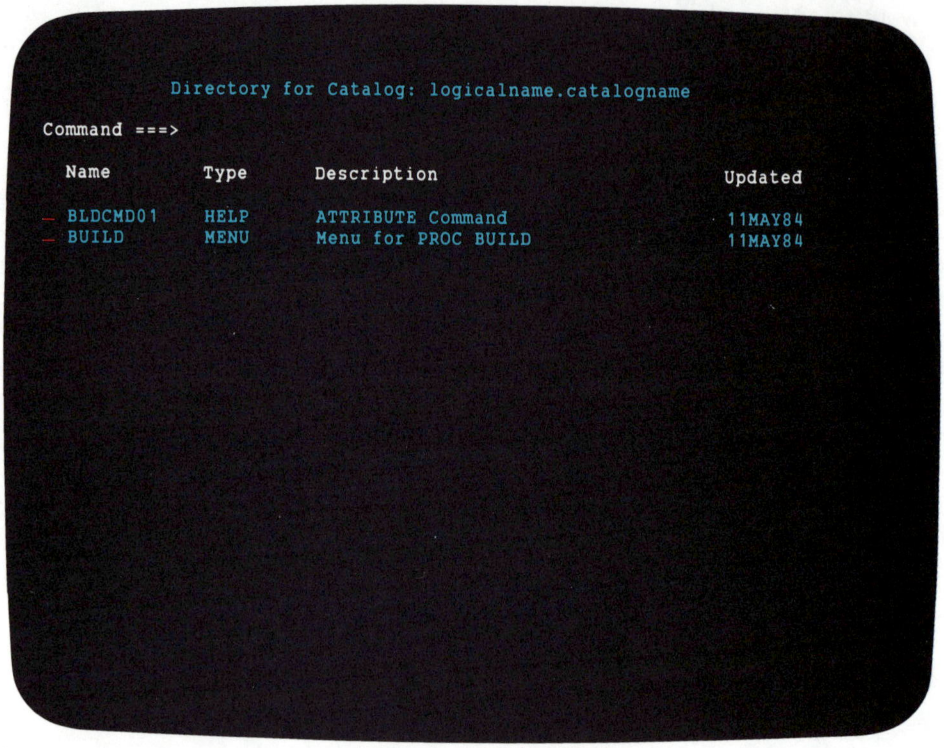

Screen 3.1 The Format of the PROC BUILD Catalog Directory

Description — is a forty-character description of the screen for CBT, HELP, MENU, and PROGRAM screens. By default, when these screens are created, the name and type appear in the description column of the screen catalog. You enter a different description while editing a screen by using the DES command on the command-line followed by up to forty-characters to describe the screen or by using the rename selection field command.

FORM and KEYS screens have no description in the catalog; for LIST screens, the description that appears is the name of the screen. The description for FORM and KEYS screens cannot be changed. You can use the rename selection field command to change LIST screen descriptions.

Updated — is the date when the screen was last modified.

Catalog Directory Commands

Command-line commands The following commands can be used on the command line of the catalog directory:

BACKWARD
: to scroll backward.

BROWSE *name.type*
to view a screen in browse mode. In browse mode, the screen displayed cannot be changed.

COPY *libref.catalog.name.type*
to copy a screen from another catalog into the current catalog.

DELETE *name.type*
to delete an entry from the catalog.

EDIT *name.type*
to display an existing screen or create a new screen in edit mode. In edit mode, changes can be executed, and the changed version can be stored.

END
to exit the catalog.

FORWARD
to scroll forward.

HELP
displays a HELP screen.

KEYS | K
displays the current function key configuration.

Selection field commands To select a screen to edit, browse, or rename, type one of the following one-letter commands in the selection field to the left of the screen name and press ENTER:

E or S	to edit a screen or any of its attributes
B	to browse a screen and any of its attributes
R	to rename an existing screen or modify its description.

CREATING SCREENS

When you enter an EDIT command on the command line or enter E or S in the selection field beside a screen in the catalog, you can create or edit any of the screen types and define their attributes. CBT, HELP, MENU, and PROGRAM screens are free-format screens with editing capabilities. FORM, KEYS, and LIST screens are described by filling in the blanks in a pre-formatted screen. These two general categories of screens are discussed separately.

Editing Screens

To create a new CBT, HELP, MENU, or PROGRAM screen, use the EDIT command. For example, if you enter the command

```
EDIT BLDCMD01.HELP
```

the screen shown in **Screen 3.2** appears.

The first time you enter an EDIT command from the catalog directory with the name and type of the screen to be created, the name and type you specify in the EDIT command appears as the description of the screen in the catalog and at the top of the screen ready for editing. You can change this description and, thus, the title of the screen using the DES command on the command line. On the command line of **Screen 3.2** if you enter the command

```
DES ATTRIBUTE Command
```

The screen shown in **Screen 3.3** appears.

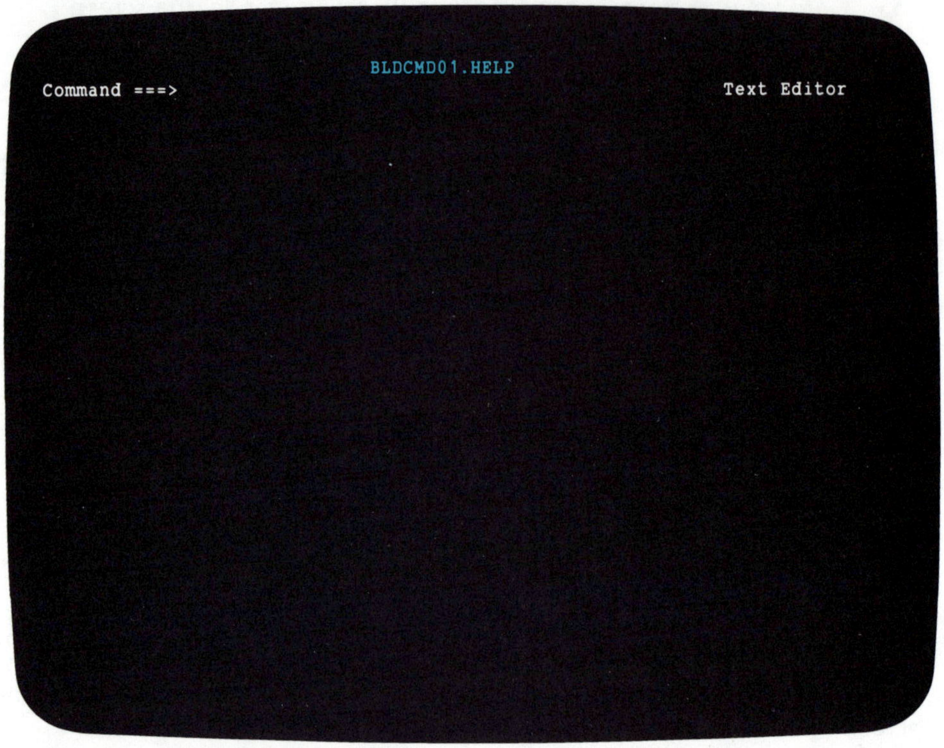

Screen 3.2 Creating a New Screen

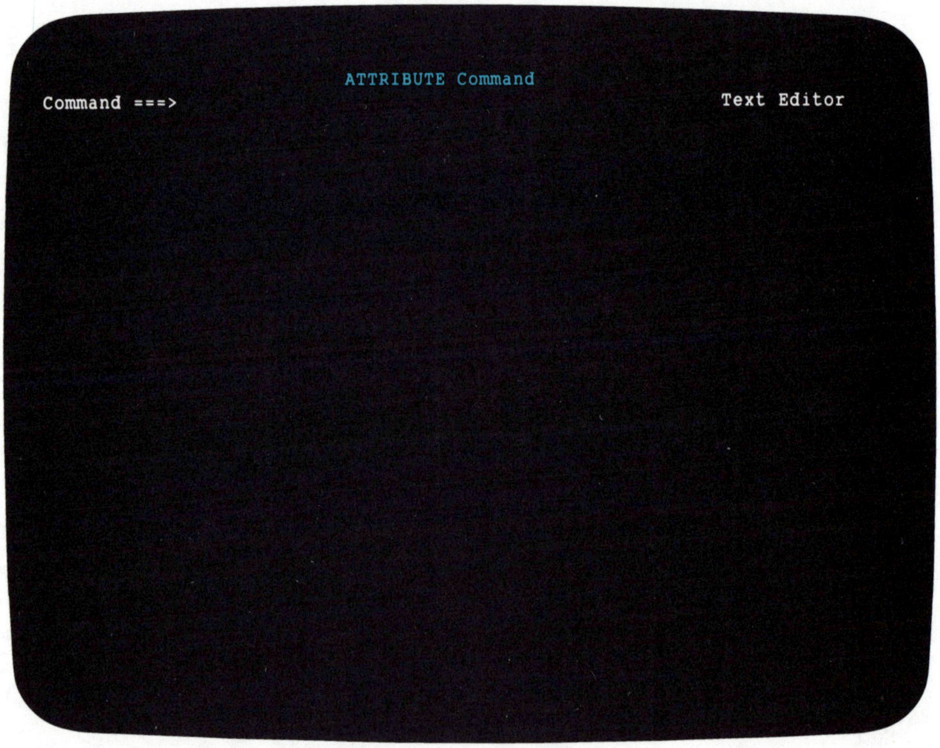

Screen 3.3 Changing the Description of the Screen

Editing Commands

The DES command is an editing command, used when creating or editing a screen. Following is a list of text editing commands that can be used on the command line when editing a new or existing screen using PROC BUILD. See the "Full-Screen Editing" appendix for a description of each command.

AUTOADD	CUNPRO	INCLUDE	TOP
BACKWARD	CURSOR	KEYS	VSCROLL
BOTTOM	DES	LEFT	
BOUNDS	END	NULLS	
CANCEL	FILL	NUMS	
CAPS	FIND	PREVCMD	
CHANGE	FORWARD	RCHANGE	
COPY	HELP	RFIND	
CPRO	HSCROLL	RIGHT	

Other text editing capabilities are available through **line commands**. When you use the NUMS command to generate line numbers in the first six columns of each screen line, you can type line commands over these numbers for additional editing. See the "Full-Screen Editing" appendix for more information.

The following commands are also available while editing a single screen in PROC BUILD:

ATTR
: displays a screen's attributes. The information you specify in the attributes panel is saved with the screen. You can change information in the attributes panel at any time.

  You can control where the screen splits when the attributes panel is displayed by moving the cursor to the location on the screen where you want the split to occur before you press ENTER or by positioning the cursor and then pressing the ATTR function key. Otherwise, the attributes panel occupies the entire display area, masking all of the current screen from view.

BROWSE *name.type*
: opens another screen in browse mode. In browse mode, the screen displayed cannot be changed.

  When you are browsing, all command-line commands are available to you except those that alter or store text. For example, you can scroll, change colors, view the attribute screen, search for character strings, and enter host-level commands with the X command. See **Multiple Screens**, below.

DMS OFF | ON
: allows you to view the log screen of display manager when a job is submitted to the SAS System from a PROGRAM screen through PROC DISPLAY. Use the DMS ON command when building a PROGRAM screen in PROC BUILD. Executing DMS ON is useful for debugging purposes when you are executing program screens under PROC DISPLAY. The default is DMS OFF.

EDIT *name.type*
displays an existing screen or creates a new screen in edit mode. In edit mode, changes can be executed, and the changed version can be stored. See **Multiple Screens**, below.

HELPNAME *name.type*
specifies a screen in the same catalog that contains help information for the screen you are building. When this screen is viewed with PROC DISPLAY, the screen specified with the HELPNAME command is displayed whenever the HELP key is pressed or the HELP command is issued.

Note: you use the HELPNAME command to designate a HELP screen for another screen when you are building screens with PROC BUILD, but the HELPNAME command has no effect until the screen is displayed with PROC DISPLAY.

SAVE *name.type*
saves the contents of a screen without exiting from that screen. (The END command saves the screen and returns you to the catalog directory.)

If you anticipate a long session in one screen, enter the SAVE command occasionally to prevent losing all of your entered data and changes if the system goes down.

Screen Attributes

When you use the ATTR command to display the attributes of the screen you are creating, the format of the display depends on the type of screen you are creating. For example, a HELP screen's only attributes are the name and type of its parent screen. A MENU screen's attributes are its parent screen and any subpanels, which are also other screens. A CBT screen's attributes are its parent screen and one child screen. A PROGRAM screen's attributes are the attributes of any user fields in the program.

Commands on the attributes display Some text-editing commands are available when you are creating or changing the attributes of a screen. These commands are listed below and are described in the "Full-Screen Editing" appendix.

BACKWARD
CANCEL
END
FORWARD
HELP

In addition, these commands can be used on the command line of the attribute panel:

DUPLICATE is used on the attribute panel of a PROGRAM screen to duplicate in another field a field value that you designate with the SELECT command. The SELECT and DUPLICATE commands are designed to be used as function keys. Place the cursor on the field value you want to be duplicated and press the SELECT key. Then position the cursor on the field where you want that value duplicated and press the DUPLICATE key.

KEYFIELD is used on the attribute panel to designate the field whose value you want to search for with the LOCATE and NEXT commands. The KEYFIELD command is designed to be used as a function key. Place the cursor on the appropriate field and press the KEYFIELD key. Then use the LOCATE command to designate the value you are searching for, and use the NEXT command to find the next occurrence of that field value. See the LOCATE and NEXT commands.

LOCATE
: is used on certain attribute panels to find a keyfield by specifying its field name. For example, in the attribute screen of a program or system screen, you can specify a LOCATE command in the form

  LOCATE *keyfieldname*

  such as

```
LOCATE FIELD1
```

  The cursor moves to the field entry area of FIELD1.

NEXT
: is used on the attribute panel to find the next occurrence of a user field of the same type. The NEXT command is designed to be assigned to a function key. Position the cursor on a user field and press the NEXT function key; the cursor moves to the next occurrence of the same user field.

SELECT
: is used on the attribute panel to designate a field value that you want to be duplicated in another field. The SELECT and DUPLICATE commands are designed to be used as function keys. Place the cursor on the field value you want to be duplicated and press the SELECT key. Then position the cursor on the field where you want that value duplicated and press the DUPLICATE key.

Multiple Screens

Within PROC BUILD, you can edit multiple screens or their attributes that are in the same catalog at the same time. The active screen is the one the cursor is on.

Opening another screen You can have more than one screen of your SAS catalog open at one time for editing or browsing. Enter the EDIT or BROWSE command from the command line of an edit screen. If you type

```
EDIT name.type
```

on the command line and press ENTER, the new screen is displayed over the screen you were editing.

If you move the cursor from the command line and position it elsewhere on the screen before pressing ENTER, the screen splits and the new screen is displayed at the cursor location. This gives you two screens sharing the display area.

If you enter

```
EDIT
```

and press ENTER without specifying a screen in the SAS catalog, the catalog directory appears, and you can place an S in the selection field of the screen you want to edit. The screen you choose appears on the screen. The first screen you were editing is still open; it is simply masked by the second screen you called. If the new screen is overlaid on the old screen, you can jump between the two screens using the JUMP command described below.

You can have many screens open at one time, either by splitting the screen and having several screens share the display area or by allowing the active screen to occupy the full screen and mask the presence of the other members. See **Managing multiple-screen display** for a discussion on managing a multiple screen session.

Commands for multiple screens The following commands can be used to manipulate and move between multiple screens. The commands can be entered on the command line of a screen being edited or its attribute display, or the commands can be assigned to function keys.

JUMP [UP | DOWN]
: is used when editing multiple screens in order to move to a screen "behind" or "in front of" the screen currently occupying the display area. When more than two screens are open at one time, you can specify UP or DOWN to indicate which screen you want to bring to the display area.

SPLIT [UP | DOWN]
: is used to designate where you want the split between multiple screens to occur. Enter the SPLIT command and place the cursor where you want the split to occur before pressing ENTER, or position the cursor and press the SPLIT function key.

SWAP [UP | DOWN]
: is used when you split your screen into multiple panels to move the cursor from one screen to the command line of another screen. You can execute the SWAP command from the command line or with a function key assigned to execute the SWAP command.

ZOOM
: is used when you split the screen into multiple panels to make one panel fill the entire screen, masking the presence of the other screens. Enter the ZOOM command again to return the enlarged panel to its original size and position on the screen.

Moving the cursor When you have several screens displayed at the same time, you can move the cursor between them using the cursor movement keys or the SWAP command. Use the UP or DOWN option on the SWAP command to move the cursor to the screen "above" or "below" the currently active screen.

Changing the location of the split For convenience in viewing and editing, you may alter the location of the split in the display area. Two or more screens can divide the display area, or each can occupy the entire display area, one masking the presence of the other. To alter the location of the split, use the SPLIT, SPLIT UP, or SPLIT DOWN command. You can use SPLIT alone if there are only two screens. You must specify UP or DOWN if more than two windows are displayed on the screen. Then position the cursor where you want the split to occur before pressing ENTER or the SPLIT key.

Managing multiple-screen display When two or more screens share the display area, you may find it more convenient to allow one screen to occupy the entire display area, masking the presence of the other windows. Use the ZOOM command to bring one of the screens to the entire display.

You can visualize the way open screens are viewed and accessed by imagining a file cabinet containing several drawers. Each drawer represents a screen. The files in each drawer represent other screens behind the first screen in the drawer.

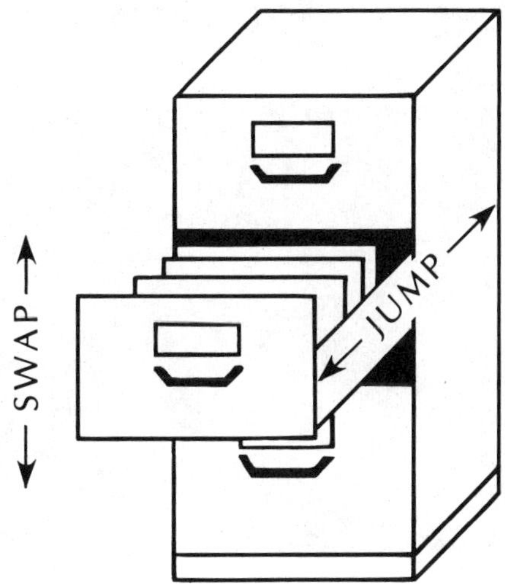

Figure 3.1 Managing Multiple Screens

You make more than one drawer visible on the screen using the SPLIT command to add another drawer. You move among drawers displayed using the SWAP command or key. The SWAP command is for moving among screens in a vertical direction.

To have a single drawer fill the entire display, use the ZOOM command. To move among files in a single drawer, use the JUMP command. The JUMP command moves among screens in a horizontal direction.

Building HELP Screens

HELP screens consist of text and are used to document or clarify features in other screens. For example, the HELP screen shown in **Screen 3.4** explains the ATTRIBUTE command.

If you access a HELP screen from a MENU or CBT screen or from the PROC DISPLAY statement, the HELP screen's parent screen determines the next screen the system accesses when you exit from the HELP screen. To specify a parent panel, enter ATTR on the command line from the HELP screen you are building and press ENTER. A panel for naming the parent screen is displayed (**Screen 3.5**). The asterisk (*) beside Libref and Catalog indicates that the parent screen resides in the same catalog as the current panel. Enter the name and type of the parent screen in the blanks provided. For example, if you want the user to return to the menu screen named BUILD after exiting from the HELP screen above, enter BUILD and MENU in the spaces provided.

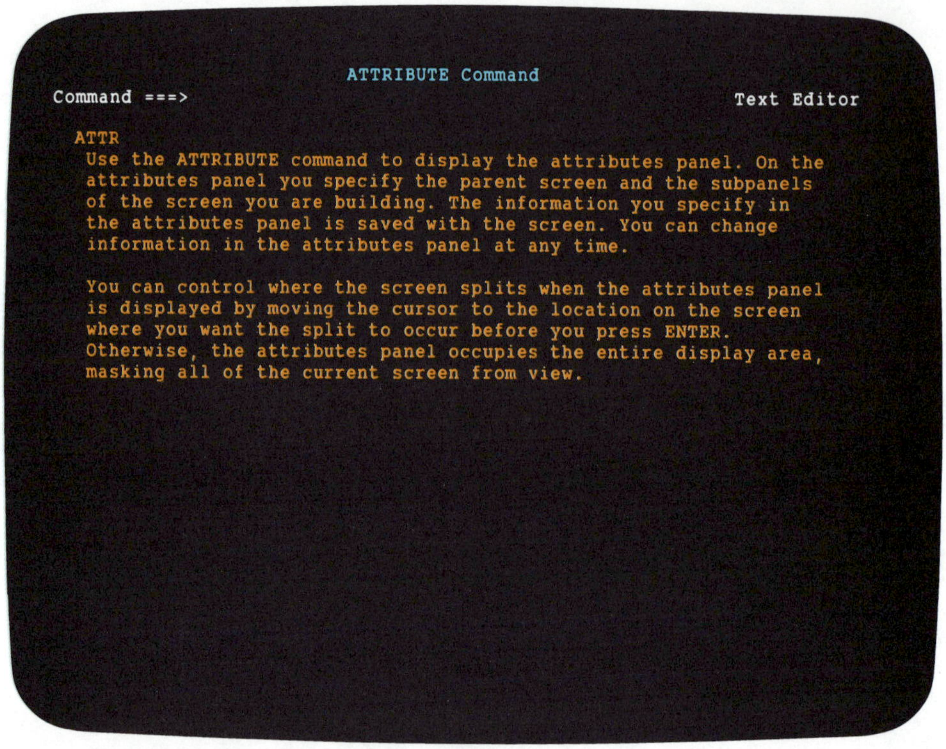

Screen 3.4 A HELP Screen

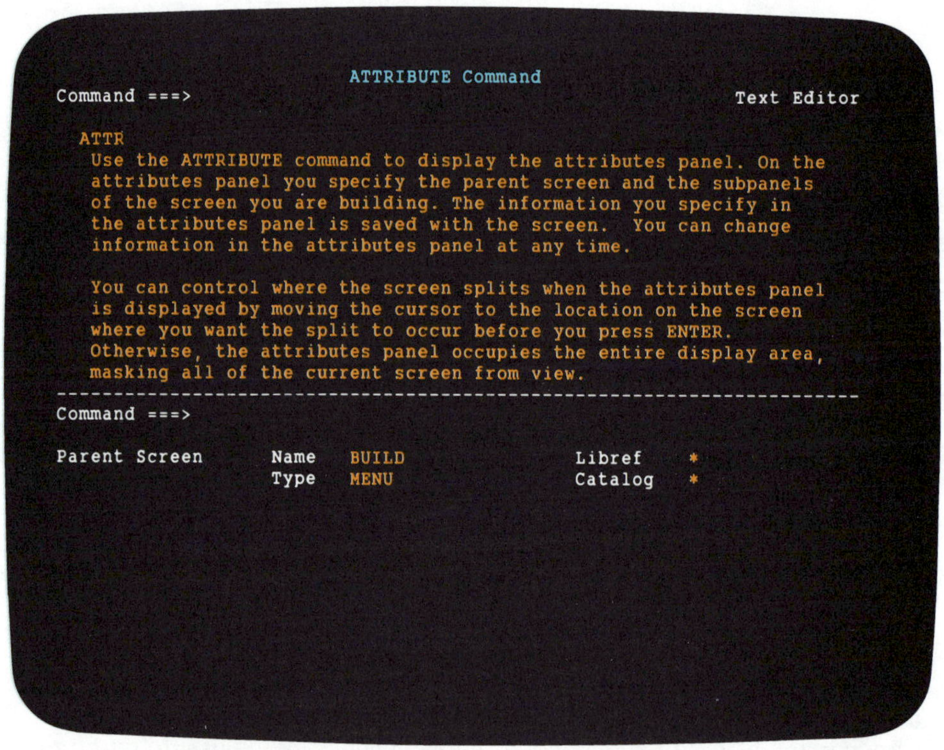

Screen 3.5 Specifying the Parent Screen

Building MENU Screens

MENU screens provide a selection of activities. They are usually used to simplify an end-user application. For example, suppose you want to build a MENU screen from which the bookkeeping staff can select jobs. Such a MENU screen is shown in **Screen 3.6**.

Each item in the list corresponds to a path of screens that allow the user to perform various activities. The path is made up of subpanels defined using ATTR in **Screen 3.7**. To specify subpanels and a parent screen, enter the command ATTR on the command line and press ENTER. In **Screen 3.7**, enter the option number or character from the MENU screen, any function key alias, and the name and type of the screen you want displayed to the user when that item is selected from the menu. If the menu contains alphabetic selections rather than numbers, the attribute panel should use the corresponding letter. Type the character of the menu item over the number in the Option column on the attribute panel. Any function key definitions that you specify on this screen automatically override any default or previously defined function key settings in effect.

In this example, you can choose "Pay bills" from the menu by entering a 1 on the command line or by pressing function key 13. The menu has no parent. Function keys 13 through 17, respectively, are set up to call the five subpanels. Note that subpanels can be CBT, HELP, MENU, or PROGRAM screens.

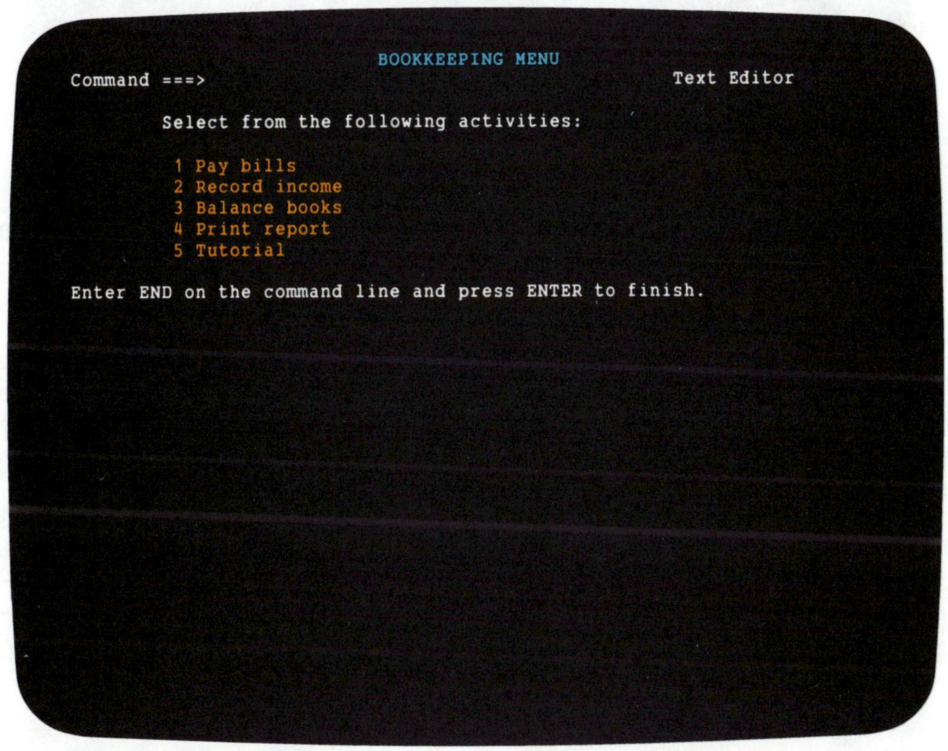

Screen 3.6 A MENU Screen

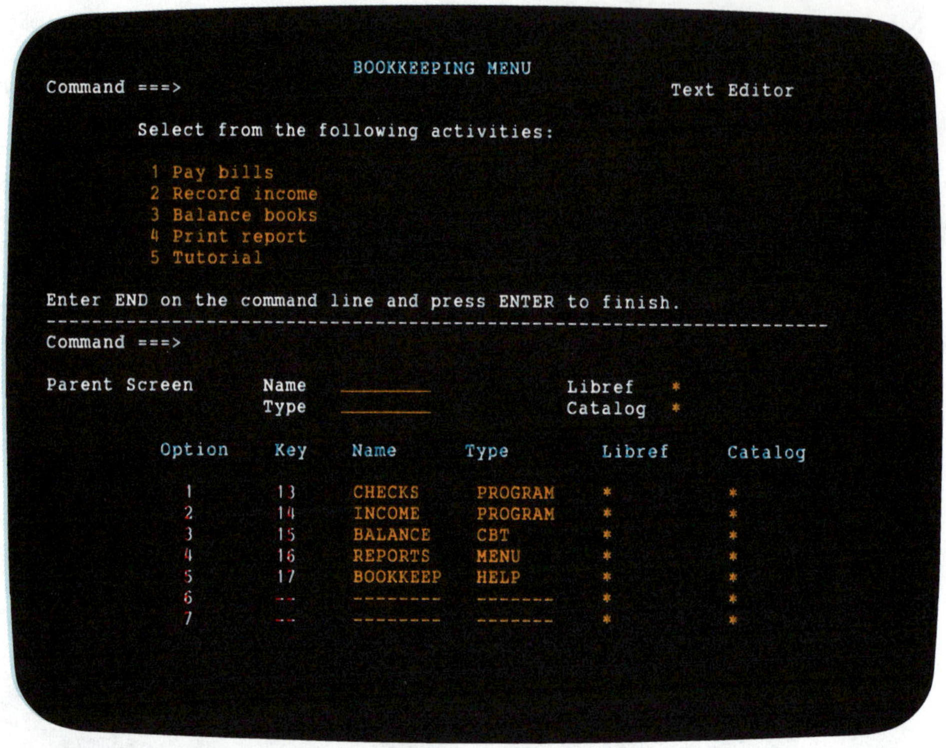

Screen 3.7 MENU Screen Attributes

Building PROGRAM Screens

PROGRAM screens have two sections. The top portion is optional. If present, it consists of text and blanks to be filled in; they are displayed by PROC DISPLAY. The user supplies responses to the blanks. These responses are then supplied to the bottom portion of the screen, and SAS code is generated and submitted to the SAS System for processing. The two portions of the screen are divided by a dashed line. Only the top portion is displayed with PROC DISPLAY. If there are no user fields, nothing is displayed, and the SAS code is automatically pushed to the SAS System. (See the Protect attribute below for a way to display text when no user input is needed.)

Screen 3.8 is a sample PROGRAM screen named PRINT.PROGRAM that prints the observations in a SAS data set. The ampersand (&) indicates the start of an unprotected user field. The dashed line marks the end of the fill-in-the-blank portion of the screen and the start of the SAS program that is submitted to the SAS System when the user enters END on the command line from PROC DISPLAY.

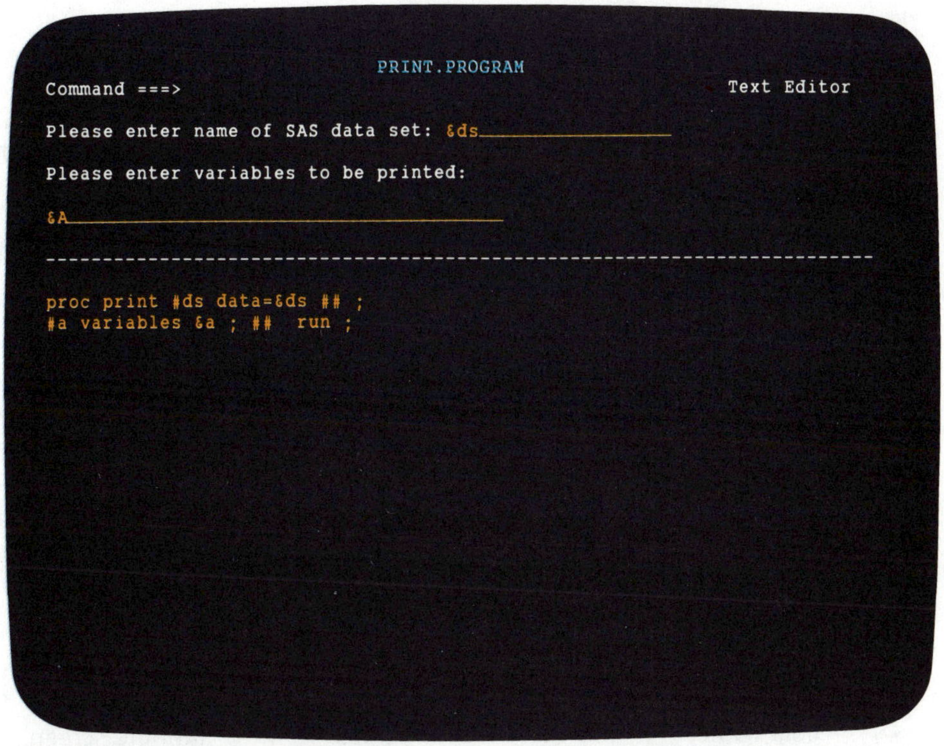

Screen 3.8 A Sample PROGRAM Screen in PROC BUILD

From PROC DISPLAY, **Screen 3.9** shows how the screen PRINT.PROGRAM appears.

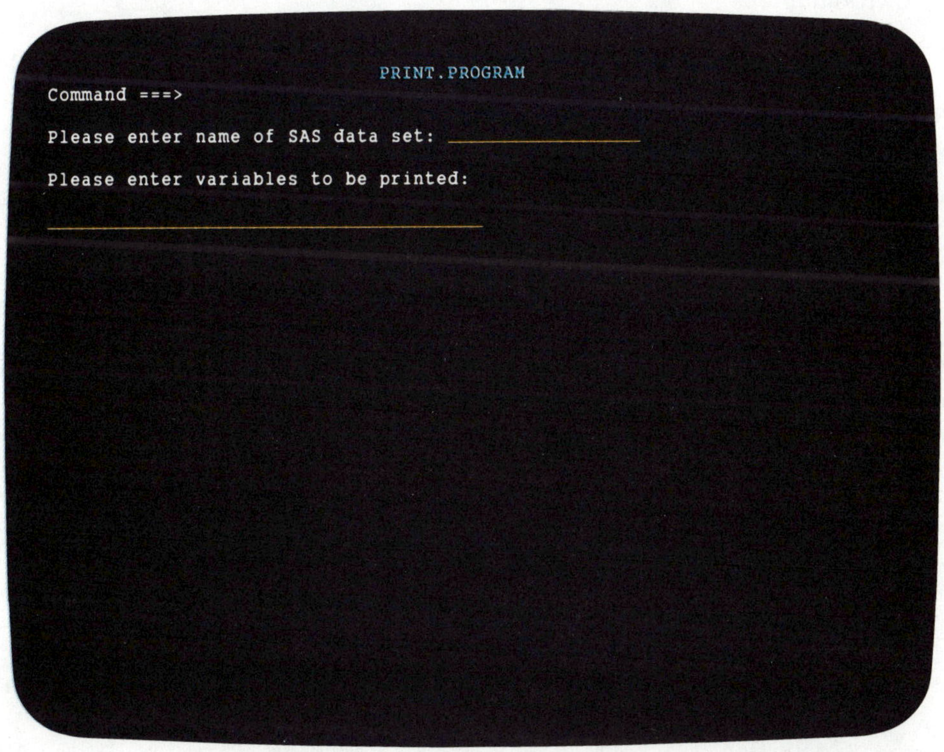

Screen 3.9 A Sample PROGRAM Screen Viewed from PROC DISPLAY

User Field Portion

The top portion of the screen contains text, questions, and user fields. In this portion of the screen, you can control what is displayed to the user by entering three not signs (¬¬¬) in columns 1-3. This indicator tells the system that text above the ¬¬¬ should remain displayed even if scrolling is necessary. Thus, if the user field portion of the PROGRAM screen must be scrolled in order to view it all, anything above the ¬¬¬ always remains displayed.

Each user field has a unique name associated with it. In **Screen 3.8** the two fields have the names DS and A. If no name is given, then the system assigns default names of FIELD*n* where *n* is the *n*th user field on the screen.

Field Attributes

Each user field in the top portion of a PROGRAM screen has associated with it several field attributes. These attributes are defined on the attribute definition panel that is displayed when you specify the ATTR command from the PROGRAM screen. Following is a list of the attributes for each user field in a PROGRAM screen:

Field Name
: can be up to eight characters in length. You specify the name in the top portion of the screen as &name followed by as many underscores as necessary. If the & is not followed by a name, the system assigns a name of the form FIELD*n* where *n* represents the *n*th field listed on the screen. Do **NOT** use FIELD as a prefix to the field name. This field cannot be modified from the attribute screen.

Length
: is the length of the field and is the number of characters on the screen including the ampersand, the field name, and any underscores. This field cannot be modified from the attribute screen.

Row,Column
: is the row and column of the screen on which the field (the ampersand) starts. This field cannot be modified from the attribute screen.

Type
: is the type of each field. Each field can be one of the following types:

  NAME
  : is any valid SAS name.

  NUM
  : is a standard SAS numeric field.

  CHAR
  : is a standard SAS character field.

  FIXED
  : is a field in which you can enter only integer numeric values.

  ACTION
  : is a one-character field that can accept either a blank or nonblank value. Any nonblank value typed into this field is automatically converted to an uppercase X. Any field that is one character in length (only an & appears for the field on the user-entry screen) is by default named FIELD*n* and assumed to be of type ACTION.

  INPUT
  : is a field containing any valid name of an existing SAS data set.

VARLIST | VARLISTN | VARLISTC
: is a field containing SAS variables; it can be a single variable or one or more variables used in an assignment statement. VARLIST means variables can be character or numeric; VARLISTN means variables are numeric; VARLISTC means variables are character. (See the List attribute, below.)

  You can enter anything in a VARLIST, VARLISTN, or VARLISTC field and only valid SAS names are validated. For example, if the user enters

```
(X+Y)*Z
```

in the field, the variables X, Y and Z are validated.

Caps
: allows you to enter an X to translate to uppercase all characters typed into this field by the user.

Just
: allows you to specify an alignment of the field to be used when the entry is displayed. Specify L for left aligned, R for right aligned, and C for centered. If left blank, the field is displayed as entered.

Pad
: causes any character specified to be used to fill the field on the screen when the user leaves the field blank.

Protect
: allows you to enter an X to protect the field. The field appears on the screen, but nothing can be entered by the user. The Protect attribute (usually with a blank as pad character) can be used for a "dummy" user field when no input is needed from the user but you want some text to be displayed when the PROGRAM screen is accessed.

Non-display
: keeps the field from being displayed to the user. For example, a field containing passwords may use the Non-display option to prevent the field from appearing on the screen.

Format
: allows you to specify any valid SAS format to be used to display the user's field entry. Defaults are standard SAS format defaults.

Informat
: allows you to specify any valid SAS informat to be used by the system to read a user field entry. Defaults are standard SAS informat defaults.

Required
: allows you to enter an X to require the user to give a response for this field.

List
: indicates a list of valid values for the field. Use one of these methods to indicate a valid list of values:

  - Specify the list of valid values separated by blanks; for example, A B C.

- Specify a range by entering the character < followed by the range; for example, < 10 100.
- Specify an equal sign (=) followed by the name of the LIST screen that contains the list of valid values if the list of valid values is longer than forty characters. The SAS System automatically looks in that list when checking for valid values for that field. See the LIST screen description, below, for more details; for example, = XYZ1.

If the type attribute for the field is VARLIST, VARLISTN, or VARLISTC, then the list attribute can specify the name of a SAS data set that contains the variables specified in the variable list field. The data sets can be listed in one of these ways:

@ fieldname1
fieldname2
fieldname3...

means that each variable specified in the variable list field must be in at least one of the data sets whose names are given by *fieldname1*, *fieldname2*, or *fieldname3*, where *fieldname* is another user field on the PROGRAM screen of type INPUT.

fieldname1
fieldname2
fieldname3...

means that each variable in the variable list field must be in **all** of the data sets referenced by INPUT user fields *fieldname1*, *fieldname2*, and *fieldname3*.

* *libref.*
SASdataset

means that each variable specified in the variable list field must be in data set *libref.SASdataset*, a valid SAS data set.

If the list attribute is left blank, then no validation is done on the variables in the variable list field.

Help

allows you to specify the name of the HELP or MENU screen that you want displayed when the user positions the cursor on the field and presses the HELP function key. If none is specified, then the HELP specified with the HELPNAME command is displayed. The screen specified must be in the current catalog.

Associated SAS Macro Variable

allows you to give the name of a SAS macro variable, and the value specified in the user field is automatically associated with that macro variable. This feature allows you to save code and values across steps in a SAS job; the system remembers these saved values even after the SAS program below the dashed line in the PROGRAM screen has been submitted to the SAS System. When the PROGRAM screen is displayed, the value of this macro variable appears in the user field.

Program Portion

All PROGRAM screens must have a dashed line followed by some SAS statements. It is not necessary to have fill-in-the-blank areas on a PROGRAM screen. If no user input is required in order to generate statements, PROC DISPLAY generates the statements below the dashed line and submits them to the SAS System when the user requests the PROGRAM screen.

Conditional Statement Execution

In **Screen 3.8** notice below the dashed line that the statements include single and double pound signs (# and ##) sometimes followed by a field name. When #*fieldname* appears, the code after it is generated only if the user enters something in the field. The string of submitted SAS code ends at either another # or ##. A ## followed by at least one blank indicates an unconditional generation, and it is used to end the effect of a #*fieldname* or ##*fieldname* control. Note that at least one blank must precede and follow each ##, #*fieldname*, and ##*fieldname* specification. See **Table 3.1** for other possibilities.

You can precede #*fieldname* or ##*fieldname* with a not sign (¬) to indicate that the subsequent string should be executed only if the corresponding field is left blank.

Table 3.1 Conditional Statement Indicators

Indicator	Use
##*fieldname*	Submit what follows if *fieldname* is not blank.
¬##*fieldname*	Submit what follows if *fieldname* is blank.
#*fieldname*	Submit what follows if *fieldname* is not blank and a prior *fieldname* or ¬##*fieldname* has not suppressed code submission.
¬#*fieldname*	Submit what follows if *fieldname* is blank and a prior ##*fieldname* or ¬##*fieldname* has not suppressed code submission.
##	Submit what follows unconditionally.

The double pound sign indicator, ##*fieldname*, is a higher level of conditional execution that allows you to nest conditional execution indicators. When ##*fieldname* appears, it ends the effect of a #*fieldname*. However, if ##*fieldname1* is followed in the program by #*fieldname2*, #*fieldname2* is ignored if the user field *fieldname* was left blank unless a ## had ended the effect of ##*fieldname1*. (See the chapter "A Menu-Driven Application" for an example using both levels of conditional execution.)

In **Screen 3.8**, if the user enters SAS data set name MY.MAYDATA and variables NAME ID SALARY in the screen in the appropriate fields:

```
Please enter name of SAS data set: MY.MAYDATA________

Please enter variables to be printed:

NAME ID SALARY____________________________________
```

then the following SAS code is generated and passed to the SAS System for execution:

```
proc print data=my.maydata;
   variables name id salary;
run;
```

If the user enters the data set name but the variable list is left blank, then the statements

```
proc print data=my.maydata;
run;
```

are sent to the SAS System for execution. By default, the PRINT procedure prints all variables in the data set when no VARIABLES statement appears.

Output from the procedure is displayed at the screen. You may want to leave the user in SAS display manager, or you can add PROC DISPLAY and RUN statements to the program to invoke display of another screen.

Validation of variables The PROGRAM screen above contains examples of INPUT and VARLIST field types. Since the value to be entered for user field &DS is the name of a SAS data set, specify that field is of type INPUT. User field &A requires a list of numeric and character variables; this field is of type VARLIST.

The attribute panel for this PROGRAM screen is shown in **Screen 3.10**.

Note that user field &A of type VARLIST has list attribute DS. This tells SAS/AF to verify that values entered for the VARLIST field &A are in the SAS data set named in user field &DS.

The system checks SAS data set MY.MAYDATA to verify that variables NAME, ID, and SALARY exist in the data set. This checking is done when the values are entered by the user, before any statements are submitted to the SAS System.

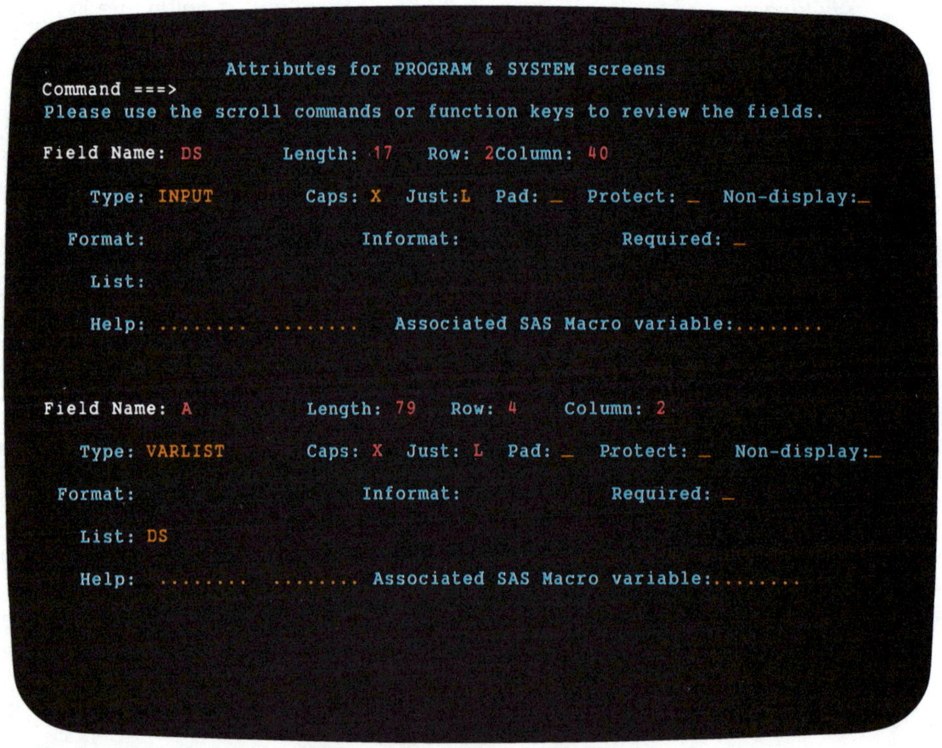

Screen 3.10 Attribute Panel for Sample PROGRAM Screen

Building CBT Screens

A screen of type CBT is a series of frames corresponding to a lesson or portion of a lesson. The screen consists of text and multiple-choice or true-false questions to be answered by the student.

Each frame of a screen corresponds to a single point to be discussed or a single question. A frame can contain up to 600 lines of text, text and a question, or just a question. A frame can also define a screen to branch to, possibly returning to the point following the branch in the lesson. No more than one question can be entered on a frame. You tell the system the correct answer to the question, the number of tries allowed for the student to get the right answer, and the feedback or screen that should be displayed when the student selects each possible answer.

A frame may be larger than what can be physically displayed on a screen at one time. The system displays to the student the portion of the frame that fits on the screen, or you can tell the system to pause at certain points within the frame. When the student presses the ENTER key, the section up to the next pause is displayed.

Below is a sample CBT screen of one frame that includes text and a question.

Frames A frame is defined to the system in one of two ways. If the frame contains only text, the first line should be a dashed line, the full width of the screen. If the frame contains a question, the first line **must** contain a question mark in column 1.

Questions Since the frame in the example above contains a question, enter a question mark (?) in column 1 of the line. Follow the question mark with the number of tries you want a student to have to get the correct answer.

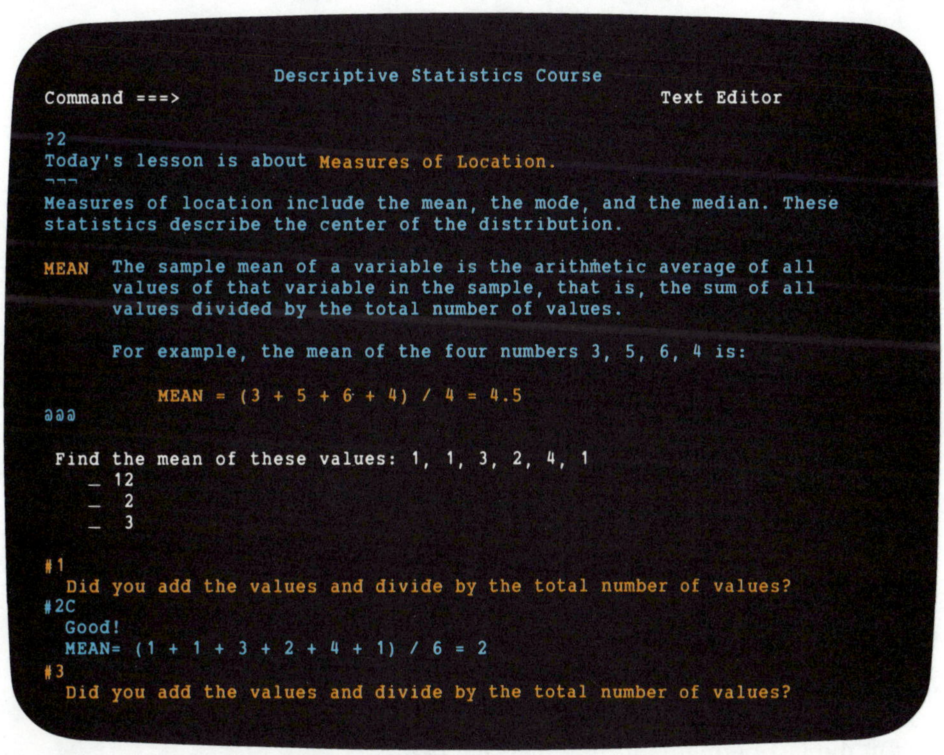

Screen 3.11 A Sample CBT Screen

Displayed text Follow the frame indicator with any text you want to appear. The three not signs (¬¬¬) in columns 1-3 immediately after the first line of text tell the system not to scroll any of the lines above the ¬¬¬. Thus, even though the frame may be scrolled to fit the screen, the line

```
Today's lesson is about Measures of Location.
```

always appears. (This feature is also available on the upper portion of PROGRAM screens.)

The three at-signs (@@@) in columns 1-3 midway down the frame tell the system to pause. The text on the line with the @@@ and all lines above it are shown when the student starts viewing the frame. The student presses ENTER to view the remainder of the frame (or down to the next pause indicator).

Answers Questions are multiple-choice or true-false with two to eight possible answers. Preceding each possible answer on the screen, enter an underscore (_). To the system the possible answers are numbered sequentially.

Feedback text For each possible answer, you can write text to be displayed as feedback when the student chooses the corresponding answer. On the line preceding the feedback text for each answer, enter a pound sign (#) in column 1 followed by the question number. Follow the question number of the correct answer with a capital C.

Feedback text for the correct answer has two parts: the first line is the congratulatory text; the remaining line is other feedback. When the student selects the correct answer, the line of text immediately following the #, question number, and capital C, is displayed with the other feedback. When the system shows the correct answer (after a student has exhausted all tries) or when the student backs up to the question after the correct answer has been indicated, the congratulatory first line is not displayed.

For example,

```
#1C
Very good!
The mean for these data is calculated as
(10 + 20 + 15)=45/3=15.
```

The line

```
Very good!
```

is only displayed when the student chooses this answer within the allotted number of tries. (All other feedback is also displayed.)

This optional line of feedback can be left blank, and the same feedback is displayed every time. In this case, begin the feedback text in the second line following the #.

The system generates a default message each time the student selects an answer. Your text is displayed with the system-generated text. For example, when the student selects a wrong answer and you have specified that more than one try is allowed, the message

```
your message here.

Press ENTER to erase old answer and try again...
```

is displayed.

On the last permitted try the message reads:

```
your message here.
```

```
Press ENTER for correct answer...
```

When the student presses ENTER, the correct answer is marked, and the second and later lines of feedback text are displayed.

If only one try is allowed, the message reads:

```
your message here.

Press ENTER to continue.
```

The correct answer is not given. When the student selects the correct answer, the following message appears

```
your complete message here.
```

Individualized instruction For optional or remedial instruction, the feedback text can be another screen. In this case, you indicate the screen name and type following a greater-than sign (>) in or after column 4 of the answer indicator line (after the capital letter C if it is the correct answer). For example, if you want the feedback text for question number 3 in the above example to be a HELP screen, say MEAN.HELP, then the answer indicator line would look like this:

```
#3 > MEAN.HELP
```

No feedback text is entered since if the user specifies answer #3, the MEAN.HELP screen is displayed. But if feedback were given, the student could see it if he came back to the main lesson and scrolled back to this frame.

Note that the screen you want to branch to can be a CBT, HELP, MENU, or PROGRAM screen in any SAS catalog in any SAS data library. Just enter the four-level name of the form

libref.catalog.name.type

following the > to point to a screen in another SAS data library. After the branch, the system marks a return point so that if the student returns to the CBT screen, he resumes the lesson immediately after the branch. If no return point should be remembered, then use two greater-than signs (>>). Checkpoints are ignored for a CBT object selected from a menu or specified in the PROC statement.

This feature of CBT screens allows you to make the lessons truly individualized for each student's expertise. For example, it allows you to skip portions of the lesson when a student's answer indicates a level of knowledge beyond the remainder of the lesson.

Note that the screen you branch to has its own parent, children, or subpanels or is programmed to lead to other screens.

Forced branching Another method of branching from a CBT screen is achieved when the frame consists of a single line that begins with "ppp" in columns 1 through 3 followed by the name and type of a CBT, MENU, PROGRAM, or HELP screen. (If the screen being branched to is a PROGRAM screen, then only the name of the screen needs to be specified.) The system remembers the location of the frame being branched from and marks a return point. The return point is the frame following the frame that caused the branch.

For example, the frame

```
-----------------------------------------------------------------
ppp NEW.CBT
-----------------------------------------------------------------
```

causes the student to branch to the screen NEW.CBT.

After branching, if the student returns to the CBT screen containing the lesson, he returns to the return point. For example, if the branches to a HELP or MENU screen whose parent is the CBT screen causing the branch, then an exit from the HELP or MENU screen returns the student to the return point in the lesson. If the screen is a PROGRAM screen, then the statements

```
PROC DISPLAY;
RUN;
```

in the SAS program cause a return to the return point in the lesson. The return point is ignored if the student restarts the lesson by selecting it from a menu or by specifying it with the CATALOG= option in a PROC DISPLAY statement.

Scoring the lesson If the name of a CBT screen contains the string 'QUIZ', then a student's score is automatically displayed on the SAS log after the lesson is complete. The score appears in the form

```
NOTE: QUIZ SCORE: x out of y
```

where *x* is the number of correct answers out of *y*, the total number of questions seen by the student.

Ending the CBT screen End each frame by entering a dashed line across the screen or by starting a new question. If you want to continue the lesson with another frame of text or a question, enter new frames by scrolling your screen with the FORWARD key. No dashed line is needed after the last frame.

The student presses ENTER to scroll through the lesson and END to finish the lesson. After the last page in the lesson, you may want to have a menu or other screen displayed.

Child screen When the user presses ENTER and there are no more frames defined in the CBT screen, the system displays the screen defined as the CBT's child screen. This subpanel is defined by entering

```
ATTR
```

on the command line to display the attributes of the screen.

Note that **Screen 3.12** is the same as the attribute panel for MENUs. However, for CBT screens only one subpanel can be specified. In the first subpanel field, you define the screen you want displayed when the student presses ENTER for the last time.

For example, suppose the last frame of the CBT screen contains the directions:

```
-----------------------------------------------------------
   Press ENTER to continue course.
   Press END to view menu of additional courses.
-----------------------------------------------------------
```

Suppose the lesson continuation is defined in the CBT screen STAT2.CBT. When the user presses ENTER while viewing the last frame, you want the first screen in STAT2.CBT to appear. Enter STAT2.CBT as the first subpanel in the attribute panel (**Screen 3.13**). (One and only one subpanel is meaningful to a CBT screen.)

Parent screen When the student presses the END key to terminate the lesson, the CBT screen's parent screen is displayed. COURSE.MENU contains a selection of courses the student can choose when he ends the current lesson by pressing END.

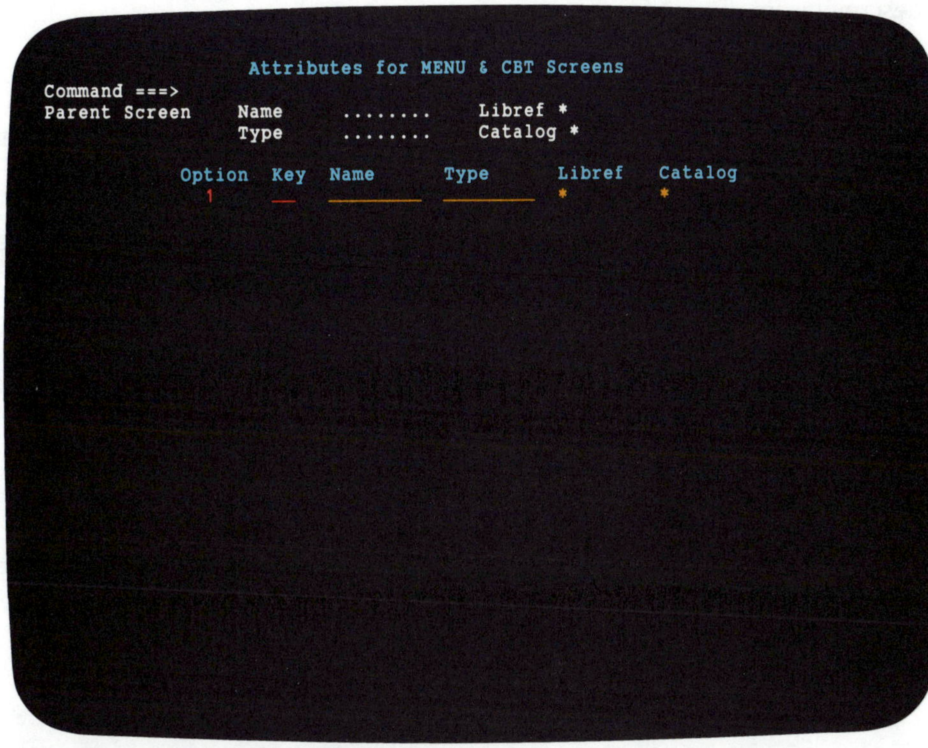

Screen 3.12 Attributes of a CBT Screen

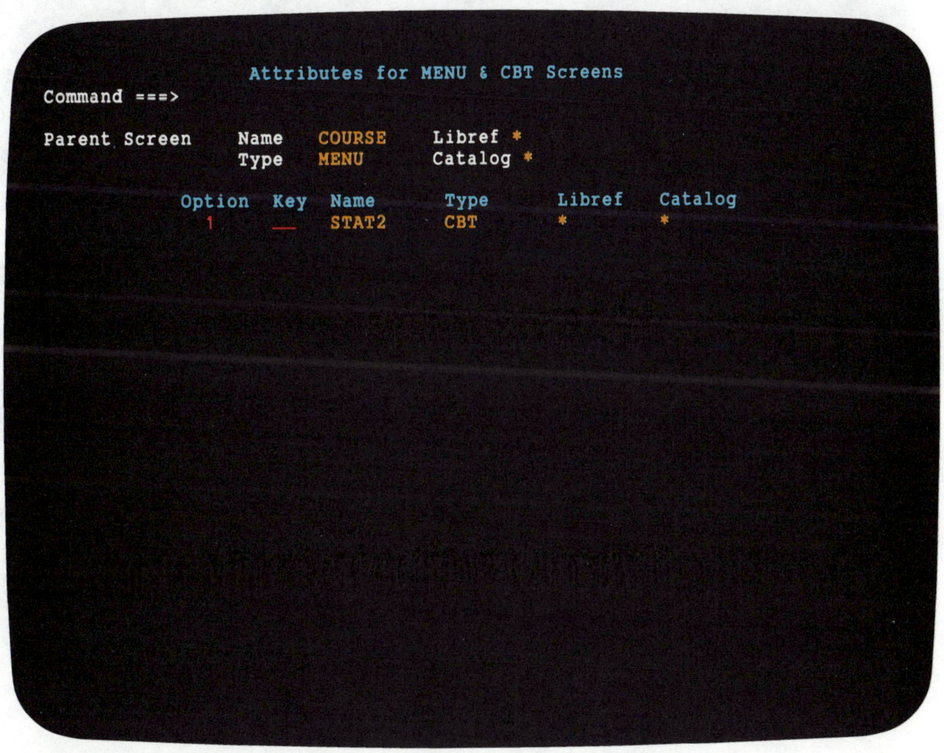

Screen 3.13 Defining the CBT's Parent and Child Screens

Students take the lesson using PROC DISPLAY. See the PROC DISPLAY description for more information.

FORM, KEYS, and LIST Screens

FORM, KEYS, and LIST screens are different from the screens discussed above because they are pre-formatted for you to fill in the blanks rather than free-form screens that you can enter with any text. Editing commands are not available when you create these screens, nor do the screens have attributes. (You are, however, asked to provide attributes of the user field to be validated when a LIST screen is first defined.) FORM and KEYS screens are stored in the user profile library allocated to your session. See a description of the user profile library in "Appendix 1: SAS User Profile."

FORM Screens

FORM screens allow you to describe the output destination and the format of letters for PROC FSLETTER and reports and screen printouts from PROC FSCALC. You can set up the FORM screen using PROC BUILD and store it in the user profile library, and it can be used as a form in SAS/FSP software. FORM screens like **Screen 3.15** have several fill-in-the-blank sections for information about your letters. The format of the FORM screen varies with output device and operating system. **Screen 3.14** is the default form screen displayed for one operating system.

Screens 3.15 and **3.16** show the other panels of a FORM screen.

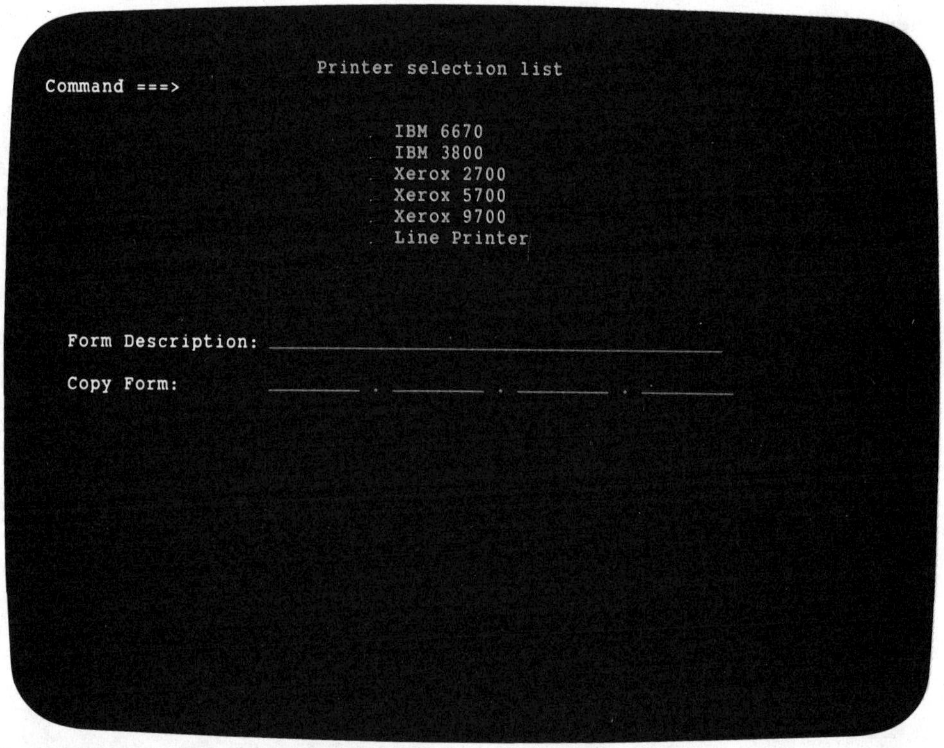

Screen 3.14 A FORM Screen

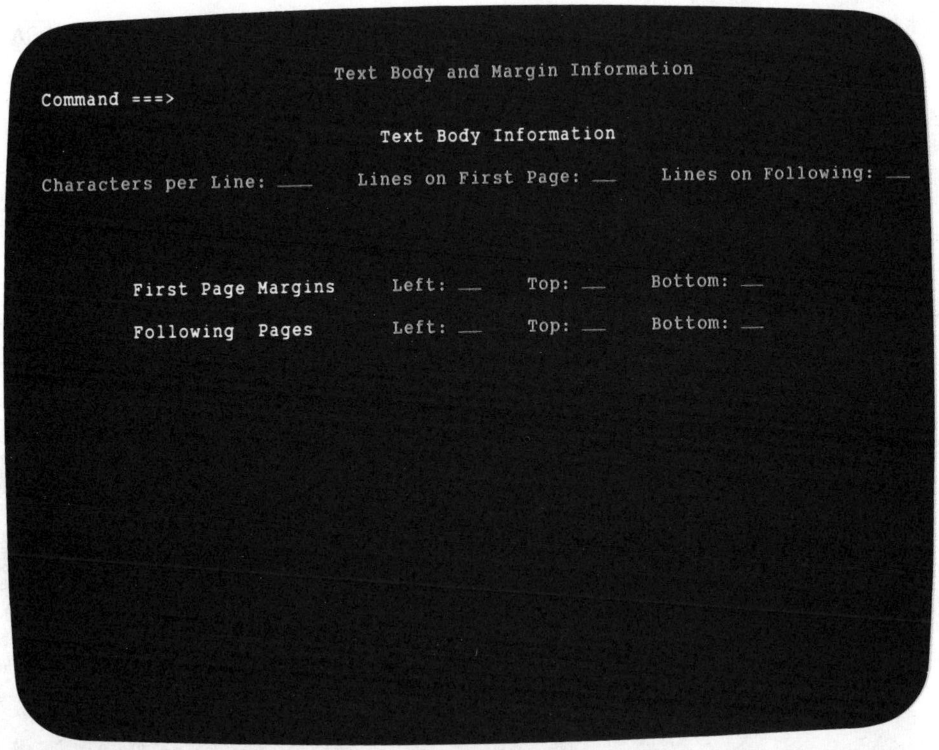
Text Body and Margin Information
Command ===>
Text Body Information
Characters per Line: ___ Lines on First Page: __ Lines on Following: __
First Page Margins Left: __ Top: __ Bottom: __
Following Pages Left: __ Top: __ Bottom: __

Screen 3.15 The Panels of the FORM Screen

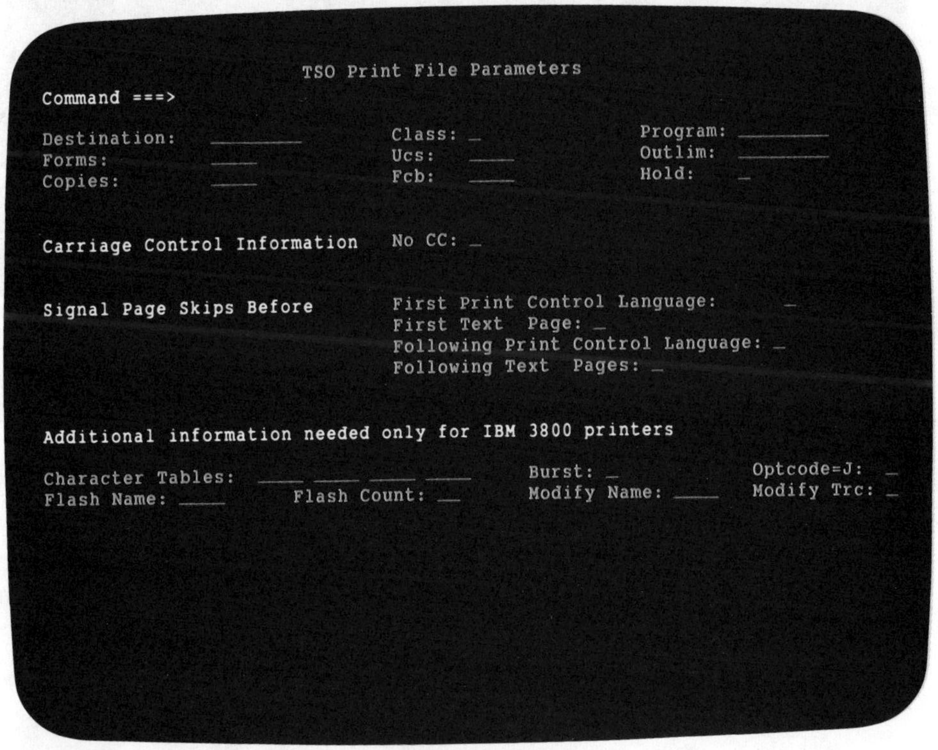
TSO Print File Parameters
Command ===>
Destination: ________ Class: _ Program: ________
Forms: ____ Ucs: ____ Outlim: ________
Copies: ____ Fcb: ____ Hold: _
Carriage Control Information No CC: _
Signal Page Skips Before First Print Control Language: _
First Text Page: _
Following Print Control Language: _
Following Text Pages: _
Additional information needed only for IBM 3800 printers
Character Tables: ____ ____ ____ ____ Burst: _ Optcode=J: _
Flash Name: ____ Flash Count: __ Modify Name: ____ Modify Trc: _

Screen 3.16 The Panels of the FORM Screen (Cont.)

KEYS Screens

KEYS screens are used to give function key definitions that can be used by SAS procedures. You fill in the function name beside the function key number.

KEYS screens are stored in the user profile library associated with your session. They become the default settings for SAS procedures. (See **Screen 3.17**).

You can define a function key to execute a command-line command or a line command. After the function key number, define the command that you want performed. The command is executed by positioning the cursor on the line of text you want to be affected by the command and pressing that function key. The commands are described in the "Full-Screen Editing" appendix.

For command-line commands, enter the name of the command beside the key number. Use the syntax in **Table 3.2** to define a function key as a line command.

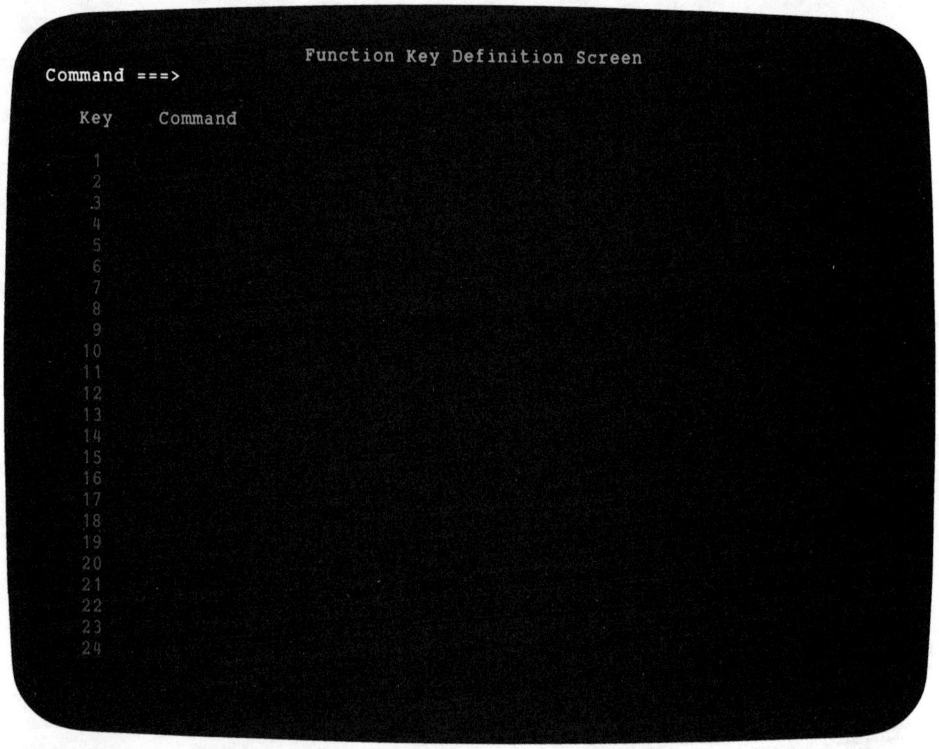

Screen 3.17 A KEYS Screen

LIST Screens

LIST screens are used to define valid values for user fields in PROGRAM screens. When you build a new LIST screen, you are asked to define attributes for the user field to be validated. See **Screen 3.18**.

The next panel displayed contains a series of blanks in which you enter the valid values in any order. The system sorts the list automatically. The LIST screen becomes the list attribute for the user field whose valid values are in the list as shown in **Screen 3.19**.

Table 3.2 Defining a Function Key as a Line Command

Function Key Definition	Line Command
:A	AFTER (target designation)
:F	FOLLOWING (target designation)
:B	BEFORE (target designation)
:P	PRIOR (target designation)
:O	OVERLAY (target designation)
:<	shift line left
:<*n*	shift line left *n* spaces
:>	shift line right
:>*n*	shift line right *n* spaces
:C	COPY
:D	DELETE
:D*n*	DELETE *n* lines
:IA	INSERT after
:IB	INSERT before
:I	INSERT
:I*n*	INSERT *n* lines
:M	MOVE
:MASK	MASK (contents of line inserted)
:R	REPEAT
:R*n*	REPEAT *n* times
:TF	TEXTFLOW
:TF*n*	sets right boundary of TEXTFLOW; a temporary override of the BOUNDS command
:TS	TEXTSPLIT
:TS*n*	TEXTSPLIT *n* lines
:CC	COPY (block command)
:DD	DELETE (block command)
:MM	MOVE (block command)
:RR	REPEAT (block command)
:<<	shift left (block command)
:<<*n*	shift left *n* spaces (block command)
:>>	shift right (block command)
:>>*n*	shift right *n* spaces (block command)

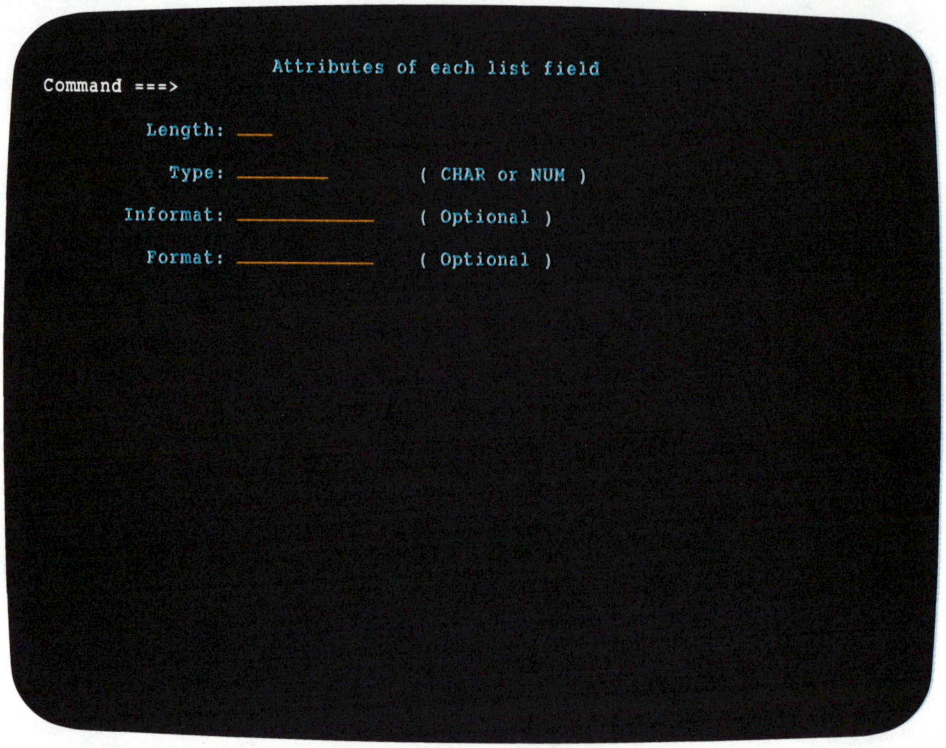

Screen 3.18 Defining Attributes of the User Field: The LIST Screen

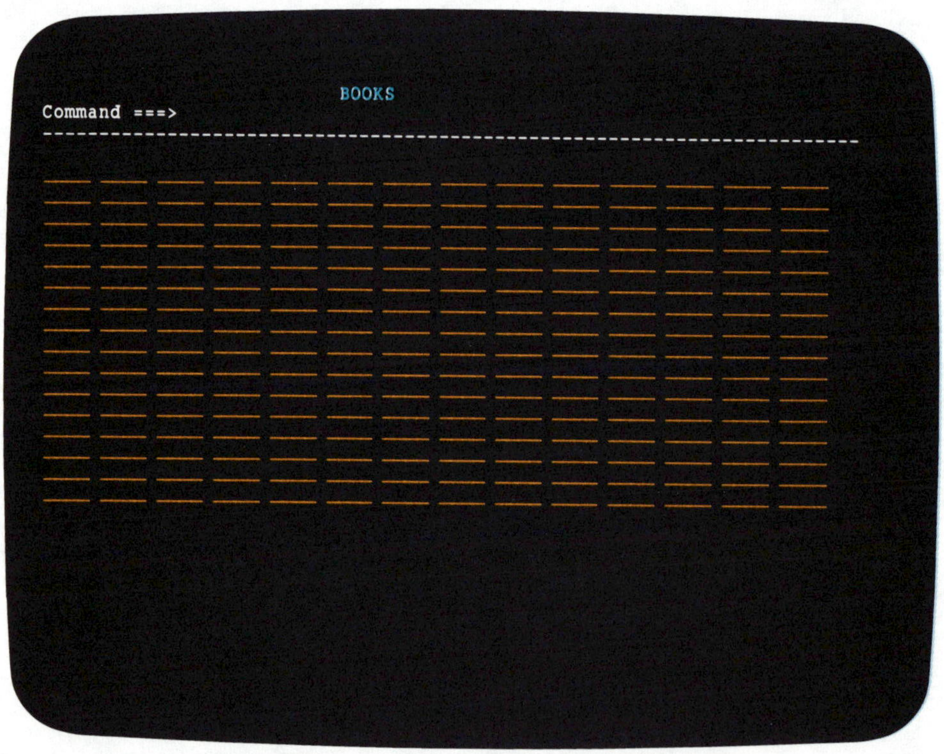

Screen 3.19 A Screen for Entering Valid Values: The LIST Screen

Chapter 4
The CPORT and CIMPORT Procedures

Operating systems: All

INTRODUCTION

The CPORT and CIMPORT procedures are used to move a SAS catalog from an IBM operating system to a Digital, Data General, or Prime system. The CPORT procedure is executed in the IBM environment to copy a catalog to a sequential file in transport format. The CIMPORT procedure is executed on the minicomputer system. The procedure reads the sequential file and builds a new catalog for the minicomputer system.

PROC CPORT

The PROC CPORT statement has the form:

PROC CPORT CATALOG=*SAScatalog***;**

The CATALOG= option **must** be specified. It gives the name of the SAS catalog that you want to transport to the minicomputer system.

Catalog names are two-level names of the form:

libref.catalog

where *libref* refers to the SAS data library where the catalog is stored and *catalog* identifies the specific SAS catalog.

When the PROC CPORT statement is executed, the system unloads the specified catalog into transport format, creating a sequential file. The control language for the SAS job that executes the CPORT procedure must reference the sequential file using the reserved fileref SASCAT. This sequential file is then moved from the IBM system to the minicomputer system using a magnetic tape. The minicomputer system reads the sequential file SASCAT and rebuilds the catalog using PROC CIMPORT.

PROC CIMPORT

CIMPORT's input is the sequential file assigned to the reserved fileref SASCAT. The PROC CIMPORT statement has the form:

PROC CIMPORT CATALOG=*SAScatalog***;**

The CATALOG= option **must** be specified. It gives the name you want the new catalog data set to have on the minicomputer system.

Catalog names are two-level names of the form:

libref.catalog

where *libref* refers to the SAS data library where the catalog is stored and *catalog* identifies the specific SAS catalog.

Chapter 5

The DISPLAY Procedure

Operating systems: All

ABSTRACT

The DISPLAY procedure can be used for a menu-driven, business or information processing application or to take a computer-based training course. These applications are composed of a variety of screens that have been built by PROC BUILD; these screens contain help facilities, menus, instructional material, fill-in-the-blank screens, and SAS programs.

INTRODUCTION

PROC DISPLAY displays screens built by PROC BUILD and stored in a SAS data library. When you invoke the DISPLAY procedure, you indicate the SAS data library and SAS catalog where the screens are stored.

You can display four types of screens with the procedure:

- CBT screens contain instructional text and questions for computer-based training.
- HELP screens explain or clarify features of an application.
- MENU screens provide a selection of tasks or activities. The items on the menu reference other screens that are part of the current application.
- PROGRAM screens are fill-in-the-blank screens. The responses are passed to a SAS program that is automatically submitted to the SAS System.

SPECIFICATIONS

The DISPLAY procedure is invoked by using the PROC DISPLAY statement followed by a RUN statement. The form of the DISPLAY procedure is:

PROC DISPLAY *options*;

PROC DISPLAY Statement

The form of the PROC DISPLAY statement is

PROC DISPLAY CATALOG=*SAScatalog.screen* [LIST];

where

CATALOG= specifies both the SAS catalog and the screen you want displayed. Normally, the name specified with the CATALOG= option references a screen that is the primary menu for an application or computer-based training course.

The full CATALOG= specification has the form *libref.catalog.name.type*:

- *libref* refers to the SAS data library where the catalog is stored.
- *catalog* identifies the specific catalog; it can be up to seven characters in length.
- *name* gives the name of the screen you want displayed.
- *type* gives the screen's type: CBT, HELP, MENU, or PROGRAM.

If the screen name is unique in the specified catalog, the screen type can be omitted.

The CATALOG= option is required the first time you invoke PROC DISPLAY in a SAS session. If the option is omitted, the most recent MENU or CBT screen is displayed. If neither a MENU nor a CBT screen has been displayed, the previously displayed HELP or PROGRAM screen is shown.

LIST tells the system to write any SAS code generated by PROGRAM screens to the SAS log.

DETAILS

When you execute PROC DISPLAY, you go directly to the screen specified in the CATALOG= option. Normally, that screen is the primary menu for an application, course curriculum, or on-line documentation system, but it can be a screen of any of the four screen types. Each screen type is discussed separately.

The CBT Screen

A CBT screen contains a lesson or portion of a lesson in a computer-based training course. When you are viewing a CBT screen from PROC DISPLAY, you can use the following commands on the command line:

- BAC scrolls toward the beginning of the CBT frame or the previous frame.
- CMD adds or removes the command line from the display.
- END returns to the CBT's parent screen.

FORWARD scrolls toward the end of the CBT frame or to the next frame.

HELP presents information about the syntax of the DISPLAY statement and some of the commands you may need with the procedure.

ID identifies the screen name and type and frame number currently displayed. This command is used primarily for testing.

KEYS displays default function key settings for the screen.

n displays the *n*th frame in the lesson.

Frames in a CBT screen correspond to a single thought or point to be made. When you enter a CBT screen from PROC DISPLAY, the screen usually consists of several frames. A frame may or may not contain a question. You can scroll through the frames of a lesson if you press ENTER, enter the FORWARD command, or press the FORWARD key. You can go directly to frame *n* of the lesson if you go to the command line and enter

```
n
```

where *n* is an integer, and press ENTER.

If you use the ENTER command to view the lesson, you cannot continue past a frame containing a question until you answer the question.

Questions and answers To answer a question, press the NEW LINE key (<---'). This key takes you directly to the first answer field. As you continue to press that key, the cursor moves to each answer field. When you decide on an answer, place an x in the answer field and press ENTER. The system tells you whether you have the correct answer and how to proceed.

For example, if you answer correctly, the system responds with feedback text and a message telling you to press ENTER to continue to the next frame.

An incorrect answer also generates feedback and one of the following messages:

```
Press ENTER to erase old answer and try again...
Press ENTER for correct answer...
Press ENTER to continue ...
```

Note that if you use FORWARD to scroll through the lesson, you can pass a question without answering it. However, that question is counted when your score is calculated. You can go back to unanswered questions using the BACKWARD, LAST, or *n* command.

Scores If the name of a CBT screen contains the character string QUIZ, for example QUIZ1 or MYQUIZ, then when you exit from the screen, your score is displayed on the SAS log in the form

```
NOTE: QUIZ SCORE x OUT OF y
```

where *x* is the number of questions you answered correctly and *y* is the number of questions you saw.

Ending the course When you are in PROC DISPLAY, each possible path is determined by parent screens, subpanels, children, programming statements, or by branching to new screens from within the CBT screen.

For example, when you are at the end of a CBT screen and you press ENTER, the next screen displayed is the child screen for the CBT screen. Usually, it will be a MENU or another CBT screen. If it is a MENU screen, you will normally be given an option to terminate the course. If it is another CBT screen, you can take the course by scrolling through the frames, or you can press END to return to the parent screen.

The HELP Screen

The HELP screen provides documentation, hints, remedial material, or additional information about the application. The following commands can be used on the command line of a HELP screen:

BAC	scrolls toward the beginning of the screen.
CANCEL	returns you to the HELP screen's parent screen or to the SAS System if no parent is defined. (CANCEL has the same effect as the END command when you issue it from the command line of a HELP screen.)
CURSOR	returns the cursor to the command line.
END	returns to the parent screen or to the SAS System if no parent is defined.
FORWARD	scrolls toward the end of the HELP screen.
HELP	displays information about HELP screens or displays the HELPNAME screen specified.
KEYS	displays current function key settings.
=X	exits to the SAS System.

There is no limit to the length of a HELP screen, and the FORWARD and BACKWARD scrolling commands are available for viewing the entire screen. When you view a HELP screen that is too long to be displayed at one time, the upper-right corner tells you to:

```
Press FORWARD to continue.
```

On the last page, the message reads:

```
Press END to return.
```

If you access a HELP screen directly by entering its name on the PROC DISPLAY statement, when you press END you return to the parent screen for the HELP screen. If no parent screen has been defined, when you press END you return to the SAS System. (Note that the CANCEL command has the same effect as the END command when you issue it from the command line of a HELP screen.)

If you access a HELP screen with the HELP command from any screen, END returns you to your previous screen or application.

The MENU Screen

A MENU screen is a screen containing a selection of activities or functions to perform. The selections all lead to other screens determined by PROC BUILD. You can scroll to view the entire screen with the FORWARD and BACKWARD commands or keys.

On the command line of a MENU screen, you can enter the number (or character) of the selection you want to make and press ENTER. This leads to a path of screens that is determined in PROC BUILD. To exit from the menu, enter CANCEL or END. The menu's parent screen is displayed.

These commands can be used on the command line of a MENU screen:

BAC scrolls toward the beginning of the screen.

CANCEL returns you to the MENU screen's parent screen or to the SAS System if no parent is defined. (CANCEL has the same effect as the END command when you issue it from the command line of a MENU screen.)

CURSOR returns the cursor to the command line.

END returns to the parent screen or to the SAS System if no parent is defined.

FORWARD scrolls the toward end of the MENU screen.

HELP displays information about MENU screens or the HELPNAME screen specified.

KEYS displays current function key settings.

=X exits to the SAS System.

The PROGRAM Screen

PROGRAM screens are screens that submit a program to the SAS System for execution. You may be asked to provide responses to some user fields before submitting the program. The following commands can be used on the command line of a PROGRAM screen:

BAC [*n* | MAX] scrolls toward the beginning of the user-entry portion of the screen.

CANCEL takes you back to the previous screen or to the return point in a CBT lesson when the PROGRAM screen is branched to form a CBT screen.

DIR requests information about the contents of a SAS data set or a SAS data library. The command

```
DIR
```

requests that the name, type, and label of variables in the last data set created during the current session be printed.

```
DIR libref.SASdataset
```

requests that the name, type, and label of variables in *libref.SASdataset* be printed.

```
DIR libref._all_
```

requests that the SAS data sets in the SAS data library referenced with *libref* be listed.

END submits a SAS program for execution and then returns to the SAS System, to a screen defined by the SAS program, or to a return point in a CBT screen when the PROGRAM screen is a branch from the CBT screen.

FORWARD [*n* | MAX] scrolls toward the end of the user-entry portion of the screen.

HELP provides information about PROGRAM screens.

KEYS displays the default function keys.

RECALL displays previous user-field responses entered during the same SAS session for user fields that do not have an associated SAS macro variable.

X allows you to enter a host-level command for execution.

When you enter a PROGRAM screen from PROC DISPLAY, sometimes a screen containing user fields is displayed. When you enter a PROGRAM screen that has been defined with no user fields, a program is automatically submitted to the SAS System.

Screens with user fields If the PROGRAM screen is defined with user fields, you can use the FORWARD and BACKWARD commands and keys to scroll through the display. The NEW LINE key (<---') moves the cursor from one user field to another for you to enter values in the fields based on the questions asked. When you press END, a SAS program is submitted to the SAS System for execution.

SAS output If the SAS program generates procedure output, the output is shown on your screen. If the DMS option is in effect (DMS ON is entered on the command line of the screen in PROC BUILD), then the output is displayed by display manager, and you can use the scrolling commands to scroll through that output. When you press END while the output is displayed, the program that was submitted may determine the next screen displayed.

Chapter 6
A Computer-based Training Application

The Human Resources Department at Acme Research and Development Company wants to set up a series of self-training modules in several subject areas. For example, employees in the administrative group are interested in familiarizing themselves with some simple statistical terminology.

Lessons in the statistical curriculum should be brief, with a way to branch out of the lesson easily at short intervals. At the end of each lesson, an employee should be given the option of going on to a new lesson or ending the session.

GETTING STARTED

SAS/AF software allows you to build a curriculum that can include an unlimited number of lessons (CBT screens) that are chosen from any number of menus (MENU screens) and that can branch to other lessons, menus, help facilities, and even SAS programs.

The best way to begin building a curriculum is to design all possible paths that a student can take. Keep in mind that most screens have parent screens, the screen that is displayed when the user exits from that screen in PROC DISPLAY, and they have subpanels or child screens, resulting in a variety of branching capabilities. The first curriculum chosen for the employees at Acme Research and Development Company is a Descriptive Statistics Curriculum that contains several lessons. It begins with a primary menu from which the student selects a lesson. See **Screen 6.1**.

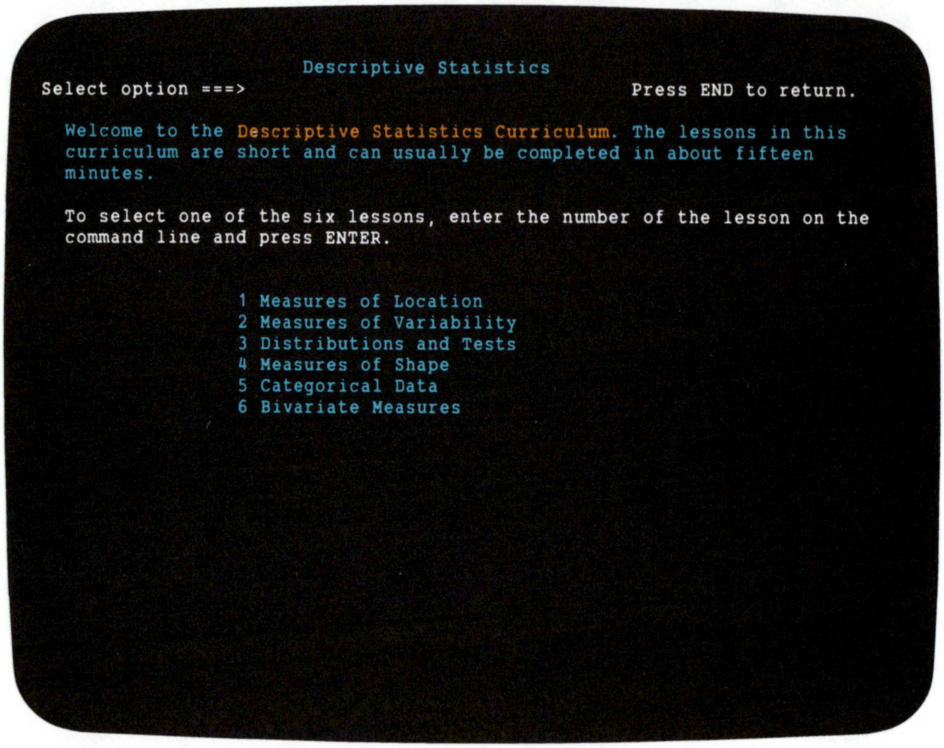

Screen 6.1 A Primary Menu for Selecting a Lesson

The system is designed in such a way that the student can begin with the first lesson and proceed through the curriculum until he has reached the end, or he can select the particular lesson he is interested in. After every lesson, the student has the option of returning to the primary menu to make another selection or of continuing the curriculum in sequence. Throughout the curriculum, the student is given other options to branch out of the lesson and return, or to exit from the system.

Flow Chart of Curriculum Organization

Figure 6.1 is an instructional flow chart that describes the choices a student can make if he selects the first lesson in the curriculum. A similar flow chart could be constructed for each lesson.

It is clear from the diagram that the paths a student takes are intertwined and that there are shortcuts and longer routes to almost every destination. The diagram indicates the screen types that make up each step.

BUILDING SCREENS

Using the diagram, you can build the screens that make up the Descriptive Statistics Curriculum. As usual, you must have access to a SAS data library where you can store the screens you build using PROC BUILD.

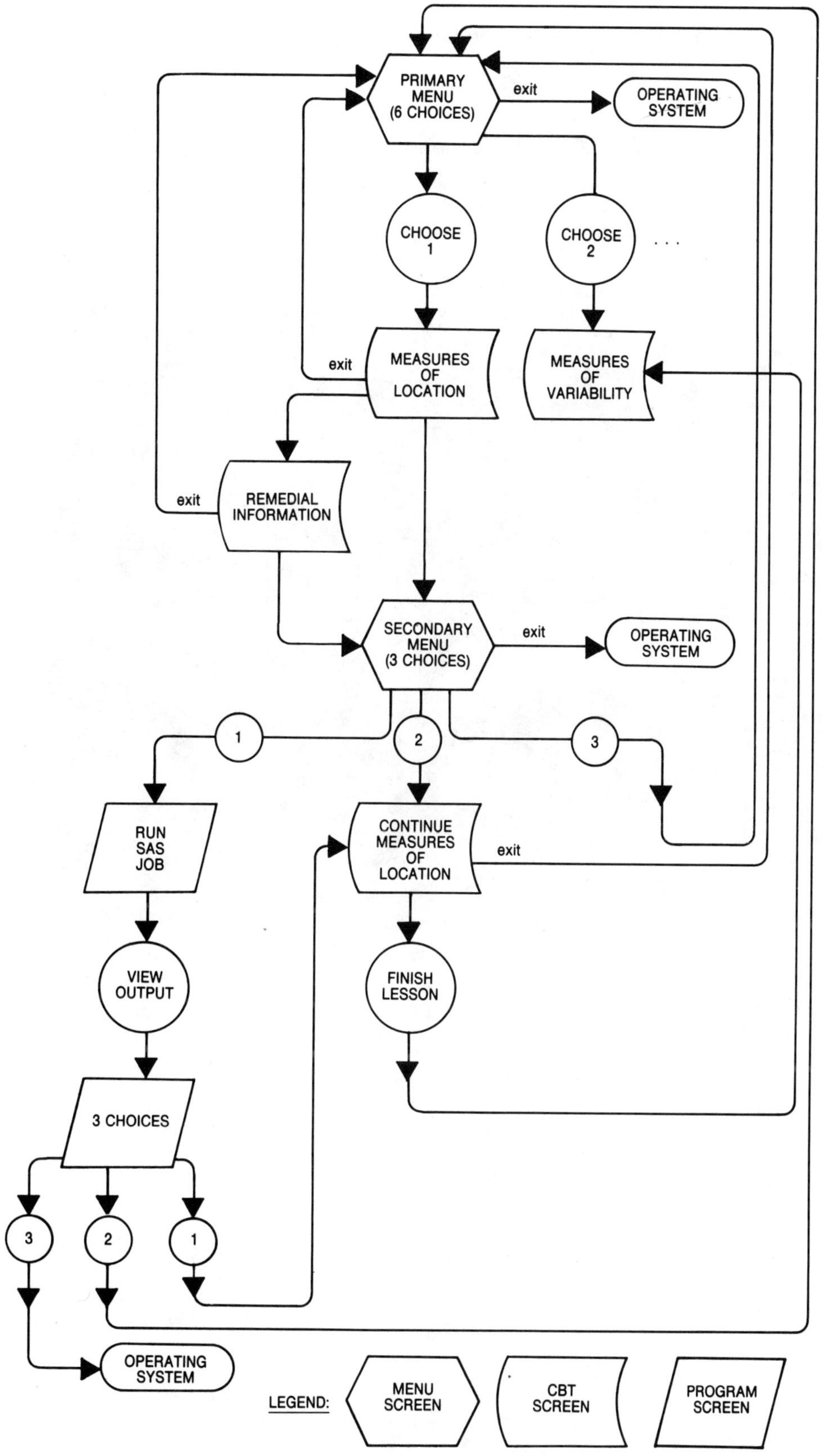

Figure 6.1 Flow Chart of Curriculum Organization

Suppose you plan to store the screens in a SAS data library referenced by libref IN. Then you can access the BUILD procedure using the following statement:

```
PROC BUILD CATALOG=IN.COURSES;
RUN;
```

As shown in **Screen 6.2** COURSES is the name of the SAS catalog where the screens that make up the Descriptive Statistics Curriculum will be stored. The catalog directory lists all the screens in the SAS catalog. In this example, you create a new SAS catalog with the PROC BUILD statements.

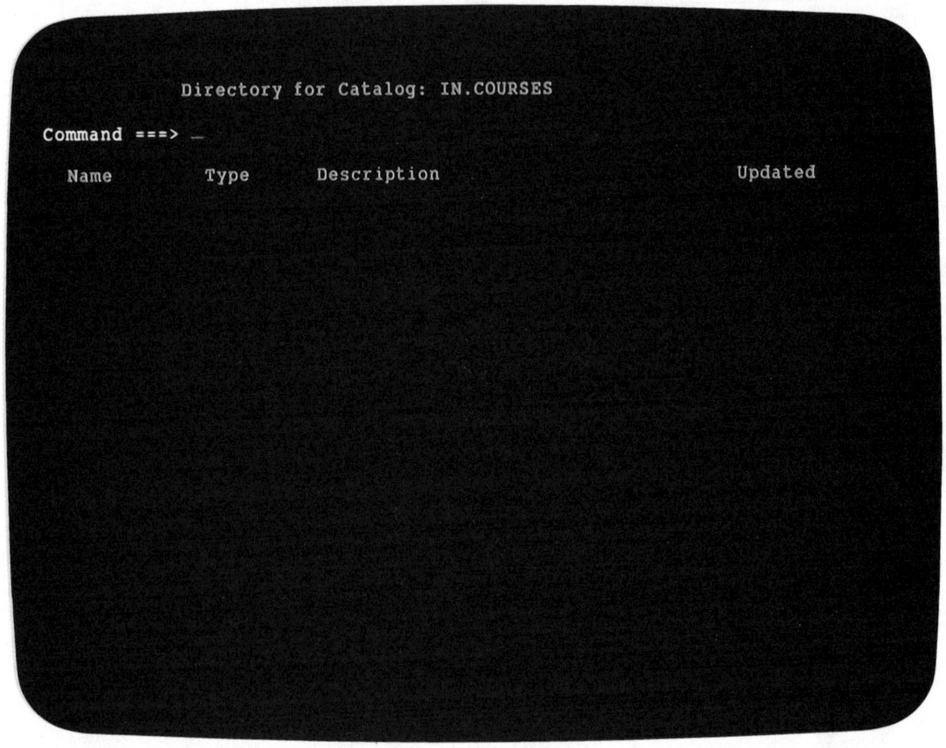

Screen 6.2 A New Catalog Directory

The first screen you want to build is the primary menu screen that contains a selection of lessons in the curriculum. To build the primary menu screen shown in **Screen 6.3**, enter the command

```
EDIT COURSE.MENU
```

on the command line and press ENTER. On the blank menu screen using editing commands, enter the text for the primary menu. The DES command

```
DES Descriptive Statistics
```

gives a title to **Screen 6.4**. This title also appears in the catalog directory as the screen's Description.

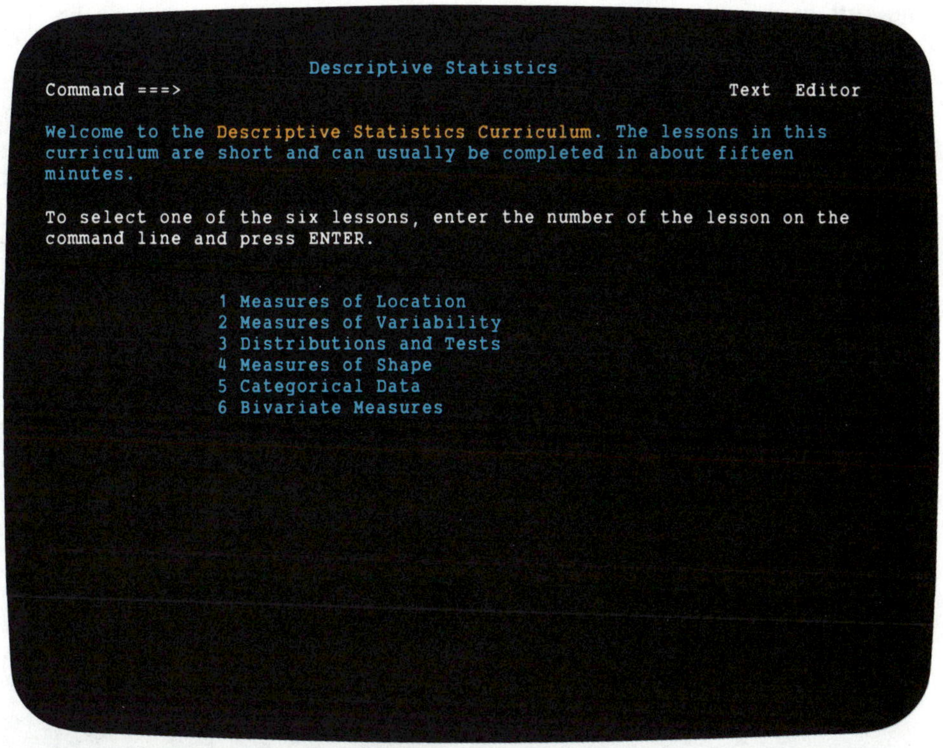

Screen 6.3 Primary Menu of Lessons

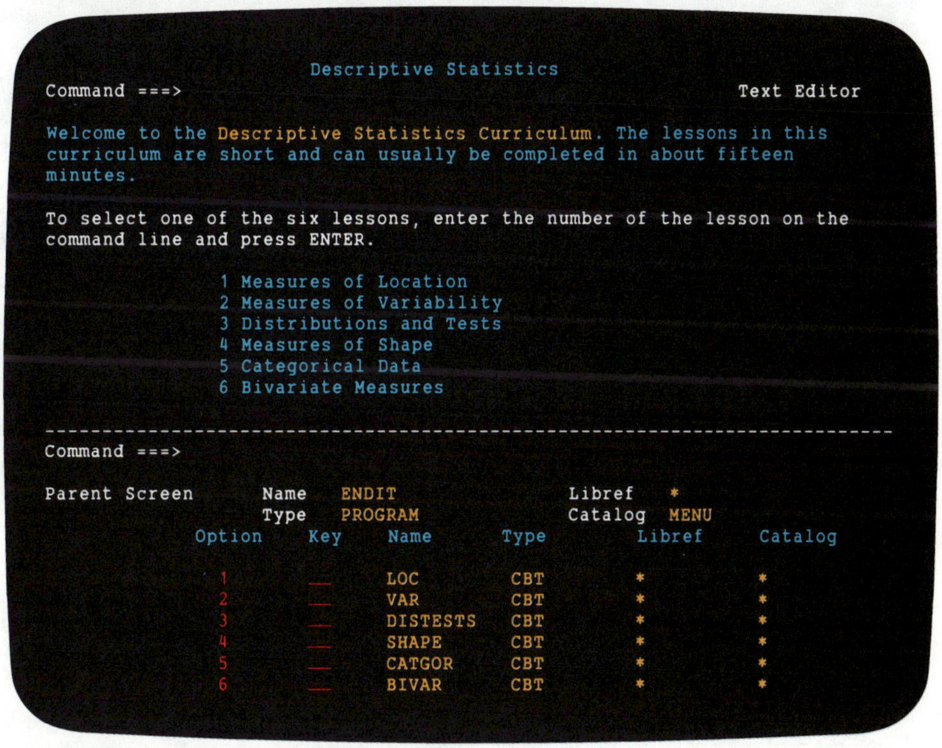

Screen 6.4 Using the ATTR Command

On the command line of the MENU screen, enter the ATTR command and move the cursor to a position below the text. Press ENTER and view the split screen containing the menu and a place to define its parent screen and subpanels:

In the spaces provided, enter the name of the screen that you want to serve as the exit from the primary menu (the parent screen). If no parent screen is given, the student returns to the SAS System after exiting from this primary menu.

In this example, you want the student to return to the operating system. Note that the parent screen ENDIT.PROGRAM is stored in a catalog named MENU that is stored in this SAS data library. The program screen ENDIT.PROGRAM is a simple program screen with no upper portion and the single SAS statement

```
endsas;
```

below the dashed line.

Name the screens that correspond to each lesson selection. In this case when a student chooses one of the six lessons, he is taken directly to a CBT screen for the lesson.

After you have built the primary menu and defined its subpanels, press END to return to the catalog directory. Note that the title, rather than the screen name and type, appears in the directory.

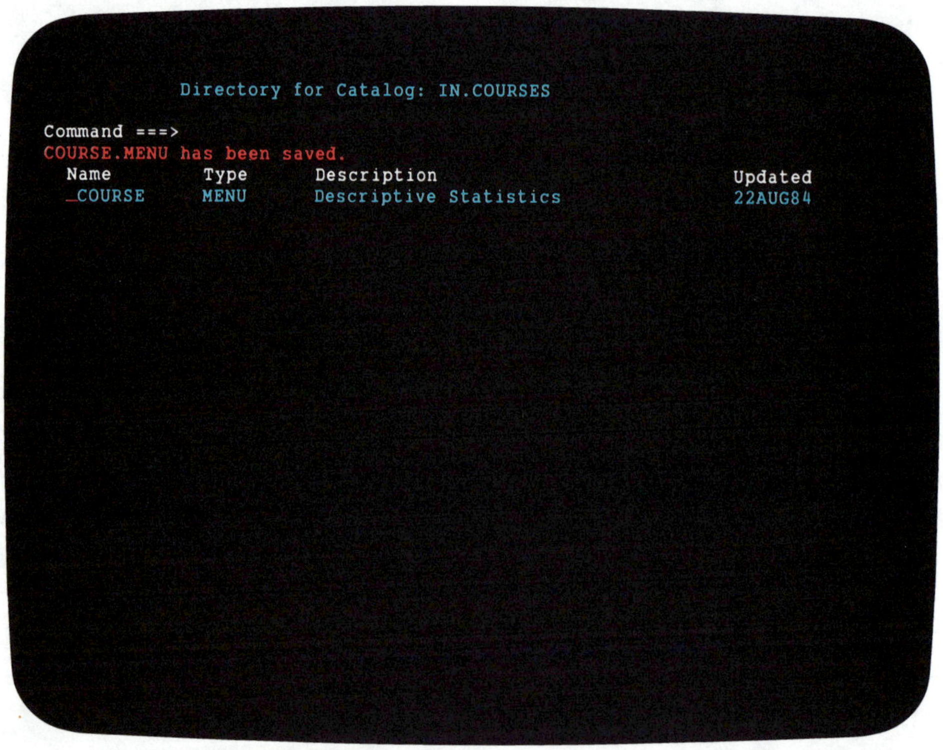

Screen 6.5 A Catalog Directory

From the catalog directory command line, you can enter an EDIT command to build the next screen in the system. The command

```
EDIT LOC.CBT
```

gives you a blank CBT screen to begin building the Measures of Location lesson.

A CBT screen is made up of frames that contain text and one question. Each frame usually corresponds to a single point to be emphasized or taught. Questions on the frames are multiple choice or true false. You tell the system the correct answer to the question, the number of tries allowed for the student to get the right answer, and the text or screen that should be displayed when the student selects each possible answer.

Screen 6.6 shows the first frame of the lesson on Measures of Location.

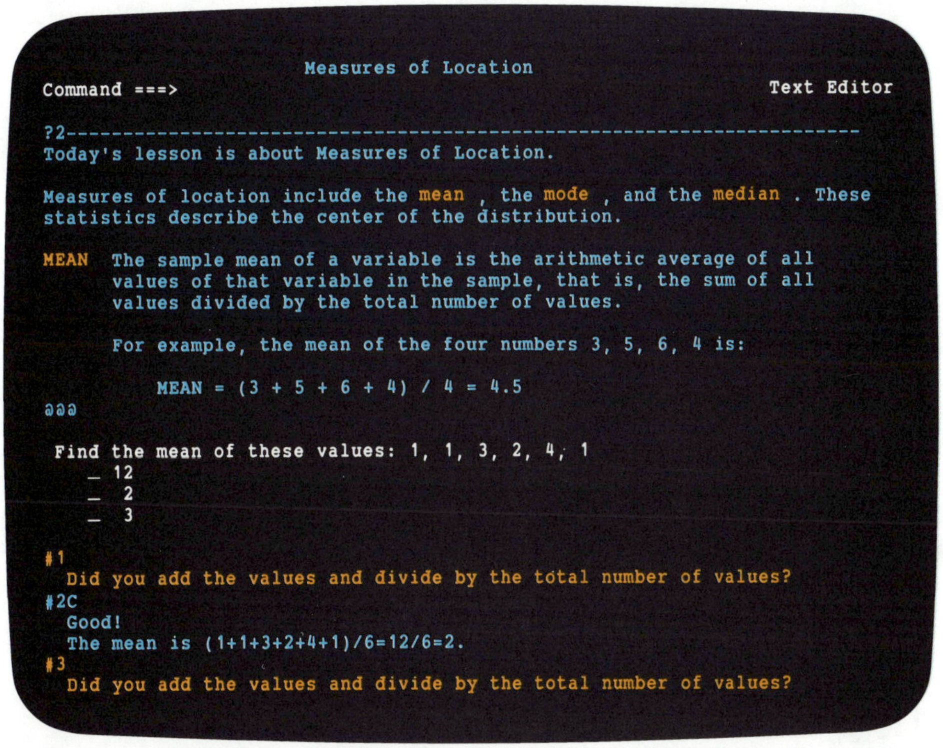

Screen 6.6 The First Frame of the Lesson on Measures of Location

Features of the CBT Screen

The first frame begins with a question mark in column 1 to tell the system that there is a question on the frame. In column 2 of the same line, specify the number of tries you want a student to have to get the correct answer. This line begins the frame and is called the frame indicator.

Follow the frame indicator with any text you want to appear on the frame. The three at signs (@@@) in columns 1-3 midway down the frame tell the system to pause. When the student views the lesson, the text above and including the line containing the at signs appears first; the remainder is displayed when the student presses ENTER. This feature allows the student to concentrate on key points in the text before the screen becomes full.

Answer fields for the possible answers to a question are preceded by an underscore (_) and a space. (The underscore must be the first nonblank character on the line.) The system numbers the answer fields for each question sequentially.

For each possible answer, you can write any feedback that you want displayed to the student when he selects that answer. Precede the text with a feedback indicator— a line containing a pound sign (#) in column 1 followed by the question number. The correct answer has a capital C in column 3 of that line. Do not put the feedback text on the line that begins with the #. Your text is displayed along with text automatically generated by the system.

Feedback for the correct answer is in two parts. The first line following the feedback indicator is for congratulatory feedback and is displayed along with the other feedback for the question only when the student selects the correct answer within the allotted number of tries. If the system supplies the correct answer, the congratulatory line is not displayed.

End the frame by entering a dashed line across the screen. If you want to continue the lesson with another frame, continue to enter new frames by scrolling your screen with the FORWARD key.

Screen 6.7 shows the entire text of the CBT screen with all its frames.

```
                           Measures of Location
Command ===>                                                  Text Editor


?2------------------------------------------------------------------
Today's lesson is about Measures of Location.

Measures of location include the mean, the mode, and the median. These
statistics describe the center of the distribution.

MEAN  The sample mean of a variable is the arithmetic average of all
      values of that variable in the sample, that is, the sum of all
      values divided by the total number of values.

      For example, the mean of the four numbers 3, 5, 6, 4 is:

          MEAN = (3 + 5 + 6 + 4) / 4 = 4.5

@@@

 Find the mean of these values: 1, 1, 3, 2, 4, 1
    _ 12
    _  2
    _  3

#1
  Did you add the values and divide by the total number of values?
#2C
  Good!
  The mean is (1+1+3+2+4+1)=12/6=2.
#3
  Did you add the values and divide by the total number of values?
?3-------------------------------------------------------------------

MODE  The mode is the value at which the density of the distribution is
      at a maximum. The sample mode is the value that occurs most often
      in the sample.
¬¬¬
      For example, the mode of the six numbers 4, 2, 4, 1, 5, 4
      is 4 since that number occurs most often.
@@@

 Find the mode of these values: 1, 1, 3, 2, 4, 1
    _ 12
    _  2
    _  1
    _  3
#1
 Did you add the numbers?
#2
 Try grouping numbers that are the same.
#3C
 That's right.
 The number 1 is the mode since it occurs three times.
#2
 Try grouping numbers that are the same.
--------------------------------------------------------------------
What happens if more than one number occurs more often than the others?
@@@
Some distributions can have more than one mode. For a distribution with
multiple modes, the common convention is to select the lowest mode for
reporting.
For example, in the group of numbers
 8, 2, 5, 5, 6, 8, 5, 8

the numbers 5 and 8 each occur three times. This distribution has two
modes.
```

(continued on next page)

(continued from previous page)

```
?1-------------------------------------------------------------------
Which SAS procedure can calculate the mode of a distribution?

_ MEANS
_ SUMMARY
_ UNIVARIATE
_ TABULATE
_ CHART

#1  > PROC.CBT

#2  > PROC.CBT

#3C > CHOOSE1.MENU

#4  > PROC.CBT

#5  > PROC.CBT
```

Screen 6.7 The Entire Text of the CBT Screen

Each frame in the screen above begins and ends with a dashed line. For pages that contain a question, it is not necessary to follow the ? and number of tries with dashes, although it is recommended for easily viewing frame breaks.

Feedback branching Notice that on the last frame of the lesson, the feedback indicator lines for questions 1 through 5 contain a greater-than sign (>) followed by the name and type of a screen that you want displayed when that answer is selected.

You can branch to a CBT, HELP, MENU, or PROGRAM screen in any catalog in any SAS data library. Just enter the four level name of the form

libref.catalog.name.type

following the > in the line that begins with #question. If the first two levels are omitted, then the system looks for the screen in the current catalog.

This feature of CBT screens allows you to make the lessons truly individualized for each student's expertise. For example, it allows you to skip portions of the lesson when a student's answer indicates a level of knowledge beyond the remainder of the lesson.

Note that the screen you branch to has its own parent, children and subpanels, or is programmed to lead to other screens.

In this example, when the student selects incorrect answers 1, 2, 4, or 5, the lesson branches to a CBT screen named PROC.CBT that contains informational text (no questions) about descriptive statistics procedures in the SAS System. If the student selects the correct answer he branches to a screen named CHOOSE1.MENU where he selects a new path. CHOOSE1.MENU is described later.

Screen 6.8 shows text for the screen PROC.CBT that is branched to when an incorrect answer is given.

```
Command ===>                                                Text Editor

                          Procedure Description

There are several SAS procedures that produce univariate descriptive
statistics. Below is a chart showing the statistics computed by each
procedure.

                                 PROCedure

 Statistic      MEANS  UNIVARIATE  SUMMARY  TABULATE  CHART
---------------------------------------------------------------------------
          mean|  X        X          X        X         X
           sum|  X        X          X        X         X
           min|  X        X          X        X
           max|  X        X          X        X
         range|  X        X          X        X
           uss|  X        X          X        X
           css|  X        X          X        X
           var|  X        X          X        X
           std|  X        X          X        X
        stderr|  X        X          X        X
            cv|  X        X          X        X
      skewness|  X        X
      kurtosis|  X        X
             t|  X        X          X        X
           prt|  X        X          X        X
        median|           X
      quantile|           X
          mode|           X

---------------------------------------------------------------------------
The UNIVARIATE procedure produces a variety of descriptive statistics about
the distribution of numeric variables.

It is the only SAS procedure that produces the mode, or most frequent
occurrence of a variable.

Other features in UNIVARIATE include:
 o detail on the extreme value of a variable
 o quantiles, such as the median
 o several plots to picture the distribution
 o frequency tables
 o a test that the data are normally distributed.

---------------------------------------------------------------------------

Press ENTER to continue...

Press END to return to primary menu.
```

Screen 6.8 Text for the PROC.CBT Screen

The path a student follows after completing the lesson contained in LOC.CBT is determined by how he answers the last question. **Screen 6.8** represents the path a student takes when he needs additional information to continue.

At the last frame in this CBT screen, the student is given two choices: he can press ENTER to continue the lesson or END to return to the primary lesson menu. These choices correspond to the CBT screen's child and parent screens, respectively. They are programmed into the system using the CBT's attribute panel. Note that at the last frame in a CBT lesson, when the student presses the ENTER key, he is branched to the screen's child; when he presses END, he is branched to the screens's parent. It is helpful to the student if you use the last frame in the lesson to describe the action of those keys.

Attribute panel If you enter the ATTR command on the command line of the CBT screen, a screen for defining the CBT screen's attributes is displayed. It is the same attribute screen displayed for MENU screens. However, for CBT screens only one subpanel can be defined. This subpanel (defined in the option 1 line) is the CBT screen's child screen. It is the screen displayed to the student when he presses ENTER from the last frame of a CBT screen. The attributes defined for CBT screen PROC.CBT are shown in **Screen 6.9**.

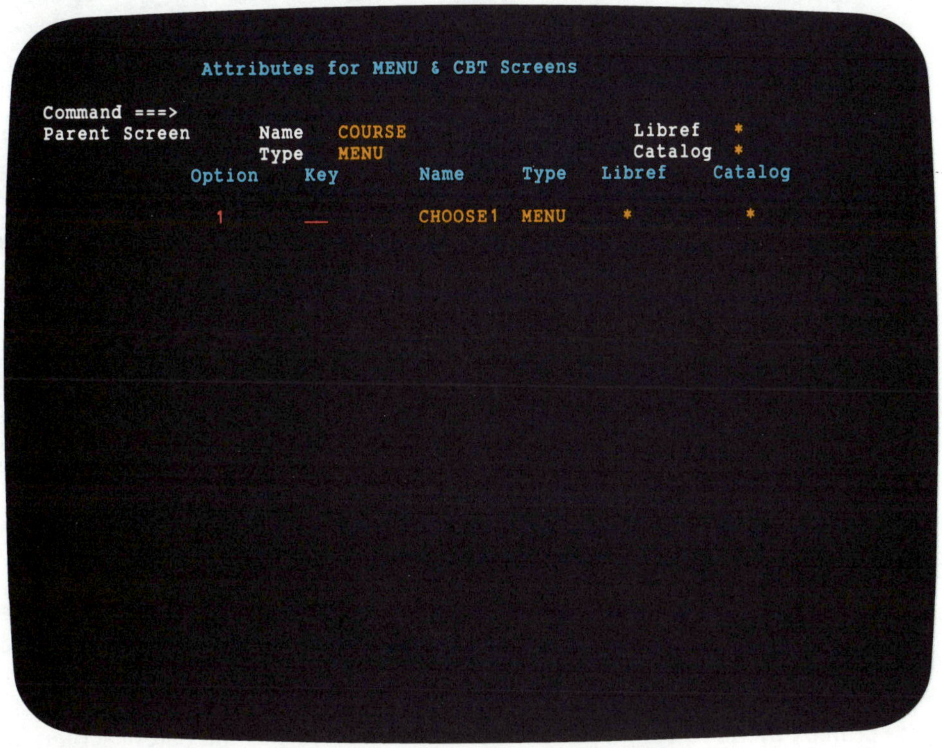

Screen 6.9 Attributes Defined for CBT Screen PROC.CBT

When the student has branched to screen PROC.CBT, he learns more about SAS procedures. He returns to the primary lesson menu (COURSE.MENU) if he presses END; he goes to a secondary menu (CHOOSE1.MENU) if he presses ENTER.

A Secondary Menu

To build CHOOSE1.MENU (**Screen 6.10**), return to the catalog directory and enter

```
EDIT CHOOSE1.MENU
```

on the command line. Then enter the text, parent, and subpanels as usual.

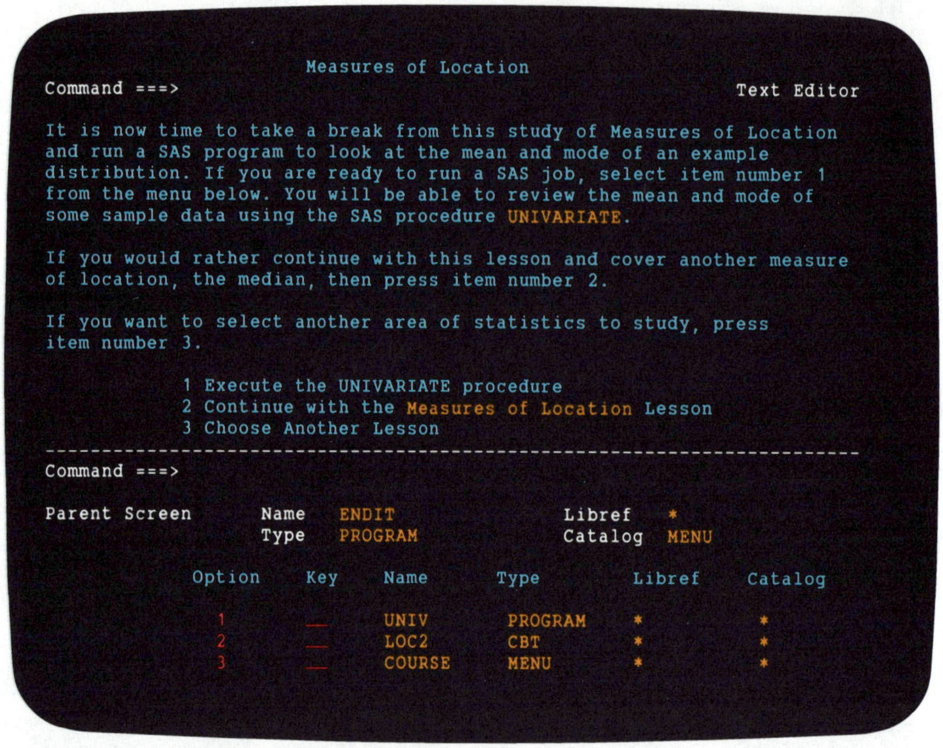

Screen 6.10 Building a Secondary Menu

The parent screen for this screen is a SAS program that causes an exit to the operating system. Note that this screen resides in a different catalog in the SAS data library. Subpanels that correspond to the item choices are a PROGRAM, CBT, and MENU screen. Note that the third choice sends the student back to the primary menu screen, COURSE.MENU, which was also the parent screen for the first portion of the lesson.

Executing a SAS Program

If a student selects item 1 from the menu above, he wants to execute a sample program to illustrate the discussion. You can create a PROGRAM screen that allows him to do that.

On the command line enter

```
EDIT UNIV.PROGRAM
```

and begin entering text. This PROGRAM screen has a user-entry portion as well as the required program portion. **Screen 6.11** shows the text for PROGRAM screen UNIV.PROGRAM.

```
                   The UNIVARIATE Procedure: Mean and Mode
Command ===>                                                   Text Editor

----------------------------------------------------------------------
Sun Bakery has collected the following data in SAS data set BAKERY.
For each working day in August, the number of customers and the
number of leftover loaves of bread are recorded:


DAY CUST BREAD   DAY CUST BREAD   DAY CUST BREAD   DAY CUST BREAD
--- ---- -----   --- ---- -----   --- ---- -----   --- ---- -----
WED  25    4     MON  18   14     MON  25   12     MON  21   12
THU  38    5     TUE  26   13     TUE  51    3     TUE  27   11
FRI  62    0     WED  38    8     WED  42    6     WED  36    9
                 THU  42    6     THU  45    5     THU  51    2
                 FRI  68    2     FRI  72    2     FRI  69    1

You will be executing the UNIVARIATE procedure. Select the numeric
variables that you want analyzed. If you want analysis on both variables
list both their names:
&var_______________

& indicates that you want to repeat the analysis by DAY.



Press FORWARD for more.





When you press END, the procedure is submitted to the SAS System at
your data center for execution and you can view the output at your
terminal.

What do you want to do next?

& continue with Measures of Location lesson
& select another lesson
& exit from the curriculum





----------------------------------------------------------------------
data sales;
input day $ cust bread @@;
cards;
WED  25    4     MON  18   14     MON  25   12     MON  21   12
THU  38    5     TUE  26   13     TUE  51    3     TUE  27   11
FRI  62    0     WED  38    8     WED  42    6     WED  36    9
THU  42    6     THU  45    5     THU  51    2
FRI  68    2     FRI  72    2     FRI  69    1
;
#field2 proc sort; by day;
##
proc univariate;
##var var &var;
#field2 by day;

##  run;
#field3 proc display catalog=in.courses.loc2.cbt;
#field4 proc display catalog=in.courses.course.menu;
#field5 proc display catalog=in.menu.endit.program;
##  run;
```

Screen 6.11 PROGRAM Screen UNIV.PROGRAM

The user-entry portion In the user-entry portion of the screen, the student reads text that describes a set of data. The student is then asked to write the names of the variables he wants to analyze. He can also indicate that he wants a detailed analysis by DAY.

The screen is designed with the amount of viewing area available to the student in mind. Since all of the user portion of the screen cannot be displayed at one time, the student must press the FORWARD key to scroll to the end of the screen. Rather than risk the student pressing END and submitting the program before he has selected his next activity, the screen tells the student to press FORWARD to continue. He then decides what he wants to do after viewing the procedure output. Note that through the use of conditional execution indicators in the program portion of the screen below the dashed line, these choices are programmed to lead to different screens and have the effect of a MENU screen.

SAS program In the program portion of the screen, the data described to the student are read into a SAS data set. If the student has indicated that he wants an analysis by DAY, the data set is sorted by DAY. Then PROC UNIVARIATE is invoked; the VAR statement is executed only if the variable field is filled in. (PROC UNIVARIATE analyzes all numeric variables by default.) A BY statement is included if the analysis is to be by DAY.

The next section of the program executes PROC DISPLAY and invokes a particular screen based on the student's choice of activities. ("The BUILD Procedure" chapter and the chapter, "A Menu-Driven Application," explain the use of conditional execution indicators in a PROGRAM screen.)

Field attributes **Screen 6.12** field attributes show that the variable VAR is a character field of length five. The remaining user fields are indicated on the user-entry screen by a single &; no field name is given. These fields are named FIELD*n* where *n* is the nth field on the screen. They are ACTION fields; anything the user enters in the single field is translated to an X and treated as an on-off switch.

```
               Attributes for PROGRAM & SYSTEM Screens
Command ===>

Please use the scroll commands or function keys to review the fields.

Field Name: VAR        Length: 20  Row: 19  Column:  2

      Type: CHAR        Caps: X  Just: L  Pad:  _ Protect: _  Non-display: _

    Format:               Informat:                             Required:    _

      List:

      Help: .....  .....             Associated SAS Macro variable .....

Field Name: FIELD2  Length:  1  Row: 21  Column:  2

      Type: ACTION      Caps: X  Just: L  Pad: _ Protect: _ Non-display: _

    Format:                 Informat:                           Required:  _

      List:

      Help: .....  .....              Associated SAS Macro Variable .....

Field Name: FIELD3  Length:  1  Row: 37  Column:  2

      Type: ACTION      Caps: X  Just: L  Pad: _ Protect: _ Non-display: _
```

Screen 6.12 Field Attributes, PROGRAM Screen

Lesson Continuation

During the lesson, the student is asked to choose whether he wants to continue the Measures of Location lesson. Lesson continuation is an option from the secondary menu and from the programmed menu in the previously described PROGRAM screen. You can build the continuation in another CBT screen named LOC2.CBT that includes many of the same features described in the CBT screen for the beginning of the lesson. **Screen 6.13** shows the text for that screen.

```
Command ===>                    LOC2.CBT
---------------------------------------------------------------------------
  MEDIAN    The median of a distribution is the value above and below which
            half of the density falls. The sample median is the middle
            value when the measurements are arranged in ascending or
            descending order. For an even number of observations, the
            midpoint between the two middle values is usually reported as
            the median.
  @@@
            For example, to calculate the median of these numbers:

            5, 6, 3, 8, 11, 4, 4, 2, 9, 8, 10

            first arrange the numbers in ascending order:

            2, 3, 4, 4, 5, 6, 8, 8, 9, 10, 11

            The middle number in the ordered list is the median of the
            group of numbers. The median is 6.

  ?2----------------------------------------------------------------------

  Find the median of these numbers:

  0, -1, -3, 5, -1.5, -8, 100, 4, -15

  _ -1
  _  0
  _  5
  _ -1.5

  #1C
      Good. You understand the median.

  #2
     Have you sorted the numbers correctly?
  #3
     Remember that negative numbers are less than zero.
  #4
     Have you sorted the numbers correctly?
  ------------------------------------------------------------------------
  ppp MEDIAN
  ------------------------------------------------------------------------
  Press ENTER to go directly to the Measures of Variability lesson.

  Press END to select another lesson.
```

Screen 6.13 Continuing the Lesson

Notice that only congratulatory feedback text is entered for the correct answer. Thus, when the system tells the user the correct answer after he has used all his tries, no feedback is displayed.

Forced branching In the screen above, notice that the frame prior to the last contains a single line and 'ppp' in columns 1 through 3 followed by the name of a PROGRAM screen. If the branch is to a CBT, HELP, or MENU screen, then the full two-level *name.type* must be given.

In this type of branching, the system remembers the frame that caused the branch and marks a check point. The student can return to that check point after completing the branch. In this example, the screen being branched to is a PROGRAM screen named MEDIAN.PROGRAM. The statements

```
PROC DISPLAY;
RUN;
```

as the last program step cause a return to **Screen 6.14**, the frame in the CBT screen that immediately follows the branching frame. (Note that a CANCEL command issued from the PROGRAM screen also results in a return to that frame.)

```
Command ===>                       MEDIAN.PROGRAM

Now use the SAS System to find the median of a set of data.

Fourteen children in the seventh grade were given a math test. Below
are the fourteen scores:

95, 72, 86, 90, 78, 62, 73, 98, 89, 92, 83, 84, 76, 82

Create a SAS data set containing these test scores. The data set
should have one variable.

DATA &dsn_____ ;
 INPUT &var_____ @@;
 CARDS;
95 72 86 90 78 62 73 98 89 92 83 84 76 82
;

Now use the UNIVARIATE procedure to calculate some statistics about the
distribution of the children's test scores. One of the statistics will be
the median test score.

PROC UNIVARIATE;
 VAR &var_____ ;
 TITLE ' &title______________________________________________________ ';

Press END to submit the program to the SAS System.
----------------------------------------------------------------------
data &dsn ;
input &var @@;
cards;
95 72 86 90 78 62 73 98 89 92 83 84 76 82
;
run;
proc univariate;
 var &var ;
 title ' &title ';
run;
proc display; run;
```

Screen 6.14 Branching to a Program Screen

After branching, if the student returns to the CBT screen containing the lesson, he returns to the return point. For example, if the branch is to a HELP or MENU screen whose parent is the CBT screen causing the branch, then an exit from the HELP or MENU screen returns the student to the return point in the lesson. If the screen is a PROGRAM screen, then the statements

```
PROC DISPLAY;
RUN;
```

in the SAS program cause a return to the return point in the lesson.

What Next?

The last frame of the CBT screen that caused the branch describes the next choice of paths. When the student presses ENTER at the last frame, he goes directly to the first frame of the next lesson on Measures of Variability. If he presses END, he returns to the primary lesson menu.

These paths are defined on the attribute panel as the child and parent screen, respectively. See **Screen 6.15**.

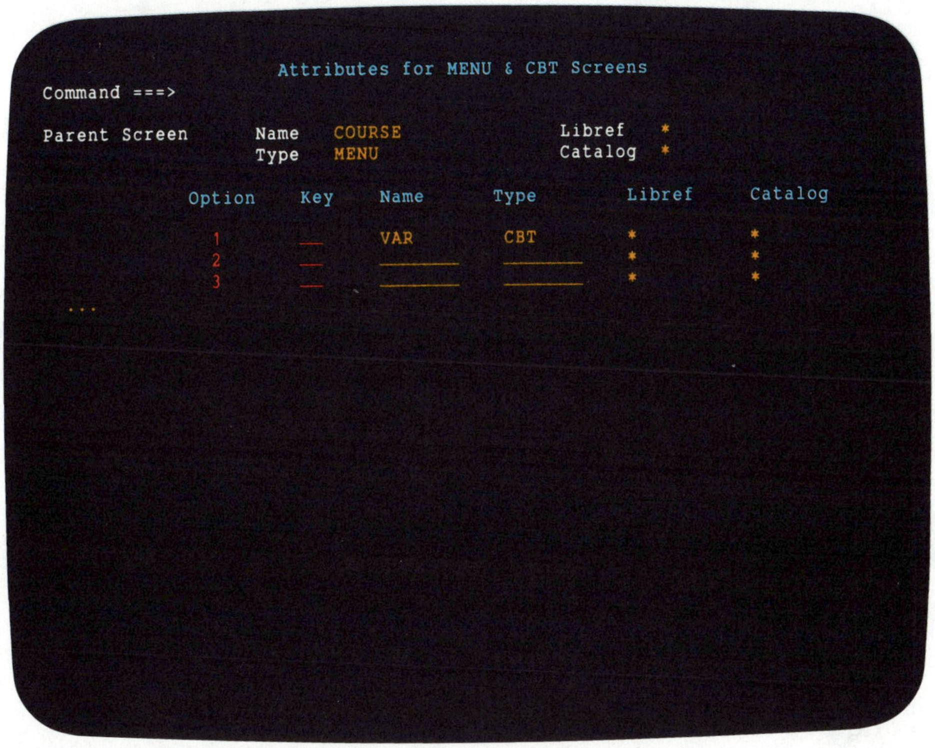

Screen 6.15 Branching Paths Defined in the Attribute Panel

Another Lesson

You can continue to build lessons in this way, branching and offering the option to exit throughout the lesson. For example, the second lesson in the curriculum (item 2 on the primary lesson menu), and also the step immediately following completion of the Measures of Location lesson, is a lesson on Measures of Variability.

The screen is named VAR.CBT and contains the text shown in **Screen 6.16**.

```
                           Measures of Variability
Command ===>                                                    Text Editor

-----------------------------------------------------------------------
Another group of statistics important for studying a variable's
distribution measures the variability, or spread of values.
Three measures of a distribution's variability are the range, the
variance, and the standard deviation.

@@@

RANGE  The simplest statistic in this category is the range, the
       difference between the highest and the lowest value. The range
       tells you nothing about the values between the maximum and the
       minimum.

       Consider the following set of values:

       21, 105, 13, 45, 22, 15, 87, 62, 27, 101, 18, 47, 37, 16

       The range of these values is 13-105 since the smallest number
       is 13 and the largest is 105.

?2
These are the high temperature for each day of August:

Day Temp   Day Temp   Day Temp   Day Temp   Day Temp   Day Temp
--------   --------   --------   --------   --------   --------
 1   85     6   82    11   77    16   73    21   70    26   88
 2   87     7   80    12   80    17   75    22   68    27   89
 3   88     8   79    13   80    18   72    23   67    28   90
 4   92     9   78    14   79    19   72    24   74    29   88
 5   90    10   77    15   76    20   71    25   80    30   87

Find the range:
_  66-93
_  67-92
_  65-87

#1
The minimum and maximum values given as the range are values that
actually occur in the distribution.

#2C
You are right!
In August, the minimum temperature was 67, the maximum, 92.

#3
Don't confuse the actual range with the temperatures on the first
and the last days of the month.
-----------------------------------------------------------------------
ppp MEANS.PROGRAM
-----------------------------------------------------------------------
VARIANCE  The variance is the expected value of the squared differences
          of the values from their mean:

                              2
          Var(x)=E(x-E(x))

          The sample variance is computed by first subtracting the sample
          mean from each value, squaring these differences, adding them
          up, then dividing the sum by the number of values minus 1.
          A sample variance computed using this formula is an unbiased
          estimate of the population variance.

           2          _ 2
          s =sum(x- x) / (n-1)

          When all the values lie close to the mean, the variance is
          small; when values are more scattered, the variance is large.
```

(continued on next page)

(continued from previous page)

```
?1
Which group of data has the largest variance?
_ A
_ B
          A:          |                      B:      |
                      |                              |
                x x   |        x                    x|x
             x x x x  | x    x x x x              xx|xx
          x x x      x|x x x         x          xxxx|xx
           x x x x x| x x x    x x x              xx|xx
                x     |  x x      x   x              |
                      |                              |
                      |                              |
                    Mean                            Mean
#1C
You are right!
The data values are farther from the mean.

#2    > VAR2.CBT
----------------------------------------------------------------------
```

Screen 6.16 VAR.CBT Screen

Its parent and child are shown in **Screen 6.17**.

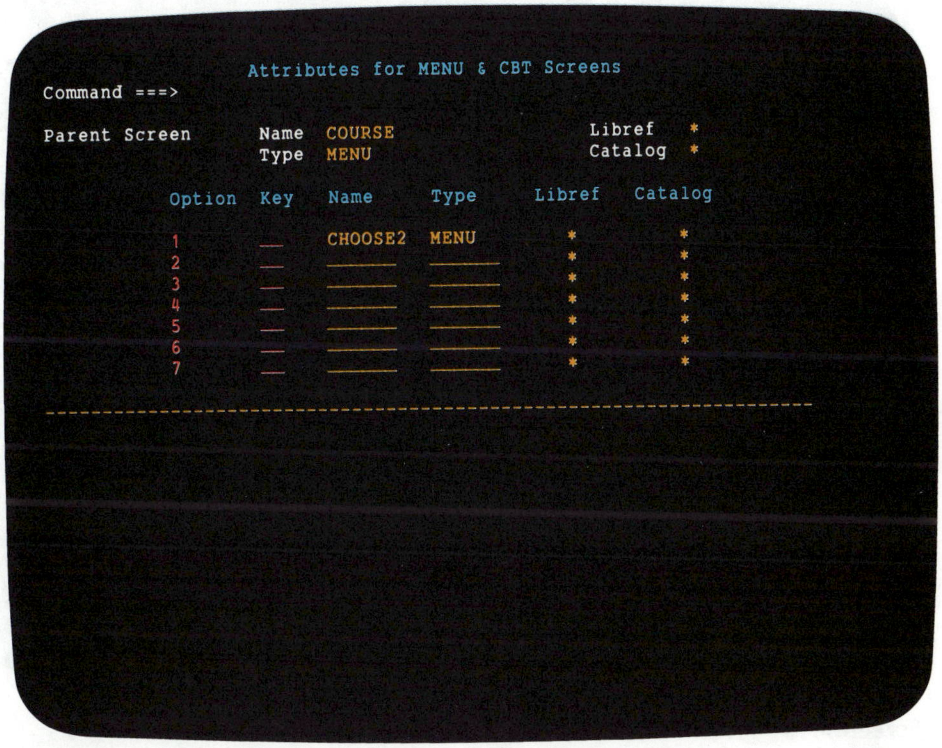

Screen 6.17 VAR.CBT Screen's Parent and Child Screens

THE STUDENT

After you have built the screens that make up the Descriptive Statistics Curriculum, you will want to test the system. Assume the role of a student ready to take a few lessons in statistics.

Getting Started

Part of building a computer-based training application is to decide how students should access the system. At Acme Research and Development Company, a student takes lessons in the Descriptive Statistics Curriculum by issuing the simple command

```
STAT
```

that displays the primary menu screen for the system.

This command represents a command procedure that contains the operating system commands and SAS statements needed to reference the catalog containing lessons in the statistics curriculum. The PROC DISPLAY statement in this command procedure has the following form:

```
PROC DISPLAY CATALOG=STUDY.COURSES.COURSE.MENU;
```

The statement references the primary menu COURSE.MENU contained in SAS catalog COURSES referenced by libref STUDY. When this DISPLAY statement followed by a RUN statement is executed, the lesson can begin!

Primary Lesson Menu

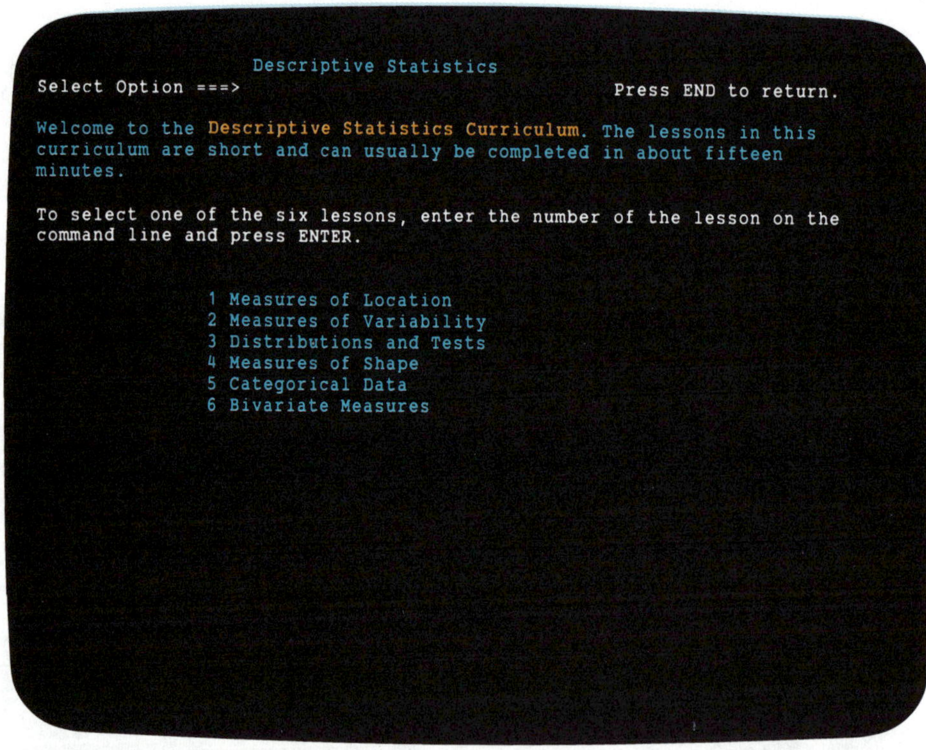

Screen 6.18 Primary Lesson Menu

You want to begin with the first lesson in the curriculum, so enter the number 1 on the command line of the primary menu and press ENTER. **Screen 6.19** appears at your terminal.

Press ENTER to continue through the lesson.

Since the frame in **Screen 6.20** contains a question, you must respond before you can continue the lesson using the ENTER key.

The NEW LINE key (<--') automatically moves the cursor to the location of answer fields on the screen. Choose your answer, place an X in the blank beside the answer, and press ENTER. The system responds.

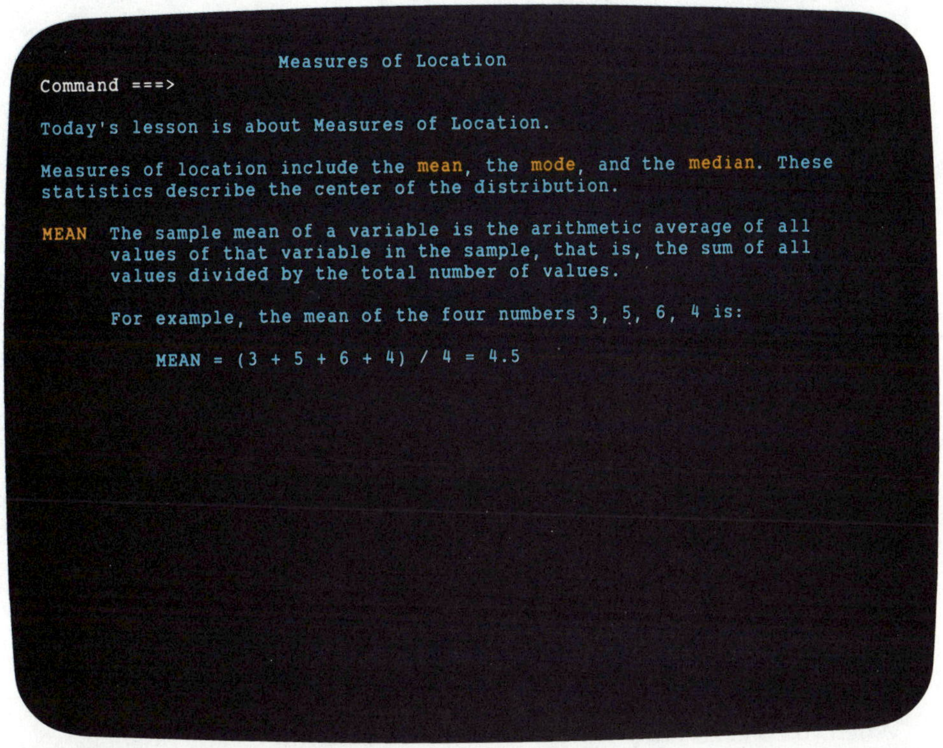

Screen 6.19 Beginning the Lesson

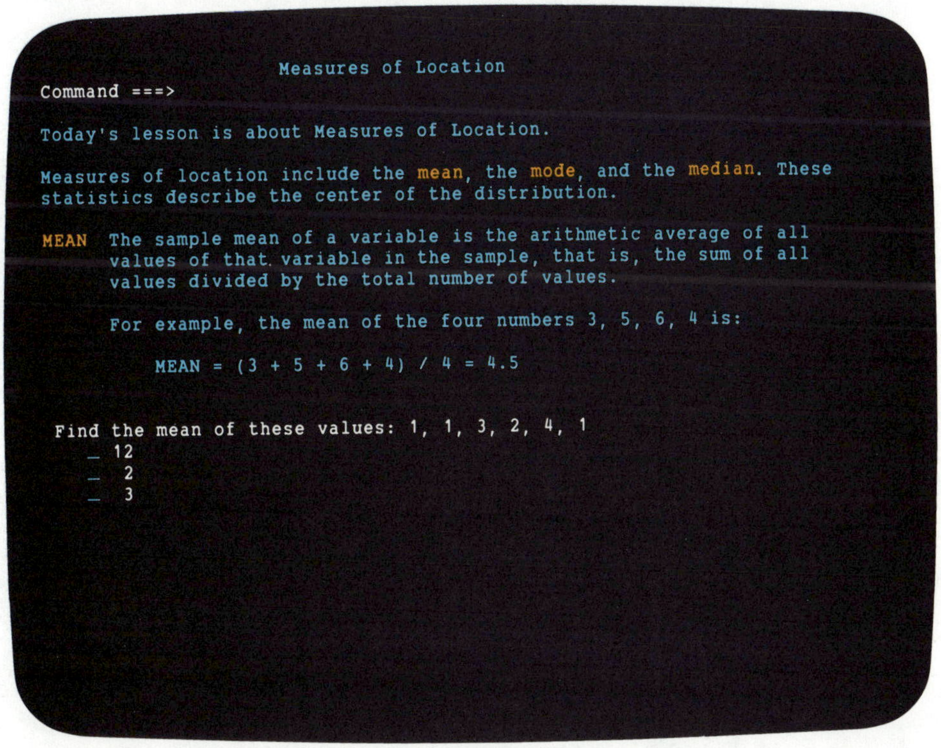

Screen 6.20 A Question Displayed on the Lesson Screen

```
                           Measures of Location
Command ===>

Today's lesson is about Measures of Location.

Measures of location include the mean, the mode, and the median. These
statistics describe the center of the distribution.

MEAN   The sample mean of a variable is the arithmetic average of all
       values of that variable in the sample, that is, the sum of all
       values divided by the total number of values.

       For example, the mean of the four numbers 3, 5, 6, 4 is:

           MEAN = (3 + 5 + 6 + 4) / 4 = 4.5


 Find the mean of these values: 1, 1, 3, 2, 4, 1
    X 12
    _  2
    _  3


  Did you add the values and divide by the total number of values?

  Press ENTER to erase old answer and try again...
```

Screen 6.21 Choosing an Incorrect Answer

When you press ENTER from **Screen 6.21**, the incorrect answer disappears; use the NEW LINE key to place an X on another answer in **Screen 6.22**.

```
                           Measures of Location
Command ===>

Today's lesson is about Measures of Location.

Measures of location include the mean, the mode, and the median. These
statistics describe the center of the distribution.

MEAN   The sample mean of a variable is the arithmetic average of all
       values of that variable in the sample, that is, the sum of all
       values divided by the total number of values.

       For example, the mean of the four numbers 3, 5, 6, 4 is:

           MEAN = (3 + 5 + 6 + 4) / 4 = 4.5


 Find the mean of these values: 1, 1, 3, 2, 4, 1
    _ 12
    X  2
    _  3

  Good!
  The mean is (1+1+3+2+4+1)=12/6=2.
```

Screen 6.22 Choosing Another Answer

Press ENTER from **Screen 6.22**, and you continue to a new frame, **Screen 6.23**.

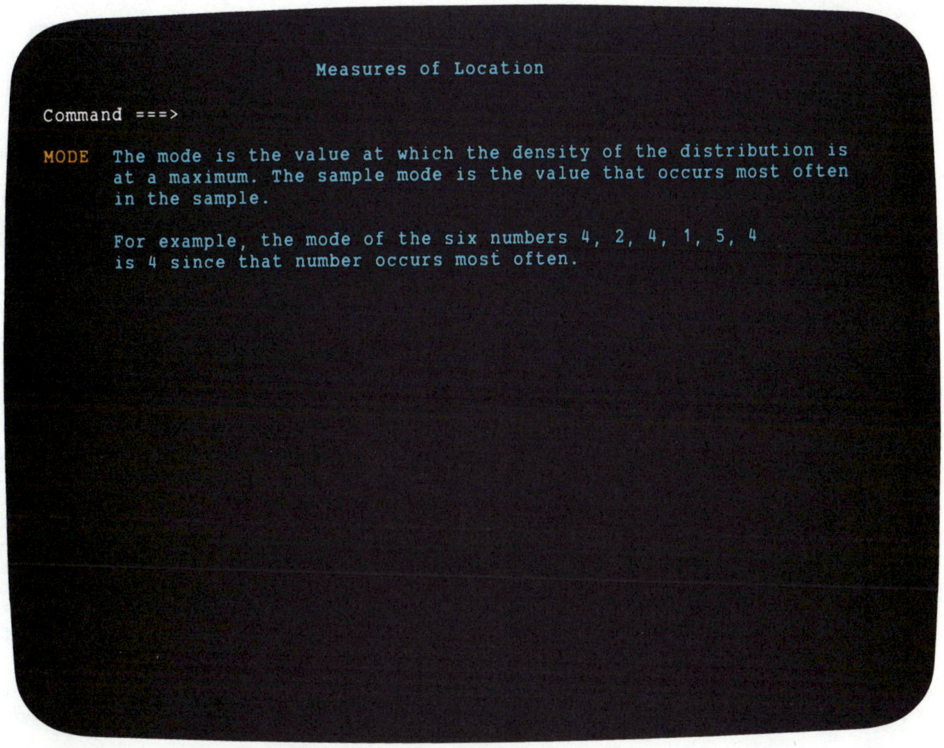

Screen 6.23 Continuing to a New Frame

Press ENTER, and **Screen 6.24** displays another question.

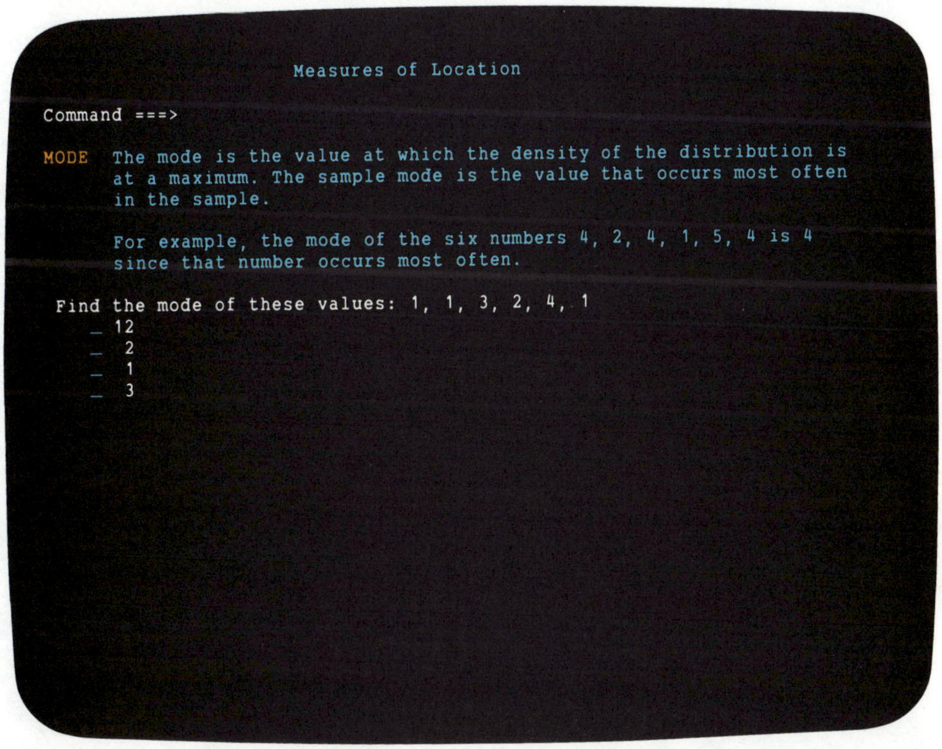

Screen 6.24 Another Question

Choose an answer as shown in **Screen 6.25** and press ENTER.

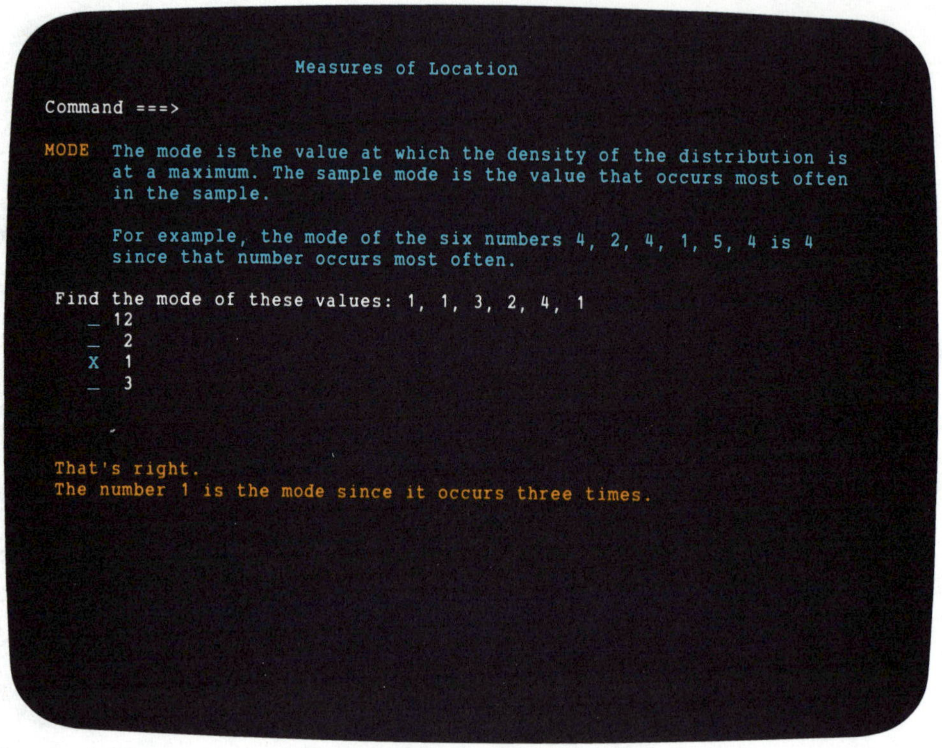

Screen 6.25. Answering the Question Correctly

ENTER lets you continue with **Screen 6.26**.

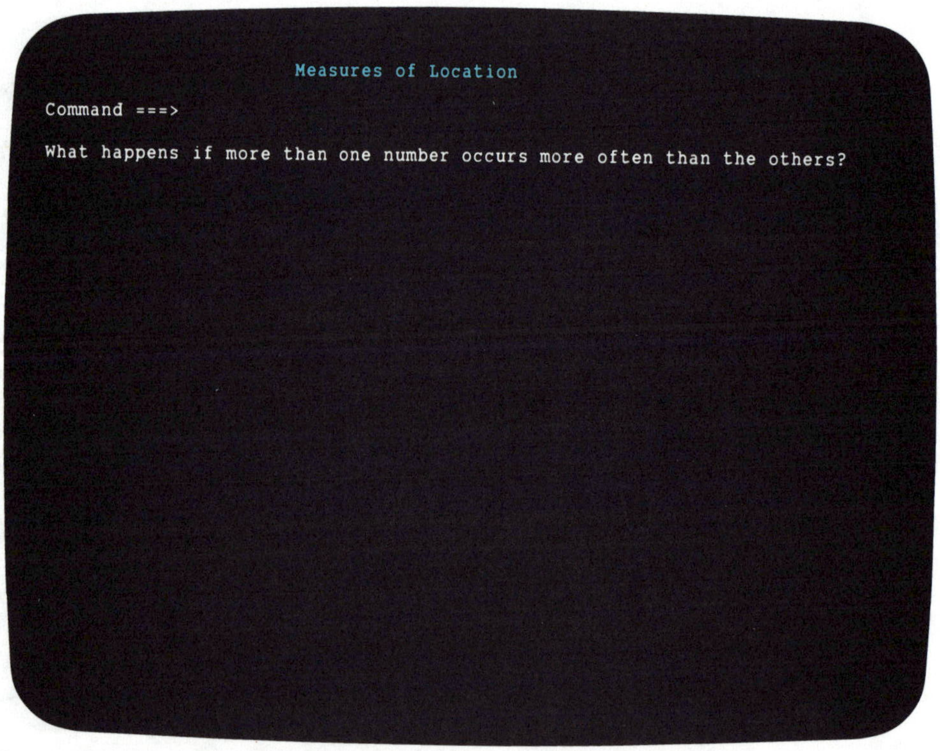

Screen 6.26 Continuing with the Lesson

Press ENTER and **Screen 6.27** is displayed.

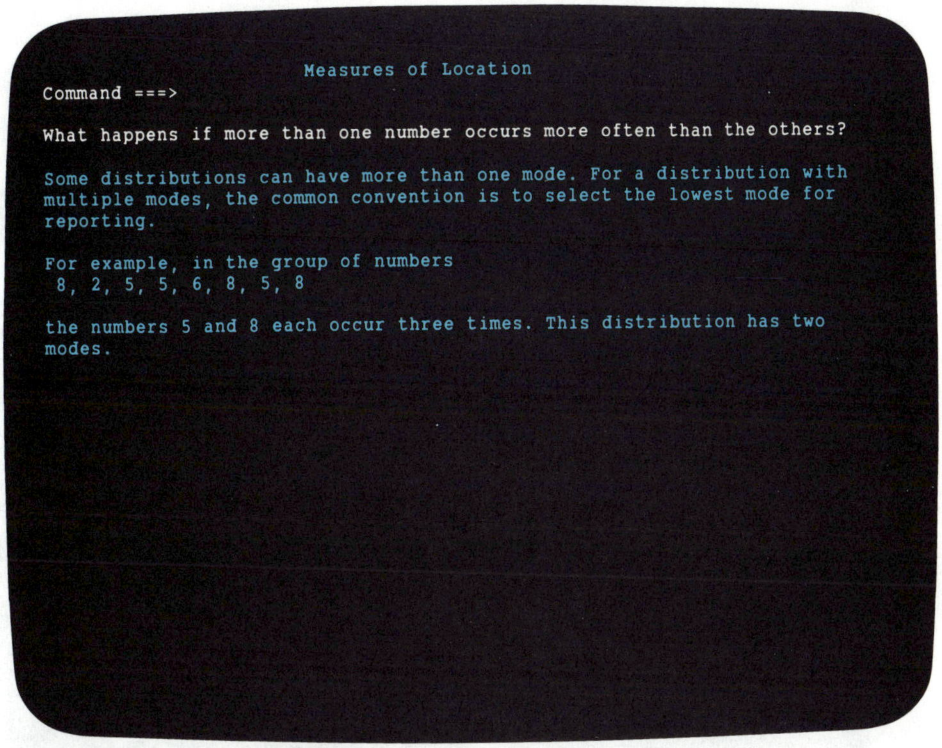

Screen 6.27 Text for the Lesson

Press ENTER to display **Screen 6.28**, another question.

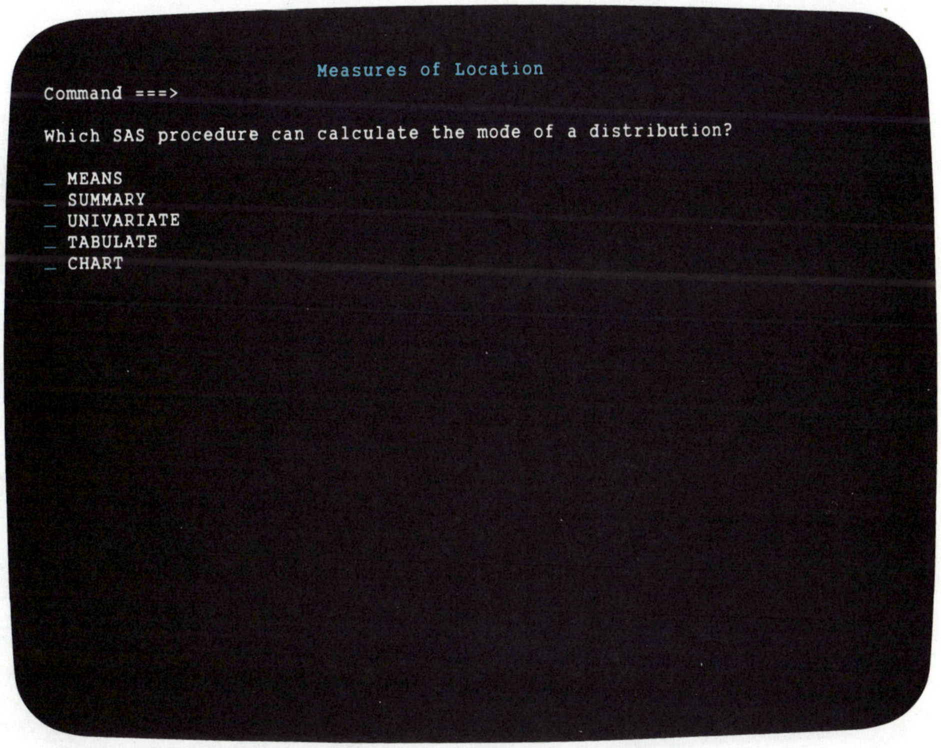

Screen 6.28 Another Question

If you choose any one of the four answers MEANS, SUMMARY, TABULATE, or CHART, then when you press ENTER **Screen 6.29** is displayed.

```
                           Procedure Description
Command ===>

There are several SAS procedures that produce univariate
descriptive statistics. Below is a chart showing the statistics computed
by each procedure.
                                      PROCedure

 Statistic       MEANS  UNIVARIATE  SUMMARY  TABULATE  CHART
------------------------------------------------------------------------
          mean|    X        X          X        X        X
           sum|    X        X          X        X        X
           min|    X        X          X        X
           max|    X        X          X        X
         range|    X        X          X        X
           uss|    X        X          X        X
           css|    X        X          X        X
           var|    X        X          X        X
           std|    X        X          X        X
        stderr|    X        X          X        X
            cv|    X        X          X        X
      skewness|    X        X
      kurtosis|    X        X
             t|    X        X          X        X
           prt|    X        X          X        X
        median|             X
      quantile|             X
          mode|             X
```

Screen 6.29 Branching from a CBT Course

Press ENTER.

```
                     Procedure Description
Command ===>

The UNIVARIATE procedure produces a variety of descriptive statistics
about the distribution of numeric variables.

It is the only SAS procedure that produces the mode, or most frequent
occurrence of a variable.

Other features in UNIVARIATE include:
 o detail on the extreme values of a variable
 o quantiles, such as the median
 o several plots to picture the distribution
 o frequency tables
 o a test that the data are normally distributed.
```

Screen 6.30 Another Frame in the Tutorial

Press ENTER again.

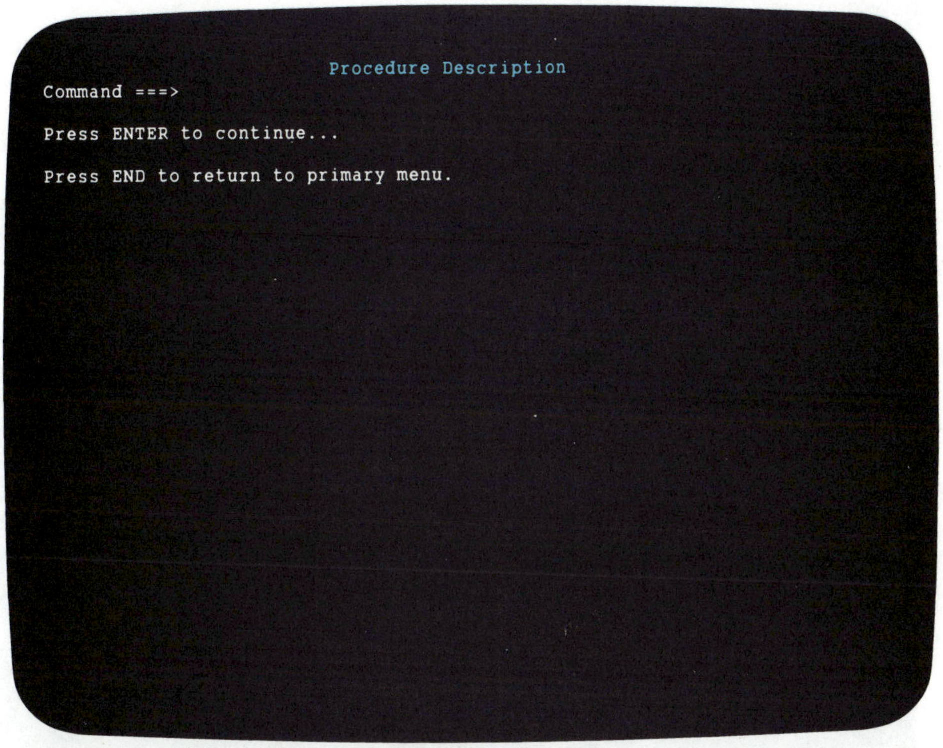

Screen 6.31 Continuing or Ending the Lesson

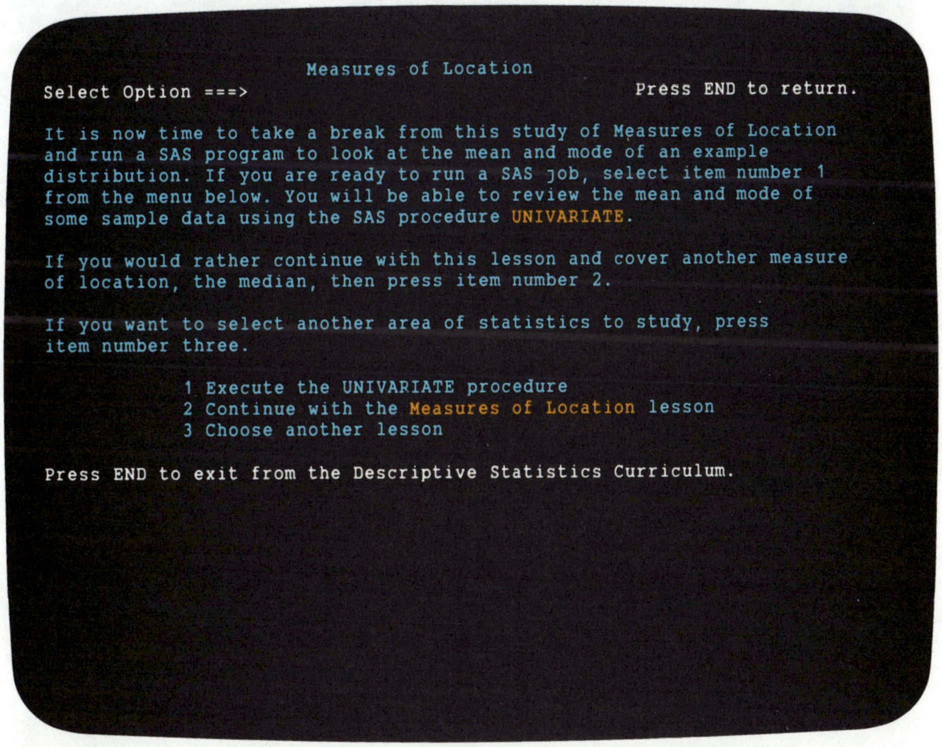

Screen 6.32 Continuing the Lesson with a Menu of New Choices

Screen 6.31 gives you instructions on how to continue. Press ENTER to continue the lesson on Measures of Location. The lesson continues with a menu of new choices.

Screen 6.32 completes a detour caused by selecting an incorrect answer to the last question in the first part of the lesson. It is the screen that would have been displayed if you had selected the answer UNIVARIATE to that question. In that case, you would not have received the short tutorial about descriptive statistics procedures in the SAS System.

You want to see an example of the output produced by the UNIVARIATE procedure, so enter 1 on the Select Option line and press ENTER. Read and complete **Screen 6.33**.

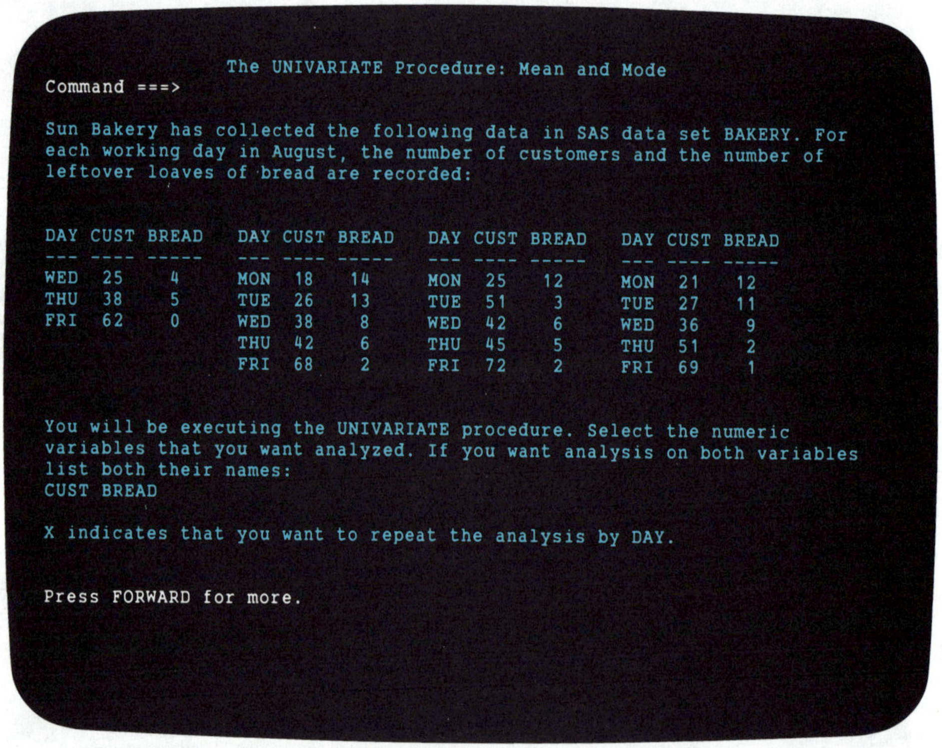

The UNIVARIATE Procedure: Mean and Mode

Command ===>

Sun Bakery has collected the following data in SAS data set BAKERY. For each working day in August, the number of customers and the number of leftover loaves of bread are recorded:

DAY	CUST	BREAD	DAY	CUST	BREAD	DAY	CUST	BREAD	DAY	CUST	BREAD
WED	25	4	MON	18	14	MON	25	12	MON	21	12
THU	38	5	TUE	26	13	TUE	51	3	TUE	27	11
FRI	62	0	WED	38	8	WED	42	6	WED	36	9
			THU	42	6	THU	45	5	THU	51	2
			FRI	68	2	FRI	72	2	FRI	69	1

You will be executing the UNIVARIATE procedure. Select the numeric variables that you want analyzed. If you want analysis on both variables list both their names:
CUST BREAD

X indicates that you want to repeat the analysis by DAY.

Press FORWARD for more.

Screen 6.33 Executing a SAS Procedure

Press FORWARD to view more of the screen. Indicate what your next step should be.

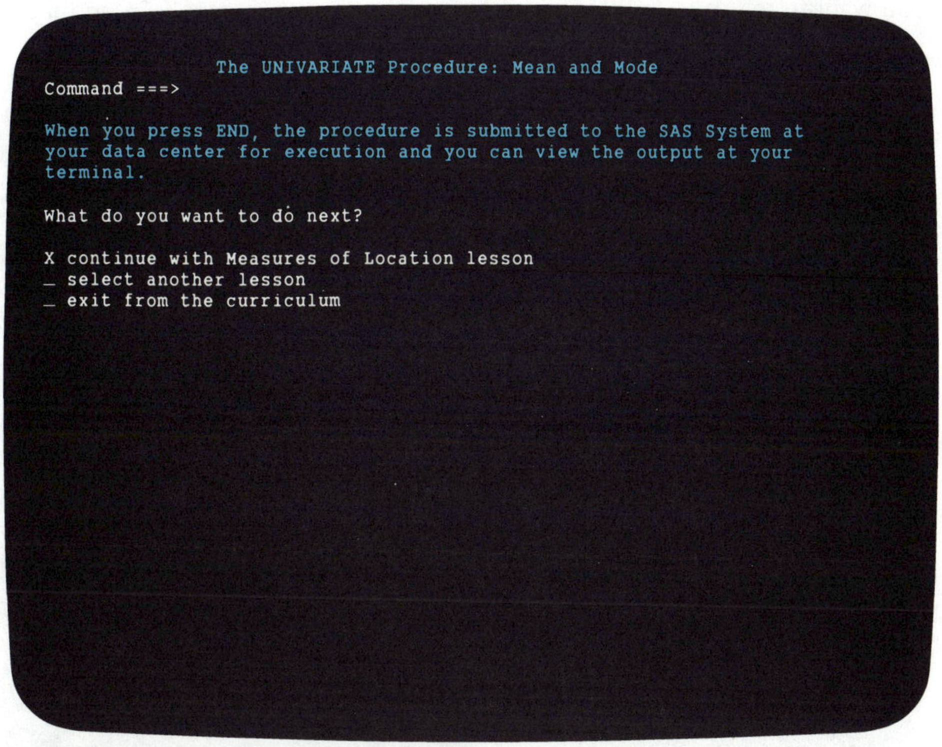

Screen 6.34 Executing a SAS Procedure

Press END to submit a program to the SAS System. The output from that program is displayed at your terminal.

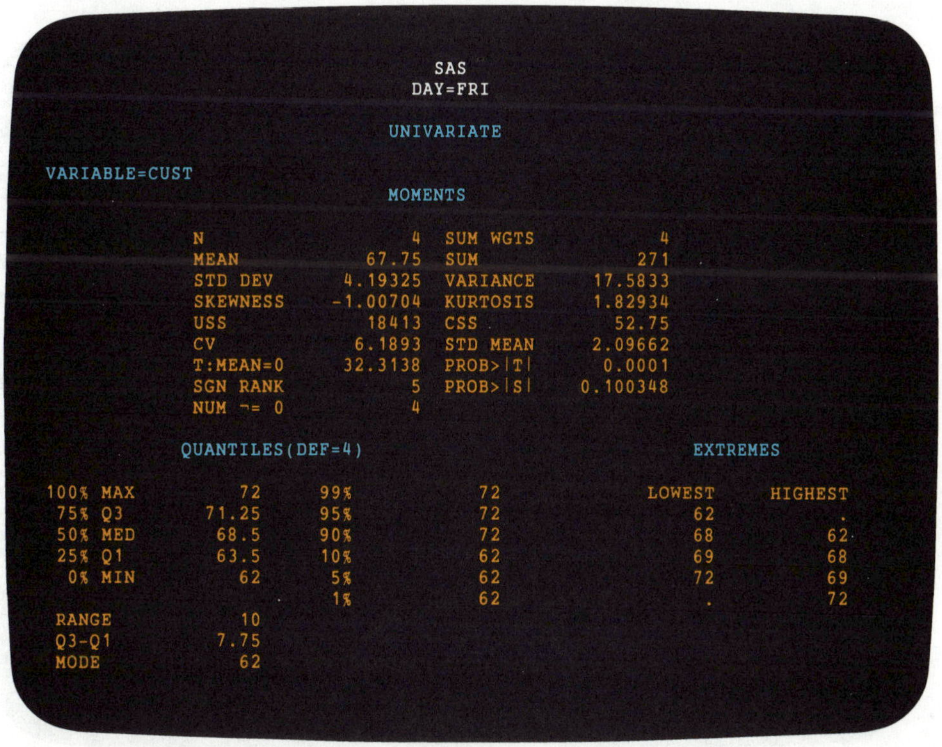

Screen 6.35 Output from a SAS Procedure

Scroll through the output using the FORWARD and BACKWARD keys. When you want to return to the lesson, press END to display **Screens 6.36** and **6.37**.

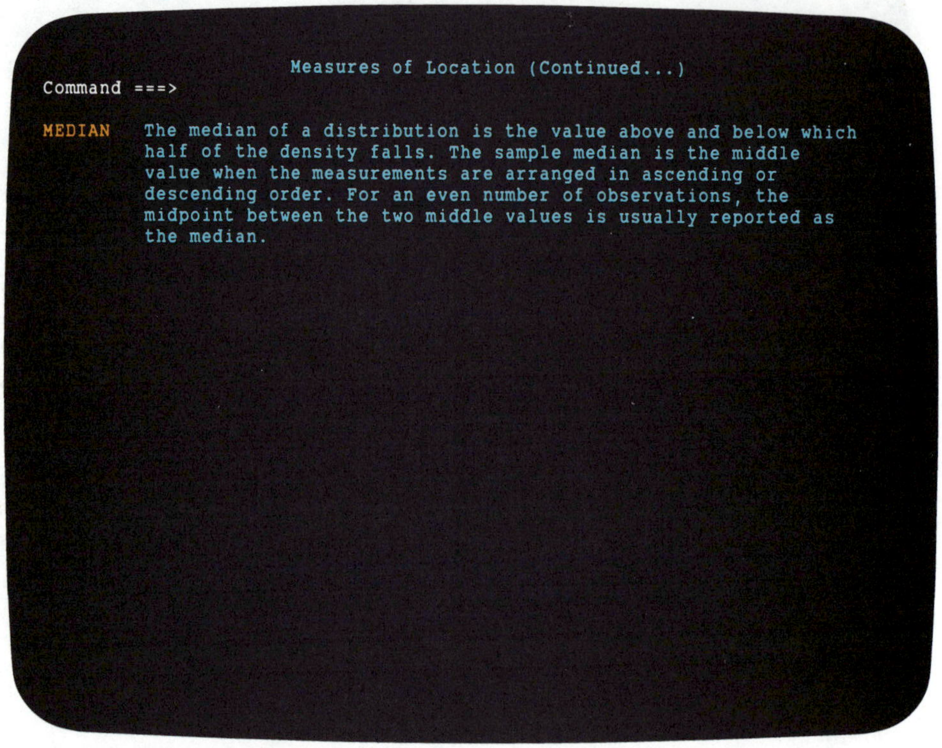

Screen 6.36 Returning to the Lesson

Press ENTER to continue.

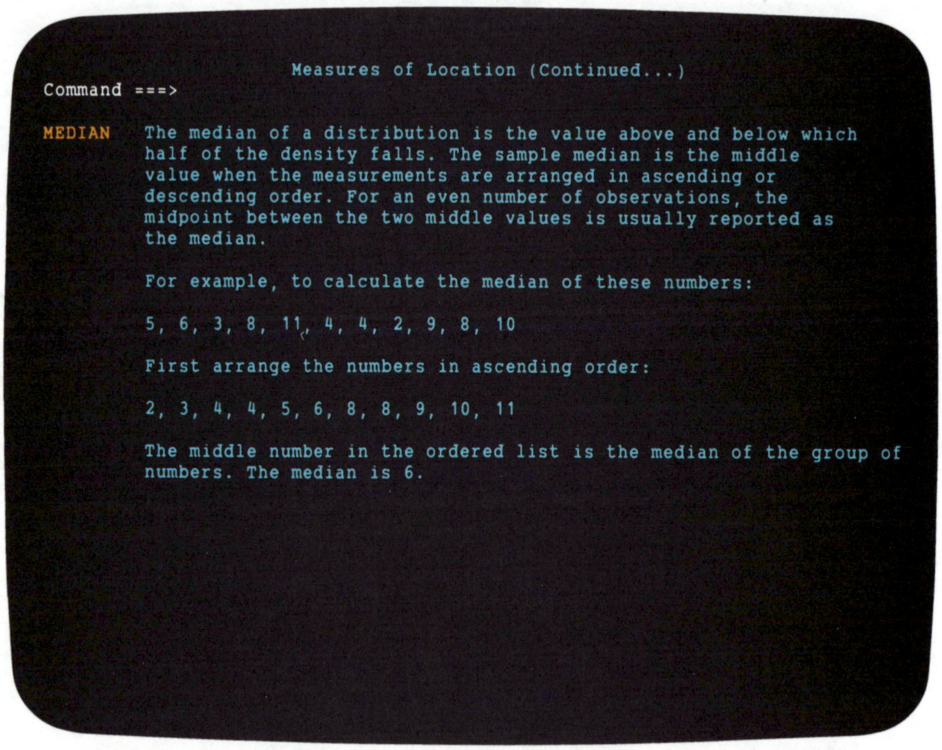

Screen 6.37 Continuing the Lesson

Press ENTER to continue. On the next screen use the NEW LINE key to move the cursor to your answer. Press ENTER again.

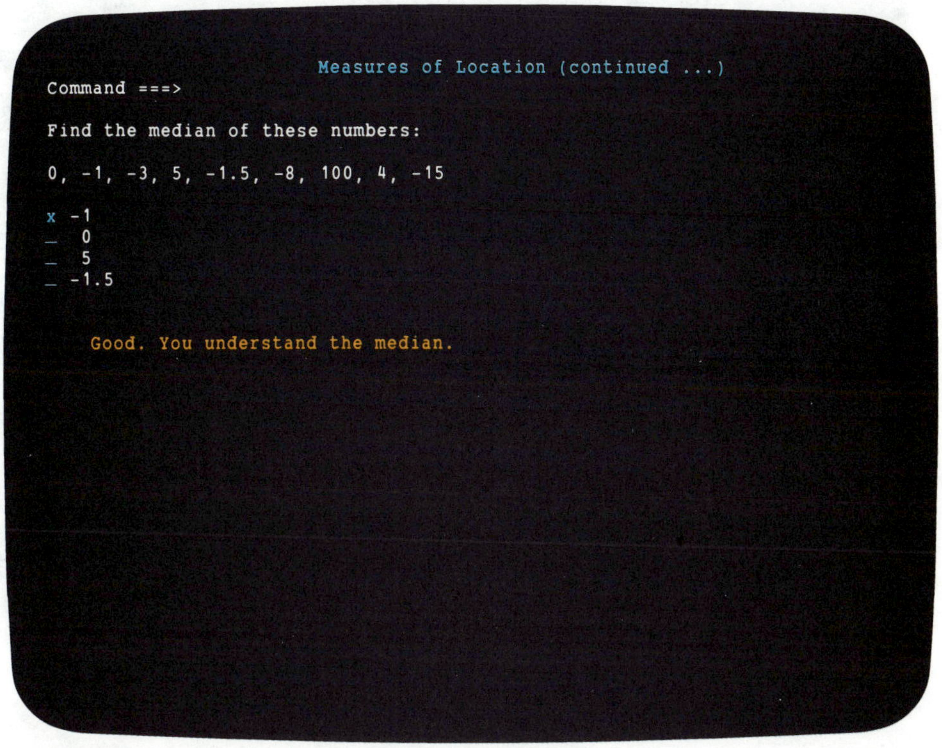

Screen 6.38 Receiving Congratulatory Feedback

Press ENTER to continue the lesson. Read and respond to the blanks in **Screen 6.38**.

Note that when you supply a variable name in the INPUT statement and press ENTER, that name is automatically inserted in the VAR statement below. Press END to submit the program in **Screen 6.39** to the SAS System. Again, the output is displayed at your terminal as shown in **Screen 6.40**.

```
                          Calculate a Median
Command ===>

Now use the SAS System to find the median of a set of data.

Fourteen children in the seventh grade were given a math test. Below are
the fourteen scores:

95, 72, 86, 90, 78, 62, 73, 98, 89, 92, 83, 84, 76, 82

Create a SAS data set containing these test scores. The data set
should have one variable.

DATA TEST ;
 INPUT SCORE @@;
 CARDS;
95 72 86 90 78 62 73 98 89 92 83 84 76 82
;

Now use the UNIVARIATE procedure to calculate some statistics about the
distribution of the children's test scores. One of the statistics will
be the median test score.

PROC UNIVARIATE;
 VAR SCORE ;
 TITLE ' Statistics on Test Scores
```

Screen 6.39 A PROGRAM Screen in the Lesson

```
                        STATISTICS ON TEST SCORES

                               UNIVARIATE

VARIABLE=SCORE
                                 MOMENTS

             N                 14  SUM WGTS           14
             MEAN         82.8571  SUM              1160
             STD DEV      9.92942  VARIANCE      98.5934
             SKEWNESS   -0.466848  KURTOSIS   -0.0542213
             USS            97396  CSS           1281.71
             CV           11.9838  STD MEAN      2.65375
             T:MEAN=0     31.2227  PROB>|T|       0.0001
             SGN RANK        52.5  PROB>|S|   0.00109705
             NUM ^= 0          14

            QUANTILES(DEF=4)                           EXTREMES

100% MAX          98     99%          98          LOWEST      HIGHEST
 75% Q3         90.5     95%          98              62           89
 50% MED        83.5     90%        96.5              72           90
 25% Q1        75.25     10%          67              73           92
  0% MIN          62      5%          62              76           95
                          1%          62              78           98
 RANGE            36
 Q3-Q1         15.25
 MODE             62
```

Screen 6.40 Output from a SAS Procedure

Press END from the procedure output display in **Screen 6.40** to return to the lesson.

You can continue to follow directions given on your screen and to enter commands to continue the lesson. Throughout the lesson, you are given the opportunity to exit or change direction.

For example, suppose that after completing the lesson on Measures of Location, you want to select another lesson. Press END from **Screen 6.41** to display the primary lesson menu.

At any time, you can exit from the statistics curriculum by returning to the primary lesson menu and pressing END. This system is designed so that when you press END from this menu, you are returned to your operating system where you exit from your session as usual.

On another day you may wish to take another lesson in the curriculum. After accessing the curriculum using the command

```
STAT
```

you can select any lesson from the primary menu displayed in **Screen 6.42**.

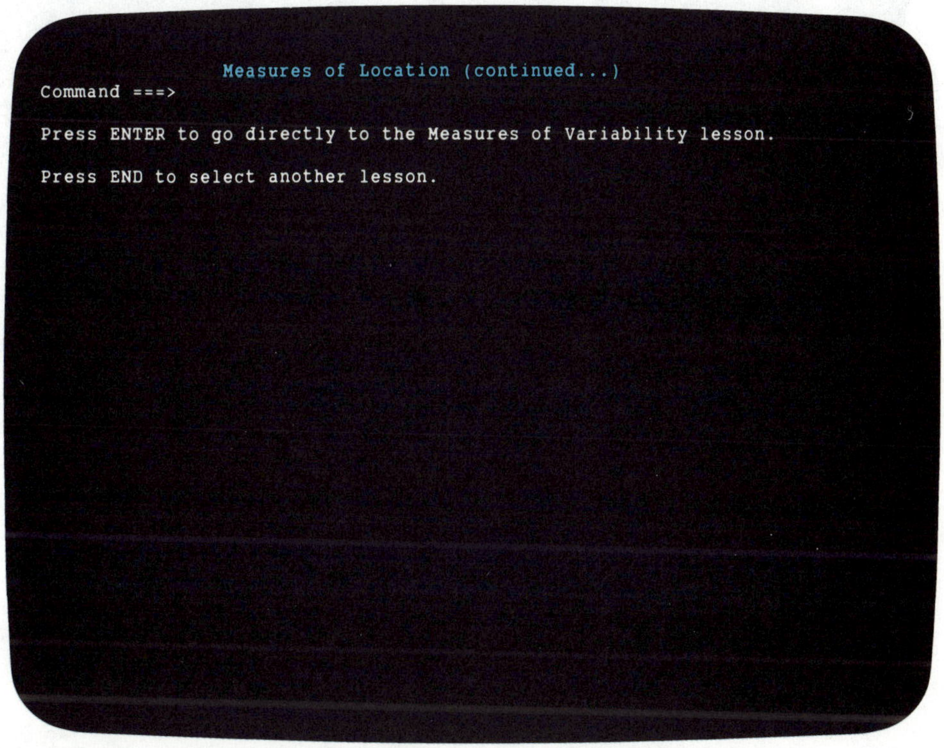

Screen 6.41 Returning to the Lesson

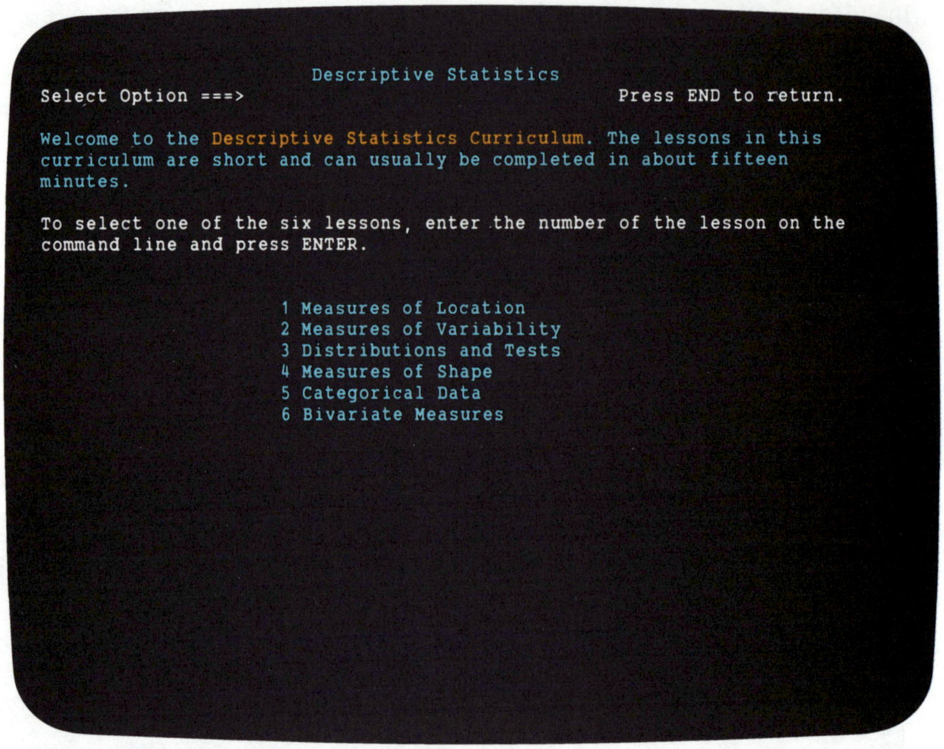

Screen 6.42 Selecting a New Lesson

Appendix 1

SAS® User Profile

INSTALLATION PROFILE
Default Forms
Default Key Definitions
INDIVIDUAL PROFILE
Defining Individual KEYS and FORM Screens

INSTALLATION PROFILE

Each version of the SAS System includes a profile library containing several catalogs. The library must be assigned libref SASUTL by the command procedure that invokes the SAS System.

Catalog	Description
SASUTL.DISPLAY	contains default information for PROC DISPLAY.
SASUTL.FSP	contains default information for SAS/FSP and SAS/AF software.
SASUTL.SAS	contains default information for the base SAS product (for example, the SAS Display Manager System and PROC DATASETS).

These catalogs contain special screens used by SAS software. In addition they contain default function key settings for the procedures and default forms for the various print devices supported by the SAS System.

Default Forms

The SASUTL.FSP catalog contains default form definitions for several of the print devices supporting SAS Institute software products. These forms can be used by SAS/FSP software to generate reports and printouts to different devices. **Table A1.1** is a listing of these default form definitions.

Default Key Definitions

The SASUTL.FSP catalog also contains the default function key definitions used by SAS/FSP and SAS/AF software. **Table A1.2** lists these screens.

The catalog SASUTL.SAS contains the default function key definitions for the SAS Display Manager System and for PROC DATASETS.

The screens in both catalogs are named with special reserved names so that the system can recognize the appropriate setting for each procedure. Your installation representative can change the default screens at your site by accessing this catalog with DISP=OLD and using PROC BUILD.

Table A1.1 Default Form Definitions for Print Devices

I3800CMS	FORM	Default form for IBM 3800 under CMS	13AUG84
I3800MVS	FORM	Default form for IBM 3800 under MVS	07AUG84
I3800VSE	FORM	Default form for IBM 3800 under VSE	14AUG84
I6670CMS	FORM	Default form for IBM 6670 under CMS	07AUG84
I6670MVS	FORM	Default form for IBM 6670 under MVS	07AUG84
I6670VSE	FORM	Default form for IBM 6670 under VSE	07AUG84
PRINTCMS	FORM	Default form for Printer under CMS	14AUG84
PRINTMVS	FORM	Default form for Printer under MVS	07AUG84
PRINTVSE	FORM	Default form for Printer under VSE	14AUG84
X2700CMS	FORM	Default form for Xerox 2700 under CMS	14AUG84
X2700MVS	FORM	Default form for Xerox 2700 under MVS	07AUG84
X2700VSE	FORM	Default form for Xerox 2700 under VSE	14AUG84
X5700CMS	FORM	Default form for Xerox 5700 under CMS	14AUG84
X5700MVS	FORM	Default form for Xerox 5700 under MVS	07AUG84
X5700VSE	FORM	Default form for Xerox 5700 under VSE	14AUG84
X9700CMS	FORM	Default form for Xerox 9700 under CMS	14AUG84
X9700MVS	FORM	Default form for Xerox 9700 under MVS	07AUG84
X9700VSE	FORM	Default form for Xerox 9700 under VSE	14AUG84

Table A1.2 Default Function Keys Used by SAS/FSP and SAS/AF Software

BUILD01	KEYS	Function Keys for BUILD Editor	07AUG84
BUILD02	KEYS	Function Keys for BUILD Attributes	07AUG84
CBT	KEYS		07AUG84
DISPLAY	KEYS		07AUG84
DPDEDIT	KEYS	Function Keys for DPD Editor	07AUG84
FSCALC01	KEYS	Function Keys for FSCALC CALC Screens	07AUG84
FSCALC02	KEYS	Function Keys for FSCALC PGM Screens	07AUG84
FSCALC03	KEYS	Function Keys for FSCALC System Screens	07AUG84
FSEDIT	KEYS	Function Keys for FSEDIT	07AUG84
FSL	KEYS	Function Keys for FSLIST	07AUG84
FSLETTER	KEYS	Function Keys for FSLETTER	07AUG84
FSPRINT	KEYS	Function Keys for FSPRINT	07AUG84
SYSTEM	KEYS	Function Keys for SYSTEM Screens	07AUG84
TEXTEDIT	KEYS	Function Keys for TEXT Editor	03SEP84

Keep in mind that any changes made to these catalogs are universal for your site; that is, the default settings are for everyone using the SAS System at your installation.

INDIVIDUAL PROFILE

In Version 5, a special catalog is also available for establishing a user profile that can be used to store customized default function key settings and form descriptions to meet individual needs and preferences. When looking for defaults, the SAS System searches the user profile for key settings and form descriptions with the appropriate names before it looks in the installation profile contained in the SASUTL library.

The individual profile is a SAS catalog named PROFILE containing KEYS and FORM screens. Function key designations for any SAS procedure can be stored in the individual profile catalog and are used by the appropriate procedure. Keep in mind that a SAS procedure looks for a KEYS designation with a specific name. In addition, FORMs can be defined and stored in the individual catalog rather than in the LETTER catalog.

PROFILE is intended to be a personal library and cannot be accessed by more than one SAS user. The catalog is stored permanently in a SAS data library with reserved libref SASUSER and is associated with an individual's user id. It should not be stored in a SAS data library that contains a catalog shared by other users. If a library named SASUSER is not referenced in your SAS job, the PROFILE catalog is stored temporarily in the WORK data library and is available only for the session. Each user should have access to his own profile. In some cases, libref SASUSER is referenced in a command procedure and is automatically accessed by the user. In other cases, the user may need to reference SASUSER each time he executes the SAS System.

The library referenced by SASUSER, unlike the library containing the profile information for the entire installation, does not exist until you create it. (You can, however, reference an existing SAS data library using libref SASUSER.) You must use a host operating system command to create a file or data set to contain a SAS data library that is associated with the reserved libref SASUSER. The system creates a PROFILE catalog automatically the first time you make a library referenced by SASUSER available to your session. Note that you must have write access to this SAS data library.

Defining Individual KEYS and FORM Screens

There are several ways to include KEYS and FORM designations in the catalog PROFILE to be used as defaults.

- By default, a KEYS screen created using a SAS full-screen procedure or the SAS Display Manager System is automatically stored with the appropriate name in the individual profile catalog.
- If you designate the name SASUSER.PROFILE as the two-level catalog name in the PROC BUILD statement:

  ```
  PROC BUILD CATALOG=SASUSER.PROFILE;
  RUN;
  ```

  you can create KEYS and FORM screens that are stored in the individual profile. Keep in mind that in order for KEYS screens to be used by a procedure, they must be named with the reserved screen name required by the procedure.

- If you specify the individual profile catalog with the LETTER= option in PROC FSLETTER, any FORM screens you create are stored there:

```
PROC FSLETTER LETTER=SASUSER.PROFILE;
RUN;
```

- You can use the EDIT command in PROC FSCALC to create KEYS and FORM screens to be stored in the individual profile.

Appendix 2
SAS® Sample Menu System

INTRODUCTION

This appendix describes a sample user-friendly front end to the SAS System. The SAS Menu System was created with SAS/AF software. It is a series of screens that allow a new SAS software user to build SAS data sets and execute SAS procedures without knowledge of the SAS System. The system can also be used as an example for creating your own interactive application systems.

THE SYSTEM

Primary Menu

The SAS Menu System consists of a primary menu from which a user can select one of the following options:

- obtain general information about the menu system
- define user profile information
- create or modify a project.

General Information

The general information section consists of MENU and HELP screens and is a tutorial on the menu system. When you access the SAS Menu System for the first time, you are sent to the general information section for an overview of how the system works before you can access the primary menu.

General Information

The general information section consists of MENU and HELP screens and is a tutorial on the menu system. When you access the SAS Menu System for the first time, you are sent to the general information section for an overview of how the system works before you can access the primary menu.

User Profile

Each user must have a user profile data set containing information to be saved from one session to the next. Examples of information stored in this user profile data set are

- whether to save each project
- whether to see the SAS code that makes up the project before the code executes
- default first title line for procedure output.

The user profile data set must be created for each user accessing the SAS Menu System and must be available to the user each time the system is accessed. Normally, access to the SAS Menu System and a user's profile are handled automatically by a command procedure.

The user profile data set has the reserved name SASUSER.MENUPROF. It is a SAS data set that is stored in the same SAS data library as the user's personal PROFILE catalog. (See the **User Profile Library** appendix for a description of the PROFILE catalog.)

The first time a user accesses the SAS Menu System, he must complete the necessary profile information. After that, the user profile section is only accessed from the primary menu when the user wants to change profile information.

Projects

Once user profile information has been established, users of the system can create projects to read and analyze their data. The first task in project creation is to define a source of input data. The SAS Menu System supports the following sources of data:

- raw data in an external file
- raw data entered at the terminal
- existing SAS data set
- data referenced by a previously defined project.

After the data are defined to the project, the user is presented with a menu of data analysis tasks to be performed.

Information about each project is stored in a SAS data set named SASUSER.SASCODE. Each time the user creates a new project, deletes an old project, or modifies an existing project, the data set SASUSER.SASCODE is automatically changed. Note that SASUSER.SASCODE is stored in the SAS data library with the user's PROFILE catalog and user profile SAS data set SASUSER.MENUPROF.

Appendix 3

Operating System Notes

INTRODUCTION

This appendix provides a general description of the basic functions of an operating system and how the operating system and the SAS System interact to execute your SAS program. You will also learn about SAS features that relate to file access.

A detailed section for each operating system includes examples to illustrate these features.

To use SAS software products, you do not need to be an expert on operating systems; however, as you learn more about your operating system, you will be able to do more with SAS. After reading this material, you should have a better idea of how the operating system and the SAS System work together and where to find more information.

THE OPERATING SYSTEM

Your SAS programs execute in an environment controlled by a set of powerful programs called an *operating system*. The operating system controls all work done by the computer, such as allocating computer resources to run programs and storing data. Because an operating system oversees activities of the computer, it is sometimes called the *host environment*.

There are different operating systems for different types of computers. However, all operating systems are designed to handle certain basic tasks:

- accept jobs for execution
- store and retrieve data files
- manage terminal sessions
- allocate resources, such as internal memory, time, and disk space, to individual jobs
- control the action of peripheral equipment, such as printers, plotters, and disk and tape drives.

In the same way that you communicate with the SAS System using the SAS language, you communicate with an operating system using the operating system's language. We refer to operating system languages generally as *control languages*. **Table A3.1** lists the types of computers and operating systems under which the SAS System runs, and it gives the commonly used names of their control languages.

INTERACTIONS BETWEEN THE OPERATING SYSTEM AND THE SAS USER

Each time a SAS program executes, many interactions between the SAS System and the operating system occur. The amount of interaction that you need to be aware of depends on your program.

Consider the following example:

```
DATA WEATHER;
   INPUT TEMP PRECIP SUNHRS;
   CARDS;
85.5 0.00 12.33
84.2 0.09 12.31
79.5 0.10 12.30
;
PROC PRINT DATA=WEATHER;
   TITLE 'WEATHER INFORMATION';
```

TABLE A3.1 Computers, Operating Systems, and Control Languages

Computers	Operating Systems	Control Language Name
Data General ECLIPSE MV	AOS/VS	Command Line interpreter (CLI)
Digital VAX	VMS	Digital Command Language (DCL)
IBM and compatible mainframes*	OS TSO (OS interactive)	Job Control Language (JCL) TSO Command Language
	CMS	CMS and CP Command Language
	VM/PC	CMS and CP Command Language
	VSE ICCF (VSE interactive)	Job Control Language (JCL) ICCF Command Language
PRIME	PRIMOS	Command Procedure Language (CPL)

*The 370, 308X, and 4300 series are examples of IBM mainframes. Amdahl 470 V6 is an example of an IBM-compatible mainframe.

Even in the simplest SAS execution, like this one, you need to be aware of two interactions:

1. *Invoking SAS.* You make a request to the operating system to use the SAS software.
2. *Receiving output.* The output from a SAS program is printed, displayed on a terminal, or written to a file.

Many of the SAS programs you write may involve no more interaction than our example. However, you need to be aware of two fairly common situations in SAS programming that require you to specify information to the operating system:

1. *Defining permanent files.* You can define a file when you want to read or write data that are stored independently from your SAS program.
2. *Rerouting output.* You can send output from a SAS program to the destination of your choice rather than to its default destination.

The following pages discuss each of these common situations in more detail.

Invoking the SAS System

In order to run a SAS program, you must issue a request to the operating system to use the SAS System. The request is made using the operating system's control language, for example, with the SAS command:

```
SAS
```

When the request is received, the operating system executes a set of instructions that makes all the components of the SAS System (such as statements, procedures, formats, and functions) available to your SAS job. The operating system also provides space in the computer's main memory in which to execute the SAS program.

You can invoke SAS to execute in *batch mode, noninteractive mode,* or *interactive mode.* The mode determines how your program executes, as described below:

Batch Mode
: Submit a group of control language statements and SAS statements to the operating system. The control language and SAS statements may be stored in a file or may be in a stack of cards. When you submit the job, the operating system schedules (enqueues) the job for execution. Once execution begins, you cannot alter the job or the execution process.

Noninteractive Mode
: Create a file containing your SAS program only (with no control language). When you enter the command to invoke SAS from your terminal, you also enter the name of the file containing your SAS program. The operating system invokes SAS, locates the file, and executes the program. This mode is similar to batch in that once execution begins, you cannot alter the execution process. However, execution does proceed immediately; the job is not enqueued.

Interactive Mode
: (also called *conversational* mode) Issue a command to invoke SAS from your terminal. One of two things happens:

- You will begin a *line-prompt session* in which SAS prompts you, usually with a line number and question mark, to enter your SAS program line by line. Your program executes one step at a time as you enter the statements.
- You will begin a *display manager session* in which you enter the SAS program on the program editor screen and issue the SUBMIT command to submit the code to SAS.

Whether your session is in line-prompt or display manager mode depends on the setting of the SAS system option DMS | NODMS and the kind of terminal you have. To use display manager, you must have a full-screen terminal and DMS must be in effect. Line-prompt mode occurs when your terminal is not full screen or when NODMS is in effect.

The **DETAILS** section for your operating system illustrates how to invoke SAS. Also see the "SAS Display Manager" appendix of this book for information on executing SAS programs in a display manager session.

Receiving the Output

The set of instructions that the operating system executes when you invoke SAS includes requests telling the operating system where to send the output from the SAS job. This is called the *default destination.* SAS output consists of two main parts: 1) the SAS log, which contains the SAS statements used in the job, notes, and error messages; and 2) the SAS procedure output. All SAS jobs output a SAS log; however, not all SAS jobs produce procedure output.

The default destination of the SAS output depends on the execution mode:

- For a batch job, the default destination is often a printer or a disk file.
- In noninteractive mode, the SAS log and procedure output are displayed on the screen after the entire job executes.

- In interactive line-prompt mode, the SAS log and procedure output are displayed on the terminal screen as each step of your program executes instead of after the entire job executes.
- In interactive display manager mode, lines written to the SAS log appear on the SAS log screen; procedure output displays on the procedure output screen unless OUTPUT OFF or DMS OFF has been specified.

You can change the default destination for SAS output by using proper control language and SAS System options. (See **Rerouting SAS Output**, below). For more information on SAS output, refer to the chapter "SAS Log and Procedure Output" in the *SAS User's Guide: Basics*.

Defining Files

In many SAS programs you will want to read or write a *permanent file* (a file that is stored for later use). For example, you may want a SAS program to read a file of data that are stored on tape in order to create a SAS data set that can be printed by PROC PRINT, or you may want to enter new data after a CARDS statement and then store the data in a permanent disk file for later use.

A permanent file resides in a storage location managed by the operating system. Thus, the SAS System must interact with the operating system to access a permanent file. You allow this interaction to take place by *defining* the permanent file(s) needed by your program.

SAS programs use two general kinds of files: *SAS files* and *external files*. SAS files are specially structured files that can be created and processed only by the SAS System. SAS data sets are the most commonly used of the SAS files. External files can be created and processed by other programming languages, as well as by SAS. For the most part, SAS procedures use SAS files.

Following is a general description of how to define permanent SAS and external files. Refer to **DETAILS** for your operating system for examples that illustrate how to define files for programs that read and create external files and SAS files.

External files To define a permanent external file, associate a fileref (short for "file reference") with the complete name of the external file. You then specify the fileref in SAS statements to refer to the external file. For example, if you are reading an external file, specify the fileref in the INFILE statement. If you are creating an external file, specify the fileref in the FILE statement.

In most cases, you must explicitly associate the fileref with the complete name of the external file.[1] The method used to associate the fileref with the file's name differs for each operating system, so be sure to see the **DETAILS** section for your operating system.

SAS files To define a permanent SAS file, associate a libref (short for "library reference") with a permanent library of SAS files, called a *SAS data library*.[2] The **DETAILS** section for your operating system includes complete instructions on how to associate a libref with a SAS data library in your environment.

After the file is defined, you use the libref as the first-level name of the SAS file's complete two-level name in any SAS statement that requests the file. For example, the name could be specified in a PROC, DATA, or SET statement.

Once defined, a libref can be used repeatedly in SAS statements in that job or session to refer to any existing SAS file in the library or to add SAS files to the library.

In most cases, librefs and filerefs must follow the rules for SAS names. Exceptions, if any, are given in **DETAILS** for your operating system. For a general discussion of SAS files, their names, and SAS data libraries, see the chapter "SAS Files" in the *SAS User's Guide: Basics*.

SAS statements used to request files The following list contains a brief description of the SAS statements that are used to request files. If you use one of these statements to request a permanent file, the file must also be defined. See the next section for a list of SAS statements used to define permanent files. All of these statements are fully described in the *SAS User's Guide: Basics*:

DATA
: initiates the DATA step and allows you to create a SAS data set. If the data set is permanent, you must define the SAS library in which to store it unless your operating system is one that defines it for you (see **Details**).

FILE
: specifies a fileref that refers to an external file. Subsequent PUT statements write to this file. Refer to **Details** for your operating system for information on how to define an external file.

%INCLUDE
: specifies a fileref that refers to an external file containing SAS statements that you want to execute. Refer to **Details** for your operating system for information on how to define an external file.

INFILE
: specifies a fileref that refers to an external file to be read by the SAS program. Refer to **Details** for your operating system for information on how to define an external file.

PROC
: uses an option to refer to a SAS library or an external file that is to be read or created. For those procedures that can read and create files in the same execution, more than one option can be specified to refer to the appropriate SAS library or external file. When the procedure uses an entire SAS library, the value of the option is a libref. The value is a two-level permanent SAS file name when the procedure uses a SAS file within the library. If the procedure reads from or writes to an external file, the value of the option is a fileref.

SET
MERGE
UPDATE
: read and manipulate observations in SAS data sets. If a data set being accessed by one of these statements is permanent, you must define the SAS library in which it is stored unless your operating system is one that defines the library for you (see **Details**).

SAS statements used to define files The following list contains a brief description of the SAS statements that are used to define permanent files. Note that under some operating systems, only control language can be used to define a file, not SAS statements. Be sure to read the **Details** section for your operating system. All of these statements are fully described in the *SAS User's Guide: Basics*:

FILENAME
: specifies a fileref with a complete file name, which includes a directory name and the name of a specific file in the directory. If the FILENAME statement does not precede a SAS statement that specifies a fileref, the SAS System uses a file in the current default directory.

LIBNAME
: associates a libref with a directory name. This statement must precede a SAS statement that specifies the libref.

LIBSEARCH establishes a search list of directories by specifying a list of librefs. Each libref listed must be associated with a directory in a LIBNAME statement. LIBSEARCH must follow LIBNAME statements that define the directories.[4]

X allows you to issue operating system commands from within your SAS program if executing in interactive or noninteractive mode.[5] If the X statement is used to issue an operating system command to define a permanent file, it must precede the statement that refers to that file (see **DETAILS**).

Rerouting SAS Output

As discussed above, the default destination of SAS output is determined by the mode of execution. You can change the default destination with the proper control language or with SAS options. For example, if you are executing SAS in display manager mode, by default the SAS log appears on the log screen and the procedure output appears on the output screen. You can copy the SAS log and procedure output with the PRINT or SAVE command of display manager.

When you reroute output, you must override default output handling . This endeavor is both operating system- and site-specific. The method you use will also depend on what you want to do. For example, you can route your output to a particular printer or terminal, or you can even route it to a permanent file. Use the following sources of information to learn how to route output:

- *SAS User's Guide: Basics*. Look for SAS system options used to reroute output on your operating system.
- SAS Companion or Technical Report for your operating system. Look for options and control language used to reroute output.
- The SAS consultant at your site.

DETAILS FOR THE AOS/VS OPERATING SYSTEM

The SAS System running under the AOS/VS operating system is documented in "Changes and Enhancements in the Base SAS and SAS/GRAPH Products under AOS/VS," SAS Technical Report P-129.

Invoking the SAS System

Enter the SAS command after you receive the) prompt:

```
) SAS
```

or

```
) SAS/options
```

or

```
) SAS filename
```

If you enter *SAS*, you will invoke the SAS System in interactive mode. Use the second method to specify valid *options* when you invoke SAS. For example, you can specify *SAS/FSDEVICE=devicename* to invoke SAS in display manager mode. With the third method, you can specify *SAS filename* to give the name of a file containing the SAS program to be executed. This method is called *noninteractive mode*.

Note that the SAS command is a CLI macro file that contains a set of control language instructions to invoke the SAS System.

Read more about the SAS command in SAS Technical Report P-129. For information on executing SAS in batch mode see P-129 and the *AOS/VS CLI User's Manual*.

Defining Files

How you define a file depends on whether the file is a SAS or non-SAS (external) file. The method that you use allows the SAS System to distinguish between SAS files and external files.

External files You can define an external file in one of the following two ways:

- with the CREATE/LINK command of the CLI control language before you invoke the SAS System
- in the FILENAME statement within your SAS program.

With either method you associate a *fileref* with a complete file name. The complete file name includes the directory name and the name of a specific file within the directory. You can also issue the CREATE/LINK command in the X statement, a SAS statement that allows you to enter CLI commands in your SAS program.

The fileref is then used in SAS statements, such as FILE and INFILE, to refer to the external file. If you specify a fileref in a SAS statement before you define the external file, the SAS System reads or creates a file in the current default directory with the following name:

```
:UDD:currentdefaultdirectory:fileref
```

where *fileref* is specified in the INFILE statement to give the name of the file that is read from the current default directory or where *fileref* is specified in the FILE statement to give the name of the file being created in the current default directory.

SAS files If you want to read or create a SAS file, you must define the appropriate directory with the LIBNAME statement. In the LIBNAME statement you associate a *libref* with a directory name only. The libref is then specified in SAS statements, such as DATA, SET, MERGE, and so on, to refer to the directory. Once you have defined a directory in the LIBNAME statement, you can use the associated libref to refer to any file in that directory.

If you do not specify the LIBNAME statement before you use the libref in a SAS statement, you will receive an error message that the directory to which you are referring cannot be found.

Note: discussion of SAS files in the following examples is limited to the most commonly used type, a **SAS data set**. A SAS data set is a SAS file containing observations and variables.

Methods for defining SAS data sets and external files are illustrated in the following sections.

Reading an External File

The following program reads an external file and includes a FILENAME statement to define the external file:

```
) SAS (invoke the SAS System)
SAS messages
1? FILENAME DAILY ':UDD:YOURDIR1:YOUR.RAW.DATA';
2? DATA WEATHER;
3?    INFILE DAILY;
more SAS statements
```

```
7? ENDSAS;
```

The FILENAME statement associates the fileref DAILY with the complete file name, and DAILY is then specified in the INFILE statement. Note that the complete file name includes a directory named YOURDIR1 and the file YOUR.RAW.DATA within the directory.

You can also use the CREATE/LINK to define the external file before you invoke the SAS System. For example:

```
CREATE/LINK DAILY :UDD:YOURDIR1:YOUR.RAW.DATA
```

If you use the CREATE/LINK command, you do not need the FILENAME statement. If you chose to define the file by issuing the CREATE/LINK command with the X statement, you can simply replace the FILENAME statement in the above program with the following SAS statement:

```
X 'CREATE/LINK DAILY :UDD:YOURDIR1:YOUR.RAW.DATA';
```

Since the X statement is a SAS statement, be sure to put a semicolon at the end.

If you do not define the external file, the SAS System will read (or attempt to read) a file from the current default directory with the following name:

```
:UDD:currentdefaultdirectory:DAILY
```

Reading a SAS Data Set

Use the LIBNAME statement to define the directory containing the SAS data set to be read, as shown in the following program:

```
) SAS (invoke the SAS System)
SAS messages
1? LIBNAME REPORT ':UDD:DIR2';
2? PROC PRINT DATA=REPORT.STATION;
3?     VAR A B C;
more SAS messages
4? ENDSAS;
```

The LIBNAME statement associates the libref REPORT with the directory :UDD:DIR2. REPORT is then used as the first level of the permanent SAS data set name REPORT.STATION in the PROC PRINT statement. When this program executes, the SAS System reads a SAS data set named STATION from the directory named :UDD:DIR2 and prints the values for variables A, B, and C.

If the LIBNAME statement is omitted or does not precede the PROC PRINT statement, you will receive an error message stating that the directory cannot be found.

Creating a SAS Data Set

Use the LIBNAME statement to define a directory in which to store a newly created SAS data set. The following program creates a SAS data set using an external file as input:

```
) SAS (invoke the SAS System)
SAS messages
1? FILENAME DAILY ':UDD:YOURDIR1:YOUR.RAW.DATA';
2? LIBNAME MAP ':UDD:YOURDIR2';
3? DATA MAP.WEATHER;
4?     INFILE DAILY;
more SAS statements and messages
```

```
5? ENDSAS;
```

The LIBNAME statement associates the libref MAP with YOURDIR2, the directory in which the SAS data set WEATHER is stored. MAP is then used as the first level of the permanent SAS data set name in the DATA statement. The FILENAME statement associates DAILY with the directory YOURDIR1 and the file YOUR. RAW.DATA, the input file.

If the LIBNAME statement is omitted, you will receive an error message stating that the directory cannot be found. If you do not specify the FILENAME statement, the SAS System will search the current default directory for a file named DAILY.

Creating an External File

Since the following program creates an external file, use the FILENAME statement to associate the fileref with the complete file name. The complete file name includes the directory name and the name of the file that is created within that directory. Since the following program uses a SAS data set as input, you must use a LIBNAME statement to define the appropriate directory:

```
) SAS (invoke the SAS System)
(SAS messages)
1? LIBNAME MAP ':UDD:DIR2'
2? FILENAME FREEZE ':UDD:DIR3:COLD.RAW.DATA';
3? DATA _NULL_;
4?    SET MAP.WEATHER;
5?    FILE FREEZE;
6?    IF TEMP < 32 THEN PUT TEMP;
more SAS statements and messages
9? ENDSAS;
```

The FILENAME statement associates FREEZE with the complete file name :UDD:DIR3:COLD.RAW.DATA. FREEZE is then specified in the FILE statement. You can also issue the CREATE/LINK command (before you invoke the SAS System or in the X statement) to define the external file.

If you do not define the external file for the above program, the SAS System will create a file in the current default directory with the following name:

```
:UDD:currentdefaultdirectory:FREEZE
```

DETAILS FOR THE CMS OPERATING SYSTEM

The SAS System running under the CMS operating System is documented in the *SAS Companion for the VM/CMS Operating System.*

Invoking the SAS System

Enter the SAS command after you receive the READY or R; prompt:

```
R;   (or READY)
SAS filename (options)
```

If your SAS program is stored in a file, specify the *filename* after the SAS command. Invoking the SAS System to execute in this way is called *noninteractive mode*. If you want to invoke SAS in interactive mode do not specify a filename. If you want to specify any of the valid *options* for the SAS command, enter a right parenthesis, followed by the options. The DMS | NODMS option and the type of terminal you are using determine whether you enter a line-prompt or display manager session. If you have a full-screen terminal and DMS is in effect, you enter display manager. If your terminal is not full screen or NODMS is in effect, you enter a line-prompt interactive session.

Note that the SAS command is a CMS command created by the SAS Institute that contains a set of control language instructions to invoke the SAS System.

Read more about the SAS command in the *SAS Companion for the VM/CMS Operating System*. To learn about running a SAS job in a CMS batch machine, refer to the *IBM Virtual/System Product: CMS User's Guide*.

Defining Files

The CMS command FILEDEF is used to define files for use in SAS programs. The FILEDEF command associates a *libref* with a SAS file or a *fileref* with an external (non-SAS) file. The libref or fileref is called a *DDname* in CMS terminology. The form of the FILEDEF command is

```
FILEDEF DDname device filename filetype filemode(options)
```

where

- *DDname* serves as a SAS file's libref or an external file's fileref
- *device* indicates the file's storage medium (usually DISK or TAPE)
- *filename* and *filetype* are the names by which CMS knows the file
- *filemode* is a letter (or letter/number combination) indicating the minidisk on which the file is stored (for disk files only)
- *options* are any of a number of CMS options for the FILEDEF command.

In most cases, you do not have to issue the FILEDEF explicitly to define a SAS file because the SAS System issues the FILEDEF automatically. You must explicitly issue the FILEDEF for an external file.

A FILEDEF can be issued before the SAS System is invoked or after SAS is invoked in an X or CMS statement. In any case, the FILEDEF must be issued before the SAS statement that references the file.

Special Naming Conventions

Although the SAS System allows you to use an underscore (_) in SAS names, CMS does not. Therefore, do not use an underscore character in a libref or a fileref.

Reading an External File

Issue a FILEDEF command to associate a fileref with the external file to be read. Then, use the fileref in the INFILE statement of your SAS program. For example, suppose you write a DATA step that reads the external disk file CLIMATE DATA, which is stored on your A-disk, and you want to use DAILY as the fileref:

```
R;
FILEDEF DAILY DISK CLIMATE DATA A
R;
SAS (invoke the SAS System)
(SAS messages)
1?
DATA WEATHER;
2?
INFILE DAILY;
3?
INPUT TEMP PRECIP SUNHRS;
```

```
4?
more SAS statements
```

The fileref DAILY points to the CMS file CLIMATE DATA A.

Reading a SAS Data Set

Under most circumstances you do not need to define a libref explicitly for a SAS file because SAS makes the association automatically. To access an existing SAS file on any minidisk, just use the file's two-level name in the appropriate SAS statement. SAS searches all accessed minidisks for the file you have specified and issues the appropriate FILEDEF when it finds the file. For example, suppose the SAS data set FOOD.PRICES is stored on your B-disk. When SAS reads this statement:

```
SET FOOD.PRICES;
```

it searches all accessed minidisks for a data set with filename PRICES and filetype FOOD. When it finds PRICES FOOD B, this FILEDEF is automatically issued:

```
FILEDEF FOOD DISK PRICES FOOD B
```

Note: if you have multiple SAS files with the same filename and filetype on different minidisks, SAS will find only the file on the minidisk that is first in the search order. For example, if you have a PRICES FOOD A and a PRICES FOOD B, SAS will find PRICES FOOD A. You must issue a FILEDEF for PRICES FOOD B explicitly if you want to access it.

Creating a SAS Data Set

Under most circumstances, you do not need to define a libref explicitly to create a SAS file because SAS makes the association automatically. When you are creating a new SAS file and you specify a two-level SAS name, SAS automatically issues a FILEDEF using the libref (first-level name) for the DDname parameter **and** for the filetype unless a FILEDEF with that DDname is already in effect. By default, the data set will be written to your A-disk. For example, suppose you are creating a SAS data set called FOOD.PRICES:

```
DATA FOOD.PRICES;
  INPUT ... ;
more SAS statements
```

When SAS reads the name FOOD.PRICES, it checks to see if a FILEDEF with DDname FOOD has been issued. If there is no such FILEDEF, SAS issues one automatically, using FOOD for both the DDname and filetype, PRICES as the filename, and A as the filemode:

```
FILEDEF FOOD DISK PRICES FOOD A
```

Note: do not use the same filetype for SAS files and external (non-SAS) files.

If you want a new SAS data set to be stored on a disk other than your A-disk, you must issue the appropriate FILEDEF explicitly. Specify the appropriate values for the DDname and filemode parameters. You can specify any value for filename and filetype; SAS will substitute the libref (first-level name) and data set name (second-level name) for filetype and filename, respectively. For example, if you want to store FOOD.PRICES on a B-disk, your FILEDEF could be:

```
FILEDEF FOOD DISK DUMMY DUMMY B
```

Notice that CMS and SAS identify the file by the same two names, but the order is reversed. For example, SAS calls the data set FOOD.PRICES, and CMS calls it PRICES FOOD.

Creating an External File

To create an external file in a SAS program, first issue a FILEDEF command to associate a fileref with the name of the external file to be created. Then use the fileref in the FILE statement of your SAS program. For example, suppose you write a DATA step that reads the external disk file CLIMATE DATA, (which is stored on your A-disk) and creates a second external file called COLD TEMPS A. You use the filerefs DAILY and FREEZE to reference the files:

```
R;
FILEDEF DAILY DISK CLIMATE DATA A
R;
FILEDEF FREEZE DISK COLD TEMPS A
R;
SAS
1?
DATA _NULL_;
2?
INFILE DAILY;
3?
INPUT TEMP PRECIP SUNHRS;
4?
FILE FREEZE;
5?
more SAS statements
```

DETAILS FOR THE OS OPERATING SYSTEM AND TSO

The SAS System running under the OS operating system is documented in the *SAS Companion for the OS Operating System and TSO.*

OS Batch

Invoking the SAS System Use the EXEC statement in your JCL:

```
// EXEC SAS,OPTIONS='options'
```

In this case, the OS cataloged procedure named *SAS* contains all the job control language instructions to invoke the SAS System in batch mode. The *OPTIONS=* parameter can be used to specify valid SAS system options.

Read more about the SAS cataloged procedure in the *SAS Companion for OS Operating System and TSO.*

Defining files Use the DD (Data Definition) statement to define permanent files, both SAS and external files. The DD statement associates a *fileref* with a permanent external file or a *libref* with a permanent library of SAS files. In OS terminology the fileref or the libref is called a *DDname.*

The external file can be an OS sequential data set or a partitioned data set (PDS). A sequential data set contains records stored in a sequence under a unique name. If the external file is a sequential data set, you associate a fileref with the sequential data set name in the DD statement, as follows:

```
//fileref DD DSN=external.file.name,DISP=disposition
```

The *fileref* is then specified in SAS statements, such as INFILE and FILE, to refer to the external file. For example,

```
INFILE fileref;
```

A PDS contains a group of data sets called members. The PDS has a name that identifies the group. Each member within the PDS has a unique name. You can identify one member by enclosing the member name in parentheses and including it as the last level of the PDS name. For example, if you want to define an external file that is a member of a PDS, you must specify the DD statement as follows:

```
//fileref DD DSN=external.file.name(member),DISP=disposition
```

In this case you only have access to the member specified. Then, you use the fileref in SAS statements, such as INFILE and FILE, to refer to that member.

To have access to all members of the PDS, use the PDS name only (without a member name) in the DD statement, as follows:

```
//fileref DD DSN=external.file.name,DISP=disposition
```

When you define the PDS in this way, you include the member name in parentheses after the fileref to refer to the specific member in the PDS. For example,

```
INFILE fileref(member1);
FILE fileref(member2);
```

The above statements refer to two members of the same PDS.

If you use a fileref in a SAS statement that is not associated with an external file in the DD statement, you will receive an error message indicating that the file to which you are referring has not been defined.

A group of SAS files is called a *SAS data library*. Once defined, all SAS files within the library are accessible. For example,

```
//libref DD DSN=SAS.library.name,DISP=disposition
```

Then use the *libref* in SAS statements, such as DATA, SET, and MERGE, to refer to the SAS library. You refer to a specific file within the library by including the SAS file name after the libref. The libref and the SAS file name are always separated by a period. For example,

```
DATA libref.SASname;
```

In some SAS statements, such as certain PROC statements, you use only the libref to refer to the entire SAS library. The utility procedure DATASETS is a good example:

```
PROC DATASETS LIBRARY=libref;
```

All of the SAS files in the library referred to by the libref are available to be processed by the DATASETS procedure.

A SAS library can contain several different types of SAS files. The discussion of SAS files in this section is limited to the most commonly used type, a **SAS data set**. A SAS data set is a SAS file that contains observations and variables.

If you use a libref in a SAS statement that is not associated with a SAS library in the DD statement, you will receive an error message indicating that the file to which you are referring has not been defined.

The DISP= parameter Each of the DD statement examples includes a DISP= parameter. DISP= specifies a disposition (status) for the file at the beginning and end of the job. The disposition also implies an access method. (Refer to the *SAS Companion for OS Operating Systems and TSO* for details on specifying the DISP= parameter in the DD statement.) All of the examples in the following sections use existing files and, therefore, specify either DISP=OLD to obtain exclusive access to an existing file or DISP=SHR to obtain shared access to an existing file.

If your SAS program writes to an existing SAS library, you must specify DISP=OLD in the DD statement because you are updating the library. You must have exclusive access to a SAS library to update it. The need to specify DISP=OLD is noted for the following examples, where appropriate.

Methods for defining SAS libraries and external files are illustrated in the following sections.

Reading an external file To read an external file you must include a DD statement in the JCL used to invoke the SAS System. In the following job:

```
//jobname JOB accountinginformation
// EXEC SAS
//DAILY DD DSN=YOUR.RAW.DATA(MON),DISP=SHR
//SYSIN  DD  *
DATA WEATHER;
   INFILE DAILY;
   INPUT TEMP PRECIP SUNHRS;
more SAS statements
```

the DD statement associates the fileref DAILY with the external file YOUR.RAW. DATA(MON). Notice that the external file is a PDS and the member MON is specified. DAILY is then used in the INFILE statement to refer to the external file.

Reading a SAS data set You also use the DD statement to define a permanent SAS library. The DD statement in the following job associates the libref REPORT with the SAS library named YOUR.SAS.LIB: REPORT is then specified as the first level of a permanent SAS data set name in the PROC PRINT statement.

```
//jobname JOB accountinginformation
// EXEC SAS
//REPORT DD DSN=YOUR.SAS.LIB,DISP=SHR
//SYSIN DD *
PROC PRINT DATA=REPORT.STATION;
   VAR A B C;
```

The association is necessary to allow the SAS System to read a SAS data set named STATION from the SAS library YOUR.SAS.LIB. When the program executes, PROC PRINT locates STATION and prints the values of the variables A, B, and C.

Note: in the DD statement YOUR.SAS.LIB is an existing SAS library defined with DISP=SHR to allow for shared use of the SAS library that is being read.

Creating a SAS data set The following program creates a SAS data set using an external file as input. Use the DD statement to define the existing SAS library in which to store the SAS data set created by this program. You must also define the external file in a DD statement:

```
//jobname JOB accountinginformation
// EXEC SAS
//DAILY DD DSN=YOUR.RAW.DATA(MON),DISP=SHR
//MAP DD DSN=YOUR.SAS.LIB,DISP=OLD
//SYSIN DD *
DATA MAP.WEATHER;
   INFILE DAILY;
more SAS statements
```

The first DD statement associates the fileref DAILY with the permanent external file named YOUR.RAW.DATA(MON). Notice that you again refer to a specific member of a PDS. The second DD statement associates the libref MAP with the existing SAS library named YOUR.SAS.LIB. MAP is then used as the first level of the permanent SAS data set name in the DATA statement. The SAS data set WEATHER created by this program is stored in YOUR.SAS.LIB.

Note: in contrast to the previous example, the SAS library must be defined with DISP=OLD because it is existing and because the SAS System will not allow you to write to a SAS library defined with shared access (DISP=SHR). Remember, if your program updates a SAS library, you must have exclusive access to the library.

Creating an external file If your SAS program creates an external file, you must use a DD statement to define the file. The following program creates an external file using a SAS data set as input; therefore, you must include two DD statements in the JCL used to invoke the SAS System:

```
//jobname JOB accountinginformation
// EXEC SAS
//MAP DD DSN=YOUR.SAS.LIB,DISP=SHR
//FREEZE DD DSN=COLD.RAW.DATA,DISP=OLD
//SYSIN  DD  *
DATA _NULL_;
   SET MAP.WEATHER;
   FILE FREEZE(JAN);
   IF TEMP < 32 THEN PUT TEMP;
more SAS statements
```

In this case the libref MAP refers to a file named YOUR.SAS.LIB, and MAP is then used as the first level of the permanent SAS data set name in the SET statement. The fileref FREEZE refers to a PDS named COLD.RAW.DATA. The member of the PDS (JAN) created by this program is specified in the FILE statement. FREEZE is then used in the FILE statement. When this program executes, the PUT statement writes all TEMP values less than 32 to the external file COLD.RAW. DATA(JAN).

TSO (OS Interactive)

Invoking the SAS System Enter the TSO command after you receive the READY prompt:

```
READY
SAS OPTIONS('options')
```

or

```
SAS INPUT('''filename''')
```

Enter *SAS OPTIONS('options')* to invoke SAS in interactive mode and specify valid SAS *options*. The DMS | NODMS option and the type of terminal you use determine whether you enter a line-prompt or display manager session. If you use a full-screen terminal and if DMS is in effect, you enter a display manager session. If your terminal is not full screen or if NODMS is in effect, you enter a line-prompt session.

Enter *SAS INPUT('''filename''') to invoke SAS in noninteractive mode and specify filename* to give the name of the file containing the SAS program to be executed.

The SAS command is a TSO CLIST (Command LIST) that contains a set of control language instructions to invoke the SAS System.

Defining files Use the ALLOCATE command of TSO to define permanent files—SAS files and external files. The ALLOCATE command associates a *fileref* with a permanent external file or a *libref* with a permanent library of SAS files. In TSO terminology a libref or fileref is called a *DDname*.

The external file can be an OS sequential data set or a partitioned data set (PDS). A sequential data set contains records stored in a sequence under a unique name. If the external file to be defined is a sequential data set, you associate a fileref with the sequential data set name in the ALLOCATE command, as follows:

```
ALLOCATE FILE(fileref) DATASET('external.file.name')disposition
```

The *fileref* is then specified in SAS statements, such as INFILE and FILE, to refer to the external file. For example,

```
INFILE fileref;
```

A PDS contains a group of data sets called members. The PDS has a name that identifies the group. Each member within the PDS has a unique name. You can identify one member by enclosing the member name in parentheses and including it as the last level of the PDS name. For example, if you want to define an external file that is a member of a PDS, you must specify the ALLOCATE command as follows:

```
ALLOCATE FILE(fileref)DATASET('external.file.name.(member)') disposition
```

In this case you only have access to the member specified. Then you use the fileref in SAS statements, such as INFILE and FILE, to refer to that member.

To have access to all members, give the PDS name only (without a member name) in the ALLOCATE command, as follows:

```
ALLOCATE FILE(fileref) DATASET('external.file.name') disposition
```

When you use the fileref in SAS statements, such as INFILE and FILE, you include the member name in parentheses after the fileref to refer to a specific member in the PDS. For example,

```
INFILE fileref(member1);
FILE fileref(member2);
```

The above statements refer to two members of the same PDS.

If you use a fileref in a SAS statement that is not associated with an external file in the ALLOCATE command, you will receive an error message indicating that the file to which you are referring has not been defined.

A group of SAS files is called a *SAS data library*. Once defined, all SAS files within the library can be accessed. For example,

```
ALLOCATE FILE(libref) DATASET('SAS.library.name')disposition
```

Then use the *libref* in SAS statements, such as DATA, SET, and MERGE, to refer to the SAS library. You refer to a specific file within the library by including the SAS file name after the libref. The libref and the SAS file name are always separated by a period. For example,

```
DATA libref.SASname;
```

In some SAS statements, such as certain PROC statements, you use only the libref to refer to the entire SAS library. The utility procedure DATASETS is a good example:

```
PROC DATASETS LIBRARY=libref;
```

All of the SAS files in the library referred to by the libref are available to be processed by the DATASETS procedure.

A SAS library can contain several different types of SAS files. The discussion of SAS files in this section is limited to one type, SAS data sets. A SAS data set is a SAS file that contains observations and variables.

If you use a libref in a SAS statement that is not associated with a SAS library in the ALLOCATE command, you will receive an error message indicating that the file to which you are referring has not been defined.

The disposition operand Each ALLOCATE command example includes a disposition operand. *Disposition* specifies the status of the file at the beginning and end of the job and also implies an access method. (Refer to the *SAS Companion for OS Operating Systems and TSO* for details on specifying the disposition operand.) All of the examples in this section use existing files and, therefore, specify either OLD to obtain exclusive access to an existing file or SHR to obtain shared access to an existing file.

If your SAS program writes to an existing SAS library, you must specify a disposition of OLD in the ALLOCATE command because you are updating the library. You must have exclusive access to a SAS library to update it. The need to specify OLD is noted for the following examples, where appropriate.

If your TSO CLIST invokes the SASCP command, you can also issue the ALLOCATE command from within your SAS program with the X or TSO statement. If you use the X or TSO statement, be sure to include it before the SAS statement that requests the file. For example, the X statement that issues an ALLOCATE command to define an input file must be specified before the INFILE statement.

If you do not define the permanent files requested by your SAS program, you will receive an error message.

Methods for defining SAS libraries and external files are illustrated in the following sections.

Reading an external file You can enter the ALLOCATE command before you invoke the SAS System to define the file to be read by the following program:

```
ALLOCATE FILE(DAILY) DATASET('YOUR.RAW.DATA(MON)') SHR
SAS  (invoke the SAS System)
SAS messages
1? DATA WEATHER;
2?    INFILE DAILY;
more SAS statements
6? ENDSAS;
```

The ALLOCATE command associates the fileref DAILY with the permanent external file YOUR.RAW.DATA(MON). Notice that you are defining a specific member of a PDS. DAILY is then specified in the INFILE statement. You can also define the file by issuing the ALLOCATE command in the X statement, as follows:

```
X ALLOCATE FILE(DAILY) DATASET('YOUR.RAW.DATA(MON)') SHR;
```

The X statement must precede the INFILE statement in the above program; otherwise, you will receive an error message indicating that you are referring to a file that has not been defined.

Reading a SAS data set Use the ALLOCATE statement to define a permanent SAS library to be used as input. In the following example the ALLOCATE command associates the libref REPORT with the SAS library named YOUR.SAS.LIB. REPORT is then used as the first level of the permanent SAS data set name in the PROC PRINT statement:

```
SAS  (invoke the SAS System)
```

```
SAS messages
1? TSO ALLOCATE FILE(REPORT) DATASET('YOUR.SAS.LIB') SHR;
2? PROC PRINT DATA=REPORT.STATION;
3?    VAR A B C;
SAS messages
4? ENDSAS;
```

In this case, the TSO statement (the equivalent of the X statement under TSO) is used to issue the ALLOCATE command. When this program executes, PROC PRINT locates the data set named STATION and prints the values of the variables A, B, and C.

Creating a SAS data set The following program creates a SAS data set using a permanent external file as input. Therefore, you must issue the ALLOCATE command twice: once to define the external file to be used as input and once to define the SAS library in which to store WEATHER, the SAS data set created by this program:

```
ALLOCATE FILE(DAILY) DATASET('YOUR.RAW.DATA(MON)') SHR
ALLOCATE FILE(MAP) DATASET('YOUR.SAS.LIB') OLD
SAS  (invoke the SAS System)
SAS messages
1? DATA MAP.WEATHER;
2?   INFILE DAILY;
3?   INPUT TEMP PRECIP SUNHRS;
more SAS statements and messages
6? ENDSAS;
```

The first ALLOCATE command associates the fileref DAILY with the external file YOUR.RAW.DATA(MON), a specific PDS member. DAILY is then used in the INFILE statement. The second ALLOCATE command associates the libref MAP with the SAS library YOUR.SAS.LIB. MAP is then used as the first level of the permanent SAS data set name in the DATA statement. When this program executes, the permanent SAS data set WEATHER contains observations with variables TEMP, PRECIP, and SUNHRS.

Note: this program creates a new SAS data set in the SAS library YOUR.SAS.LIB and thereby updates the library. Notice that the YOUR.SAS.LIB is defined in the ALLOCATE command with a disposition of OLD.

Creating an external file The following program creates an external file using a SAS data set as input. As before, you must issue the ALLOCATE command twice: once to define the permanent external file created by the program and once to define the permanent SAS library that is used as input:

```
ALLOCATE FILE(MAP) DATASET('YOUR.SAS.LIB') SHR
ALLOCATE FILE(FREEZE) DATASET('COLD.RAW.DATA') OLD
SAS  (invoke the SAS System)
SAS messages
1? DATA _NULL_;
2?   SET MAP.WEATHER;
3?   FILE FREEZE(JAN);
4?   IF TEMP < 32 THEN PUT TEMP;
more SAS statements
8? ENDSAS;
```

The first ALLOCATE command associates the libref MAP with the SAS library named YOUR.SAS.LIB. MAP is then used in the SET statement as the first level in the permanent SAS data set name MAP.WEATHER. The second ALLOCATE command associates the fileref FREEZE with a PDS named COLD.RAW.DATA. FREEZE is then used in the FILE statement along with the PDS member JAN that is created by this program. When the program executes, the SAS data set WEATHER is read from the SAS library YOUR.SAS.LIB and all TEMP values less than 32 are written to the external file COLD.RAW.DATA(JAN).

DETAILS FOR THE PRIMOS OPERATING SYSTEM

The SAS System running under the PRIMOS operating system is documented in "Changes and Enhancements in the Base SAS and SAS/GRAPH Products under PRIMOS," SAS Technical Report P-130.

Invoking the SAS System

Enter the SAS command after you receive the OK, prompt:

```
OK, SAS
```

or

```
OK, SAS -options
```

or

```
OK, SAS filename
```

If you enter *SAS*, you will invoke the SAS System in interactive mode. Use the second method to specify valid *options* when you invoke SAS. For example, you can specify *SAS-FSDEVICE=devicename* to invoke SAS in display manager mode. With the third method, you can specify *filename* to give the name of a file containing the SAS program to be executed. This method is called *noninteractive mode*.

Read more about the SAS command in SAS Technical Report P-130.

For information on executing SAS in batch mode, refer to P-130 and *PRIMOS Command Reference Guide*.

Defining Files

How you define a file depends on whether the file is a SAS or non-SAS (external) file. The method that you use allows the SAS System to distinguish between SAS files and external files.

External files Use the FILENAME statement to define an external file. In the FILENAME statement you associate the fileref with a complete file name, which includes the directory name and a specific file within the directory. The FILENAME statement must be included in the SAS program before a SAS statement that refers to the permanent external file. For example, if your program uses an external file as input, the FILENAME statement that defines the file must precede the INFILE statement.

If you do not define the external file to be read or created by your program, the SAS System reads or creates a file in the current directory with the following name:

```
<masterfiledirectory>currentdirectory>fileref
```

where *fileref* is specified in the INFILE statement to give the name of the file that is read from the current default directory or where *fileref* is specified in the FILE statement to give the name of the file being created in the current default directory.

SAS files If you want to read or create a permanent SAS file, you must define the appropriate directory with the LIBNAME statement. In the LIBNAME statement you associate a libref with a directory name only. The libref is then used in SAS statements, such as DATA, SET, MERGE, and so on, to refer to the directory. Once you have defined a directory in the LIBNAME statement, you can use the associated libref to refer to any file in that directory.

The LIBNAME statement must precede a SAS statement that refers to the SAS files (that is, a statement that specifies the libref); otherwise, you will get an error message stating that the directory to which you are referring cannot be found.

Note: when you specify the directory name in the LIBNAME statement or the complete file name (directory name and specific file in the directory) in the FILENAME statement, consider including the master file directory name in the specification. For example,

```
LIBNAME libref '<MASTERDIR>YOURDIR';
FILENAME fileref '<MASTERDIR>YOURDIR2>INPUT.STUFF';
```

Although PRIMOS does not require this level of specification, including the name of the master file directory in a directory specification will ensure that you get the file you want.

Note: discussion of SAS files in the following examples is limited to the most commonly used type, a SAS data set. A SAS data set is a SAS file containing observations and variables.

Methods for defining SAS data sets and external files are illustrated in the following sections.

Reading an External File

Use the FILENAME statement in the SAS program to define the file to be read. The FILENAME statement associates the fileref DAILY with the complete file name <MFD>YOURDIR1>YOUR.RAW.DATA:

```
OK, SAS (invoke the SAS System)
SAS messages
1? FILENAME DAILY '<MFD>YOURDIR1>YOUR.RAW.DATA';
2? DATA WEATHER;
3?    INFILE DAILY;
more SAS statements
7? ENDSAS;
```

DAILY is then used in the INFILE statement. If you do not specify the FILENAME statement, the SAS System searches the current directory for the following file:

```
<masterfiledirectory>currentdirectory>DAILY
```

Reading a SAS Data Set

Use the LIBNAME statement to define the directory containing the SAS data set to be read:

```
OK, SAS (invoke the SAS System)
SAS messages
1? LIBNAME REPORT '<MFD>DIR2';
2? PROC PRINT DATA=REPORT.STATION;
3?    VAR A B C;
more SAS messages
4? ENDSAS;
```

In the above program the LIBNAME statement associates the libref REPORT with the directory named <MFD>DIR2. REPORT is then used as the first level of the permanent SAS data set name REPORT.STATION in the PROC PRINT statement. This association is necessary to allow PROC PRINT to locate a SAS data set named STATION in this directory and print the values of variables A, B, and C.

If the LIBNAME statement is omitted or is not included before the SAS statement that specifies the libref, the SAS System will issue an error message that the directory cannot be found.

Creating a SAS Data Set

The following program creates a permanent SAS data set named WEATHER. You must use the LIBNAME statement to define the directory in which to store WEATHER. This program also uses an external file as input:

```
OK, SAS (invoke the SAS System)
SAS messages
1? FILENAME DAILY '<MFD>YOURDIR1>YOUR.RAW.DATA';
2? LIBNAME MAP '<MFD>YOURDIR2';
3? DATA MAP.WEATHER;
4?    INFILE DAILY;
more SAS statements and messages
5? ENDSAS;
```

In this case, LIBNAME associates the libref MAP with the directory <MFD>YOURDIR2. MAP is then used as the first level of the SAS data set name in the DATA statement.

If the LIBNAME statement is omitted, you will receive an error message stating that the directory cannot be found. If you do not specify the FILENAME statement, the SAS System will search the current directory for a file named DAILY.

Creating an External File

The following program creates an external file using a SAS data set as input. Use the FILENAME statement to associate the fileref with the complete file name. The complete file name will include the directory name and the name of a file to be created in that directory. Use a LIBNAME statement to define the directory containing the SAS data set to be read:

```
OK, SAS (invoke the SAS System)
SAS messages
1? LIBNAME MAP '<MFD>YOURDIR2'
2? FILENAME FREEZE '<MFD>DIR3>COLD.RAW.DATA';
3? DATA _NULL_;
4?    SET MAP.WEATHER;
5?    FILE FREEZE;
6?    IF TEMP < 32 THEN PUT TEMP;
more SAS statements and messages
9? ENDSAS;
```

The LIBNAME statement associates the libref MAP with <MFD>YOURDIR2, the directory containing the SAS data set WEATHER. MAP is then used as the first level of a permanent SAS data set name in the SET statement.

When this program executes, all TEMP values less than 32 in the SAS data set WEATHER are written to an external file named COLD.RAW.DATA. This file is located in the directory <MFD>DIR3. If the FILENAME statement is omitted, the SAS System writes the values to a file in the current directory with the following name:

```
<masterfiledirectory>currentdirectory>FREEZE
```

DETAILS FOR THE VM/PC OPERATING SYSTEM

The SAS System running under the VM/PC operating system is documented in the *SAS Companion for the VM/CMS Operating System.*

Invoking the SAS System

Enter the SAS command after you receive the READY or R; prompt:

```
R;   (or READY)
SAS filename (options)
```

If your SAS program is stored in a file, specify the filename after the SAS command. Invoking the SAS System to execute in this way is called *noninteractive mode*. If you want to invoke SAS in interactive mode, do not specify a filename. If you want to specify any of the valid *options* for the SAS command, enter a right parenthesis, followed by the options. The DMS | NODMS option and the type of terminal you are using determine whether you enter a line-prompt or display manager session. If you are using a full-screen terminal and DMS is in effect, you enter a display manager session. If your terminal is not full screen or if NODMS is in effect, you enter a line-prompt session.

Note that the SAS command is a CMS command created by SAS Institute that contains a set of control language instructions to invoke the SAS System.

Read more about the SAS command in the *SAS Companion for the VM/CMS Operating System*.

Defining Files

The CMS command FILEDEF is used to define files for use in SAS programs. The FILEDEF command associates a libref with a SAS file or a fileref with an external (non-SAS) file. The libref or fileref is called a *DDname* in CMS terminology. The form of the FILEDEF command is

```
FILEDEF DDname device filename filetype filemode(options
```

where

- *DDname* serves as a SAS file's libref or an external file's fileref
- *device* indicates the file's storage medium (usually DISK)
- *filename* and *filetype* are the names by which CMS knows the file
- *filemode* is a letter (or letter/number combination) indicating the minidisk on which the file is stored (for disk files only)
- *options* are any of a number of CMS options for the FILEDEF command.

In most cases, you do not have to issue the FILEDEF explicitly to define a SAS file because the SAS System issues the FILEDEF automatically. You do have to issue the FILEDEF explicitly for an external file.

A FILEDEF can be issued before the SAS System is invoked or after SAS is invoked in an X or CMS statement. In any case, the FILEDEF must be issued before the SAS statement that references the file.

Special Naming Conventions

Although the SAS System allows you to use an underscore (_) in SAS names, VM/PC does not. Therefore, do not use an underscore character in a libref or a fileref.

Reading an External File

Issue a FILEDEF command to associate a fileref with the external file to be read. Then use the fileref in the INFILE statement of your SAS program. For example, suppose you write a DATA step that reads the external disk file CLIMATE DATA, which is stored on your A-disk, and you want to use DAILY as the fileref:

```
R;
FILEDEF DAILY DISK CLIMATE DATA A
R;
SAS (invoke the SAS System)
(SAS messages)
1?
DATA WEATHER;
2?
INFILE DAILY;
3?
INPUT TEMP PRECIP SUNHRS;
4?
more SAS statements
```

The fileref DAILY points to the CMS file CLIMATE DATA A.

Reading a SAS Data Set

Under most circumstances, you do not need to define a libref explicitly for a SAS file because SAS makes the association automatically. To access an existing SAS file on any minidisk, just use the file's two-level name in the appropriate SAS statement. SAS searches all accessed minidisks for the file you have specified and issues the appropriate FILEDEF when it finds the file. For example, suppose the SAS data set FOOD.PRICES is stored on your B-disk. When SAS reads this statement,

```
SET FOOD.PRICES;
```

it searches all accessed minidisks for a data set with filename PRICES and filetype FOOD. When it finds PRICES FOOD B, this FILEDEF is automatically issued:

```
FILEDEF FOOD DISK PRICES FOOD B
```

Note: if you have multiple SAS files with the same filename and filetype on different minidisks, SAS will find only the file on the minidisk that is first in the search order. For example, if you have a PRICES FOOD A and a PRICES FOOD B, SAS will find PRICES FOOD A. You must issue a FILEDEF for PRICES FOOD B explicitly if you want to access it.

Creating a SAS Data Set

Under most circumstances, you do not need to define a libref explicitly to create a SAS file because SAS makes the association automatically. When you are creating a new SAS file and you specify a two-level SAS name, SAS automatically issues a FILEDEF using the libref (first-level name) for the DDname parameter **and** for the filetype unless a FILEDEF with that DDname is already in effect. By default, the data set will be written to your A-disk. For example, suppose you are creating a SAS data set called FOOD.PRICES:

```
DATA FOOD.PRICES;
  INPUT ... ;
more SAS statements
```

When SAS reads the name FOOD.PRICES, it checks to see if a FILEDEF with DDname FOOD has been issued. If there is no such FILEDEF, SAS issues one automatically, using FOOD for both the DDname and filetype, PRICES as the filename, and A as the filemode:

```
FILEDEF FOOD DISK PRICES FOOD A
```

Note: do not use the same filetype for SAS files and external (non-SAS) files. If you want a new SAS data set to be stored on a disk other than your A-disk, you must issue the appropriate FILEDEF explicitly. Specify the appropriate values for the DDname and filemode parameters. You can specify any value for filename and filetype; SAS will substitute the libref (first-level name) and data set name (second-level name) for filetype and filename, respectively. For example, if you want to store FOOD.PRICES on a B-disk, your FILEDEF could be:

```
FILEDEF FOOD DISK DUMMY DUMMY B
```

Notice that CMS and SAS identify the file by the same two names, but the order is reversed. For example, SAS calls the data set FOOD.PRICES, and CMS calls it PRICES FOOD.

Creating an External File

To create an external file in a SAS program, first issue a FILEDEF command to associate a fileref with the name of the external file to be created. Then use the fileref in the FILE statement of your SAS program. For example, suppose you write a DATA step that reads the external disk file CLIMATE DATA (which is stored on your A-disk) and creates a second external file called COLD TEMPS A. You use the filerefs DAILY and FREEZE to reference the files:

```
R;
FILEDEF DAILY DISK CLIMATE DATA A
R;
FILEDEF FREEZE DISK COLD TEMPS A
R;
SAS
1?
DATA _NULL_;
2?
INFILE DAILY;
3?
INPUT TEMP PRECIP SUNHRS;
4?
FILE FREEZE;
5?
more SAS statements
```

DETAILS FOR THE VMS OPERATING SYSTEM

The SAS System running under the VMS operating system is documented in "Changes and Enhancements in the Base SAS and SAS/GRAPH Products under VMS," SAS Technical Report P-128.

Invoking the SAS System

Enter the SAS command after you receive the $ prompt:

```
$ SAS
```

or

```
$ SAS/options
```

or

```
$ SAS filename
```

If you enter SAS, you will invoke the SAS System in line-prompt mode. Use the second method to specify valid *options* when you invoke SAS. For example, you can specify *FSDEVICE=devicename* to invoke SAS in display manager mode. With the third method, you can specify *filename* to give the name of a file containing the SAS program to be executed. This method is called *noninteractive mode*.

Read more about the SAS command and how to execute SAS in batch mode in Technical Report P-128.

Defining Files

The method that you use to define a file depends on whether the file is a SAS or non-SAS (external) file. The method that you use allows the SAS System to distinguish between SAS files and external files.

External files You can define an external file in one of the following two ways:

- with the ASSIGN command of the DCL control language before you invoke the SAS System
- in the FILENAME statement within your SAS program.

With either method you associate the fileref with a complete file name, which includes the directory name and the name of a specific file within the directory. You can also issue the ASSIGN command in the X statement, a SAS statement that allows you to enter DCL commands in your SAS program.

The fileref is then used in SAS statements, such as INFILE and FILE, to refer to external files. If you specify a fileref in a SAS statement before you define the external file, the SAS System reads or creates a file in the current default directory with the following name:

```
[currentdefaultdirectory]fileref.extension
```

where *fileref* is specified in the INFILE statement to give the name of the file that is read from the current default directory or where *fileref* is specified in the FILE statement to give the name of the file being created in the current default directory.

Extension is a part of the file name that indicates the type of information a file contains. You must include the extension in the complete file name when you define an external file. (Refer to SAS Technical Report P-128 for more information on extension names.)

SAS files If you want to read or create a permanent SAS file, you must define the appropriate directory with the LIBNAME statement. In the LIBNAME statement you associate a libref with a directory name only. The libref is then used in SAS statements, such as DATA, SET, MERGE, and so on, to refer to the directory. Once you have defined a directory in the LIBNAME statement, you can use the associated libref to refer to any file in that directory.

If you do not include the LIBNAME statement in your program before a SAS statement that specifies the libref, you will get an error message stating that the directory to which you are referring cannot be found.

Note: discussion of SAS files in the following examples is limited to the most commonly used type, a **SAS data set**. A SAS data set is a SAS file containing observations and variables.

Methods for defining SAS data sets and external files are illustrated in the following sections.

Special Naming Conventions

Although the SAS System allows you to use an underscore (_) in SAS names, VMS does not. Therefore, do not use the underscore character in a libref or a fileref.

Reading an External File

You can use the FILENAME statement to define an external file. In the following program the FILENAME statement associates a fileref with a complete file name:

```
SAS (invoke the SAS System)
SAS messages
1? FILENAME DAILY '[YOURDIR1]YOURRAW.DAT';
2? DATA WEATHER;
3?    INFILE DAILY;
4?    INPUT TEMP PRECIP SUNHRS;
more SAS statements and messages
7? ENDSAS;
```

The FILENAME statement associates the fileref DAILY with the complete file name [YOURDIR1]YOURRAW.DAT. DAILY is then specified in the INFILE statement. Notice that the file name includes the directory name YOURDIR1 and the file YOURRAW within the directory DAT is the extension name.

You can also use the ASSIGN command to define the permanent external file before you invoke SAS. For example,

```
ASSIGN [YOURDIR1]YOURAW.DAT DAILY
```

Notice that the fileref DAILY is specified after the complete file name in the ASSIGN statement, which is opposite from the way you specify the FILENAME statement. If you chose to define the file by issuing the ASSIGN command with the X statement, you can simply replace the FILENAME statement in the above program with the following SAS statement:

```
X 'ASSIGN [YOURDIR1]YOURRAW.DAT DAILY';
```

Since the X statement is a SAS statement, be sure to put a semicolon at the end.

If you do not define the external file to be read by the above program, the SAS System will read (or attempt to read) a file from the current default directory with the following name:

```
[currentdefaultdirectory]DAILY.DAT
```

Reading a SAS Data Set

Use the LIBNAME statement to define the directory containing the SAS data set to be read, as shown in the following program:

```
SAS (invoke the SAS System)
(SAS messages)
1? LIBNAME REPORT '[DIR2]';
2? PROC PRINT DATA=REPORT.STATION;
3?    VAR A B C;
```

```
more SAS messages
4? ENDSAS;
```

The LIBNAME statement associates the libref REPORT with the directory [DIR2]. REPORT is then used as the first level of the permanent SAS data set name in the PROC PRINT statement. When this program executes, the SAS System reads a SAS data set named STATION from the directory named [DIR2], and PROC PRINT prints the values for the variables A, B, and C.

If you specify a libref that has not been associated with a directory in the LIBNAME statement, you will receive an error message that the directory cannot be found.

Creating a SAS Data Set

The following program creates a SAS data set using an external file as input. You must use the LIBNAME statement to define the directory in which to store the SAS data set. You must also use the FILENAME statement to associate a fileref with the complete file name [YOURDIR1]YOURRAW.DAT.

```
SAS (invoke the SAS System)
SAS messages
1? FILENAME DAILY '[YOURDIR1]YOURRAW.DAT';
2? LIBNAME MAP '[YOURDIR2]';
3? DATA MAP.WEATHER;
4?    INFILE DAILY;
more SAS statements and messages
5? ENDSAS;
```

The LIBNAME statement associates the libref MAP with the directory [YOURDIR2], the directory in which WEATHER is stored. MAP is then specified as the first-level name of the SAS data set in the DATA statement.

If the LIBNAME statement is not specified before a statement that specifies the libref, you will receive an error message that the directory cannot be found. If you do not specify the FILENAME statement, the SAS System will search the current default directory for a file named DAILY.DAT.

Creating an External File

When you are creating an external file, you can use the FILENAME statement or the ASSIGN command to define the complete file name. The following program uses a SAS data set as input to create an external file:

```
SAS (invoke the SAS System)
SAS messages
1? FILENAME FREEZE '[DIR3]COLDRAW.DAT';
2? LIBNAME MAP '[YOURDIR2]';
3? DATA _NULL_;
4?    SET MAP.WEATHER;
5?    FILE FREEZE;
6?    IF TEMP < 32 THEN PUT TEMP;
more SAS statements and messages
9? ENDSAS;
```

The FILENAME statement associates the fileref FREEZE with the complete file name [DIR3]COLDRAW.DAT, and the LIBNAME statement associates the libref MAP with the directory containing WEATHER, the SAS data set being used as input.

When this program executes, all TEMP values less than 32 are written to an external file named COLDRAW.DAT. This file is located in the directory [DIR3]. If you do not specify the FILENAME statement, the SAS System writes the values in a file in the current default directory. The file has the following name:

```
[currentdefaultdirectory]FREEZE.DAT
```

DETAILS FOR THE VSE OPERATING SYSTEM AND ICCF

The *SAS Companion for the VSE Operating System* and "Enhancements and Updates for the VSE Operating System," SAS Technical Report P-132, give complete information on using the SAS System with the VSE operating system and ICCF.

The examples in this section use the word SAS to invoke the SAS System.

VSE Batch

Invoking the SAS System Use the EXEC statement in your JCL:

```
// EXEC PROC=SAS
```

In this case, a VSE batch procedure named *SAS* contains all the standard job control language required to invoke the SAS System in batch mode. Refer to the *SAS Companion for the VSE Operating System* for information on how to specify options at SAS invocation.

If your installation does not support a batch procedure to invoke the SAS System, your SAS consultant can tell you how to invoke SAS.

Defining files To define files stored on disk use the following set of JCL statements: DLBL, EXTENT, and ASSGN. You must issue this set of statements for each disk file needed—SAS and non-SAS. (In this context non-SAS means an external file—a file that is not a SAS file.)

The DLBL statement associates a *fileref* with an external file or a *libref* with a library of SAS files. In VSE terminology the fileref or the libref is called a *filename*. The EXTENT statement provides information about disk space occupied by the file, names a disk volume, and assigns a logical unit. The ASSGN statement associates the logical unit with the disk volume.

For example, the following statements define an external file stored on disk:

```
// DLBL fileref,'external.file.name',expiry
// EXTENT logicalunit,volumeserial,type,seq,begin,trks/blks
// ASSGN logicalunit,DISK,VOL=volumeserial,disposition
```

Use the following statements to define a library of SAS files stored on disk:

```
// DLBL libref,'SAS.library.name',expiry
// EXTENT logicalunit,volumeserial,type,seq,begin,trks/blks
// ASSGN logicalunit,DISK,VOL=volumeserial,disposition
```

The *fileref* is then used in SAS statements, such as FILE and INFILE, to refer to a permanent external file, and the *libref* is then used in SAS statements, such as DATA, SET, MERGE, and so on, to refer to a permanent SAS library. Once defined the libref can be used repeatedly in SAS statements to read or create SAS files in the library.

These three statements must be specified in the order shown above. Notice that both DLBL statements show how to specify an expiration date (expiry), and the EXTENT statements show how to specify full extent information (type,seq, begin,trks | blks). These specifications are required when you are creating either a new SAS library or an external file, but they are not necessary for existing files. Example programs in the following sections use existing files.

Note: a SAS library can contain several different types of files. This discussion of SAS files is limited to one type, **SAS data sets**. A SAS data set is a SAS file containing observations and variables.

To define files stored on tape, use the TLBL, ASSGN, PAUSE, MTC, and UPSI statements. These statements are explained in the *SAS Companion for the VSE Operating System*, along with more detailed information on how to define tape and disk files.

If you use a libref or fileref in a SAS statement without having defined the file to which you are referring, you will receive an error message.

Special naming conventions The following information concerning fileref and libref naming conventions is summarized from the *SAS Companion for the VSE Operating System*:

- **Filerefs** or **librefs** specified in DLBL and TLBL statements must not exceed seven characters, although most SAS documentation states that as many as eight characters are allowed.
- The first letter of the **libref** specifies how the SAS library is accessed, that is, how the file is opened and whether you can write to it. Use one of the following letters as the first letter in a libref to indicate the appropriate access mode:

W	to specify a work library assumed to be a temporary file.
O	to create a new SAS library, not to be confused with writing a newly created SAS data set to an existing SAS library. The EXTENT statement must contain full extent information, as shown above.
I or S	to read a SAS file from a SAS library; the file can be used for input only.
U	(or any letter except W, O, S, or I) to specify read and write access to a SAS library.

- To access a permanent external file or SAS library stored on tape, you must use a libref or fileref ending with a 1-, 2-, or 3-digit number that matches the logical unit number specified in the control language.

These naming conventions are reflected in the following examples where appropriate. For more information on VSE naming conventions, please refer to the *SAS Companion for the VSE Operating System* and "Enhancements and Updates in SAS82.4 under VSE," SAS Technical Report P-132.

Methods for defining SAS libraries and external files are illustrated in the following sections.

Reading an external file In the following example, you must use the DLBL, EXTENT, and ASSGN statements to define the external file to be read:

```
* $$ JNM=jobname ...
* $$ LST LST= ...
* $$ LST LST= ...
// JOB jobname ...
// DLBL DAILY,'YOUR.RAW.DATA'
// EXTENT SYS050,VSE123
// ASSGN SYS050,DISK,VOL=VSE123,SHR
```

```
// EXEC  PROC=SAS
DATA WEATHER;
   INFILE DAILY RECFM=FB BLKSIZE=192 LRECL=1920;
   INPUT TEMP PRECIP SUNHRS;
more SAS statements
```

The DLBL statement associates the fileref DAILY with the file named YOUR. RAW.DATA. DAILY is then used in the INFILE statement

Note: the INFILE statement, in addition to giving fileref DAILY, must also supply the record format and block size. You must specify these two file characteristics for any file that you are reading by using the SAS options RECFM= and BLKSIZE=. You must also give the logical record length (LRECL=) if the file's record format is FB (fixed blocked) or VB (variable blocked).

Reading a SAS data set Use DLBL, EXTENT, and ASSGN statements to define a SAS library. In the following job, the DLBL statement associates the libref REPORT with a SAS library named YOUR.SAS.LIB. REPORT is then used in the PROC PRINT statement as the first level of the permanent SAS data set name:

```
* $$ JNM=jobname ...
* $$ LST LST= ...
* $$ LST LST= ...
// JOB jobname ...
// DLBL REPORT,'YOUR.SAS.LIB'
// EXTENT SYS050,VSE123
// ASSGN SYS050,DISK,VOL=VSE123,SHR
// EXEC  PROC=SAS
PROC PRINT DATA=REPORT.STATION;
   VAR A B C;
more SAS statements
```

When this program executes, the SAS data set named STATION is read from the SAS library YOUR.SAS.LIB, and PROC PRINT prints all the values for variables A, B, and C.

Note: if you specify a libref beginning with the letter I or S in this example, you have read-only access to the SAS library. For example, if YOUR.SAS.LIB is protected and allows only read access, you must specify IREPORT instead of REPORT. Remember that a libref beginning with a letter other than W, I, S, or O requests read and write access.

Creating a SAS data set The following program creates a permanent SAS data set using an external file as input. Therefore, you must use two sets of DLBL, EXTENT, and ASSGN statements: one set to define the SAS library that will store the newly created SAS data set and one to define the external file to be read.

```
* $$ JNM=jobname ...
* $$ LST LST= ...
* $$ LST LST= ...
// JOB jobname ...
// DLBL DAILY,'YOUR.RAW.DATA'
// EXTENT SYS050,VSE123
// ASSGN SYS050,DISK,VOL=VSE123,SHR
// DLBL MAP,'YOUR.SAS.LIB'
// EXTENT SYS067,ABC321
// ASSGN SYS067,DISK,VOL=ABC321,SHR
// EXEC  PROC=SAS
DATA MAP.WEATHER;
```

```
    INFILE DAILY RECFM=recfmBLKSIZE=blksizeLRECL=lrecl;
    INPUT TEMP PRECIP SUNHRS;
more SAS statements
```

The first DLBL statement associates the fileref DAILY with the permanent external file YOUR.RAW.DATA. DAILY is then used in the INFILE statement. The second DLBL statement associates the libref MAP with the SAS library YOUR.SAS.LIB. MAP is then used as the first level of the permanent SAS data set name in the DATA statement. When this program executes the new SAS data set WEATHER is stored in YOUR.SAS.LIB. Observations in WEATHER will contain the variables TEMP, PRECIP, and SUNHRS.

Creating an external file The following program creates an external file using a SAS data set as input. Again, you must include one set of JCL statements to define the SAS library to be used as input and one set to define the external file that is created by this program.

```
* $$ JNM=jobname ...
* $$ LST LST= ...
* $$ LST LST= ...
// JOB jobname ...
// DLBL MAP,'YOUR.SAS.LIB'
// EXTENT SYS051,VSE123
// ASSGN SYS051,DISK,VOL=VSE123,SHR
// DLBL FREEZE,'COLD.RAW.DATA',99/365
// EXTENT SYS050,VSE123,1,0,5280,300
// ASSGN SYS050,DISK,VOL=VSE123,SHR
// EXEC  PROC=SAS
DATA _NULL_;
   SET MAP.WEATHER;
   FILE FREEZE;
   IF TEMP < 32 THEN PUT TEMP;
   more SAS statements
```

The first DLBL statement associates the libref MAP with the SAS library YOUR.SAS.LIB. MAP is then used in the SET statement as the first level of the permanent SAS data set name. The second DLBL statement associates the fileref FREEZE with the permanent external file COLD.RAW.DATA. FREEZE is then used in the FILE statement. When this program executes, all TEMP values less then 32 that are read from the SAS data set WEATHER are written to the file COLD.RAW.DATA. These values replace existing information in the file.

ICCF (VSE Interactive)

Invoking the SAS System Enter the ICCF proc (short for procedure) after you receive the *READY prompt:

```
*READY
SAS
```

The ICCF proc (named *SAS,* in this case) contains the standard job control language used to invoke the SAS System. If you are using a full-screen terminal, display manager mode is default; otherwise, line-prompt mode is the default. Refer to the *SAS Companion for the VSE Operating System* for information on how to specify options at SAS invocation.

If your installation does not support a proc to invoke the SAS System, your SAS consultant can tell you how to invoke SAS.

Defining files In the ICCF proc that is used to invoke the SAS System, you must include a /FILE statement to define each permanent file—SAS and non-SAS. In this context non-SAS means an external file—any file that is not a SAS file.

In the /FILE statement you associate a *fileref* with a permanent external file and a *libref* with a library of SAS files. In ICCF terminology the fileref or the libref is called a *filename*. For example, to define an external file include the /FILE statement in the ICCF proc:

```
/FILE NAME=fileref,ID'external.file.name',UNITS=logicalunit,
/  SERIAL=volumeserial,DATE=expiry,LOC=begin,trks|blks
```

The *fileref* is then used in SAS statements, such as FILE and INFILE, to refer to the external file.

To define a SAS data library, include the following /FILE statement in the ICCF proc:

```
/FILE NAME=libref,ID'SAS.library.name',UNITS=logicalunit,
/  SERIAL=volumeserial,DATE=expiry,LOC=begin,trks|blks
```

The *libref* is then used in SAS statements, such as DATA, SET, MERGE, and so on, to refer to the library of SAS files.

The /FILE statements shown above include parameters for specifying an expiration date (DATE=expiry), beginning tracks, and number of tracks or blocks used (LOC=begin,trks | blks). This information is required if you are creating a new SAS library or a new external file, but it is not necessary if you are using an existing library.

Note: UNITS must specify a logical unit that was assigned to the disk volume *volumeserial* in the ICCF start-up JCL. See your systems personnel for more information on logical units.

You cannot use tape files with the SAS System running under ICCF.

If you use a libref or fileref in a SAS statement without having defined the file to which you are referring, you will receive an error message.

Note: a SAS library can contain several different types of files. This discussion of SAS files is limited the most commmonly used type, a **SAS data set**. A SAS data set is a SAS file containing observations and variables.

Special naming conventions The following information concerning fileref and libref naming conventions is summarized from the *SAS Companion for the VSE Operating System*:

- Filerefs or librefs specified in /FILE statements must not exceed seven characters, although most SAS documentation states that as many as eight characters are allowed.
- The first letter of the **libref** specifies how the SAS library is accessed, that is, how the file is opened and whether you can write to it. Use the following letters as the first letter in a libref to indicate the appropriate access mode:

W	to specify a work library assumed to be a temporary file.
O	to create a new SAS library, not to be confused with writing a newly created SAS data set to an existing SAS library. Remember to include the DATE= and LOC= parameters in the /FILE statement, as shown above.
I or S	to read a SAS file from a SAS library; the file is used for input only.

U (or any letter except W, O, S, or I) to specify read and write access to a SAS library.

These naming conventions are reflected in the following examples where appropriate. For more information on VSE naming conventions, please refer to the *SAS Companion for the VSE Operating System* and "Enhancements and Updates in SAS82.4 under VSE," SAS Technical Report P-132.

Methods for defining SAS libraries and external files are illustrated in the following sections.

Reading an external file If your SAS program reads an external file, you must define that file by including the /FILE statement in the ICCF proc. Assume that the file to be read is an existing file named YOUR.RAW.DATA. Include the following statement:

```
/FILE NAME=DAILY,ID'YOUR.RAW.DATA',UNITS=SYS050,SERIAL=VSE123
```

The /FILE statement associates the fileref DAILY with the external file YOUR. RAW.DATA, an existing file.

Now, invoke the SAS System and enter your program. You will use the fileref DAILY in the INFILE statement to refer to the external file:

```
SAS (invoke the SAS System)
SAS messages
*ENTER DATA?
DATA WEATHER;
*ENTER DATA?
INFILE DAILY RECFM=recfm BLKSIZE=blksize LRECL=lrecl;
*ENTER DATA?
INPUT TEMP PRECIP SUNHRS;
more SAS statements and messages
*ENTER DATA?
ENDSAS;
```

Note: the INFILE statement, in addition to fileref DAILY, must also supply the record format and block size. You must specify these two file characteristics for any file that you are reading by using the SAS options RECFM= and BLKSIZE=. You must also give the logical record length (LRECL=) if the file's record format is FB (fixed blocked) or VB (variable blocked).

Reading a SAS data set The following program reads a SAS data set from an existing SAS library. You must define the library by including a /FILE statement in the ICCF proc:

```
/FILE NAME=REPORT,ID'YOUR.SAS.LIB',UNITS=SYS050,SERIAL=VSE123
```

The /FILE statement associates the libref REPORT with the SAS library named YOUR.SAS.LIB.

You are now ready to invoke the SAS System and enter the program:

```
SAS (invoke the SAS System)
SAS messages
*ENTER DATA?
PROC PRINT DATA=REPORT.STATION;
*ENTER DATA?
VAR A B C;
      more SAS messages
*ENTER DATA?
ENDSAS;
```

The libref REPORT is used in the PROC PRINT statement as the first level of the permanent SAS data set name. When this program executes the SAS data set named STATION is read from the SAS library YOUR.SAS.LIB, and PROC PRINT prints all values for variables A, B, and C.

Note: if you specify a libref beginning with the letter I or S, you have read-only access to the SAS library. For example, if you specify IREPORT instead of REPORT in this example, you have read-only access to YOUR.SAS.LIB. Remember that a libref beginning with a letter other than W, I, S, or O requests read and write access.

Creating a SAS data set The following program creates a SAS data set using an external file as input. Therefore, you include two /FILE statements in the ICCF proc: one to define the SAS library that will store the newly created SAS data set and one to define the external file to be used as input:

```
/FILE NAME=DAILY,ID'YOUR.RAW.DATA',UNITS=SYS050,SERIAL=VSE123
/FILE NAME=MAP,ID'YOUR.SAS.LIB',UNITS=SYS067,SERIAL=ABC321
```

The first /FILE statement associates the fileref DAILY with the permanent external file YOUR.RAW.DATA. The second /FILE statement associates the fileref MAP with the permanent SAS data library YOUR.SAS.LIB, an existing SAS library.

You are now ready to invoke the SAS System and enter the program statements:

```
SAS (invoke the SAS System)
SAS messages
*ENTER DATA?
DATA MAP.WEATHER;
*ENTER DATA?
INFILE DAILY RECFM=recfm BLKSIZE=blksize LRECL=lrecl;
*ENTER DATA?
INPUT TEMP PRECIP SUNHRS;
more SAS statements and messages
*ENTER DATA?
ENDSAS;
```

DAILY is used in the INFILE statement to refer to the external file. MAP is used as the first level of the permanent SAS data set name in the DATA statement. When this program executes, it creates the new SAS data set WEATHER in YOUR. SAS.LIB. Observations in WEATHER will contain the variables TEMP, PRECIP, and SUNHRS.

Creating an external file The following program creates an external file using a SAS data set as input. Again, in the ICCF proc you must include one /FILE statement to define the SAS library to be used as input and another /FILE statement to define the external file that is created by this program:

```
/FILE NAME=MAP,ID'YOUR.SAS.LIB',UNITS=SAS051,SERIAL=VSE123
/FILE NAME=FREEZE,ID'COLD.RAW.DATA',UNITS=SYS050,SERIAL=VSE789
```

The first /FILE statement associates the libref MAP with an existing SAS library, YOUR.SAS.LIB. The second /FILE statement associates the fileref FREEZE with the external file COLD.RAW.DATA, also existing.

You are now ready to invoke the SAS System and enter the program:

```
SAS (invoke the SAS System)
SAS messages
*ENTER DATA?
DATA _NULL_;
*ENTER DATA?
```

```
SET MAP.WEATHER;
*ENTER DATA?
FILE FREEZE;
*ENTER DATA?
IF TEMP < 32 THEN PUT TEMP;
more SAS statements and messages
*ENTER DATA?
8? ENDSAS;
```

The libref MAP is used as the first level of the permanent SAS data set name in the SET statement. The fileref FREEZE is used in the FILE statement. When this program executes, all TEMP values less then 32 that are read from the SAS data set WEATHER are written to the file COLD.RAW.DATA. These values replace existing information in the external file.

NOTES

1. **AOS/VS, PRIMOS, VMS**: If you do not define the external file to be read or created by your SAS program, the SAS System uses a file in the current default directory with the following name:

```
AOS/VS   :UDD:currentdefaultdirectory:fileref
PRIMOS   <masterdirectory>currentdirectory>fileref
VMS      [currentdefaultdirectory]fileref.DAT
```

2. **AOS/VS, PRIMOS, VMS**: A SAS data library is a logical concept, not a physical entity. All permanent SAS files in a directory belong to the same SAS data library.

CMS, VM/PC: A SAS data library is a logical concept, not a physical entity. All SAS files with the same filetype and filemode make up a logical SAS data library.

OS, VSE: A SAS data library is a physical data set— an OS or VSE data set that contains one or more SAS files.

3. **AOS/VS, PRIMOS, VMS**: The LIBNAME statement is available if you are running the SAS System under one of these operating systems.

4. **AOS/VS, PRIMOS, VMS**: The LIBSEARCH statement is available if you are running the SAS System under one of these operating systems.

5. **CMS, OS**: Under TSO you can use the SAS TSO statement to issue TSO commands from within your SAS program. Under CMS you can use the SAS CMS statement to issue CMS commands from within your SAS program. The X statement is used like a CMS statement under CMS and like a TSO statement under TSO.

Appendix 4
Full-Screen Editing

INTRODUCTION

This appendix shows you how to enter information if you are using the SAS System with a full-screen terminal. Use the editing features described here with the SAS Display Manager System for entering SAS program statements. These editing features can also be used to enter text in other full-screen SAS software products, for example, to enter FSLETTER text in the SAS/FSP software product or to compose screen applications with the SAS/AF software product. You can also set your terminal keys to convenient functions with the SAS user profile facility.

The display manager examples shown in **Screens A4.1-A4.6** illustrate full-screen editing capabilities that are available wherever you need them in the SAS System.

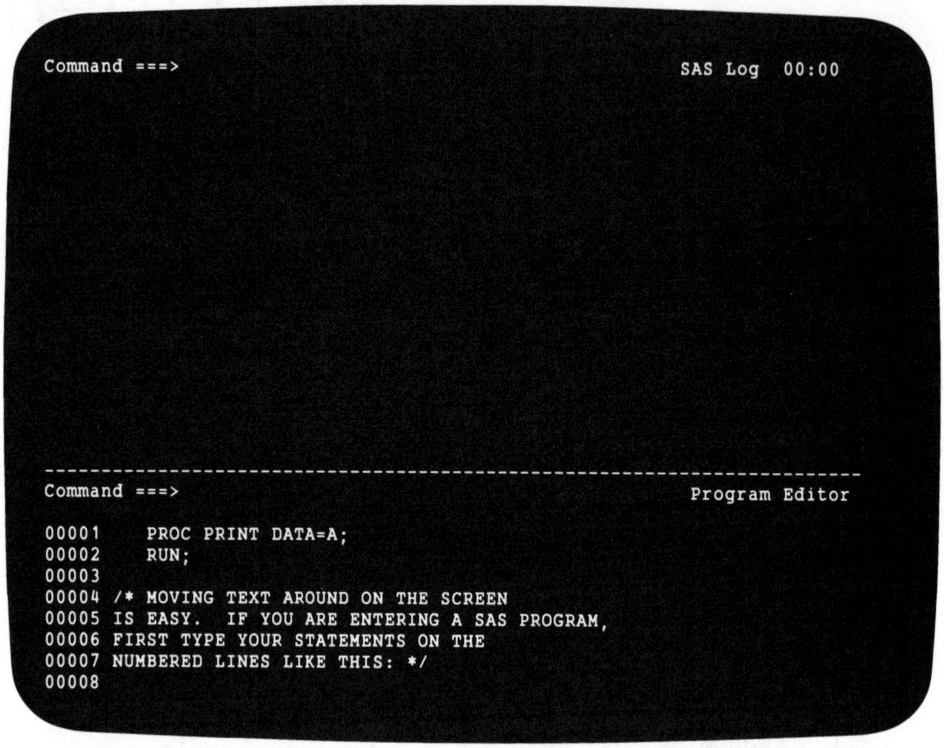

Screen A4.1 Entering Text

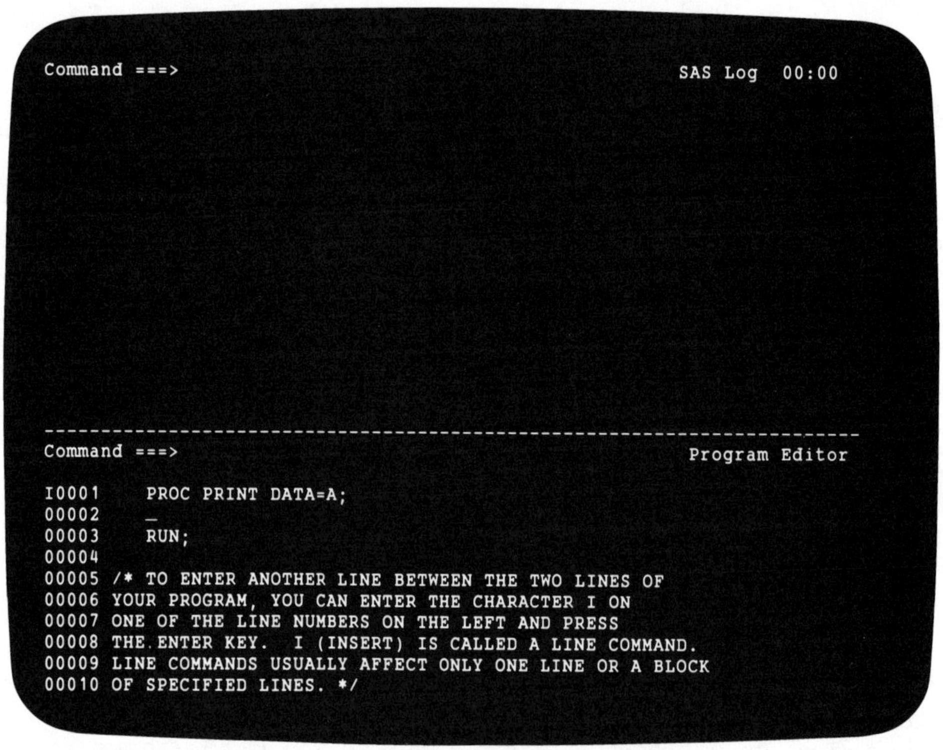

Screen A4.2 Inserting Lines with a Line Command

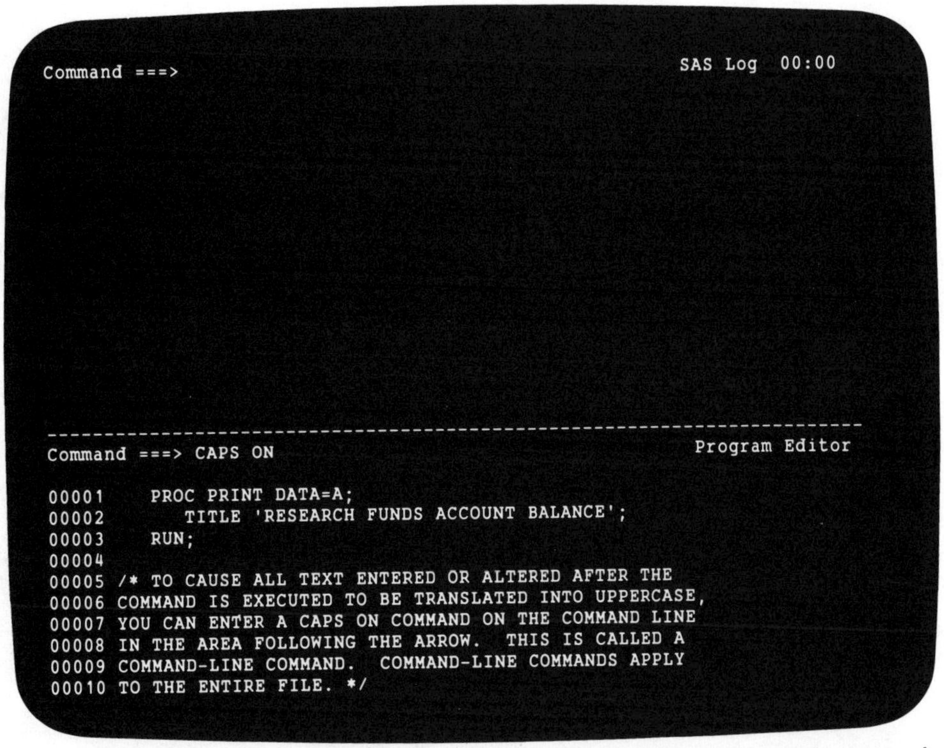

Screen A4.3 Translating Text into Uppercase with a Command-Line Command

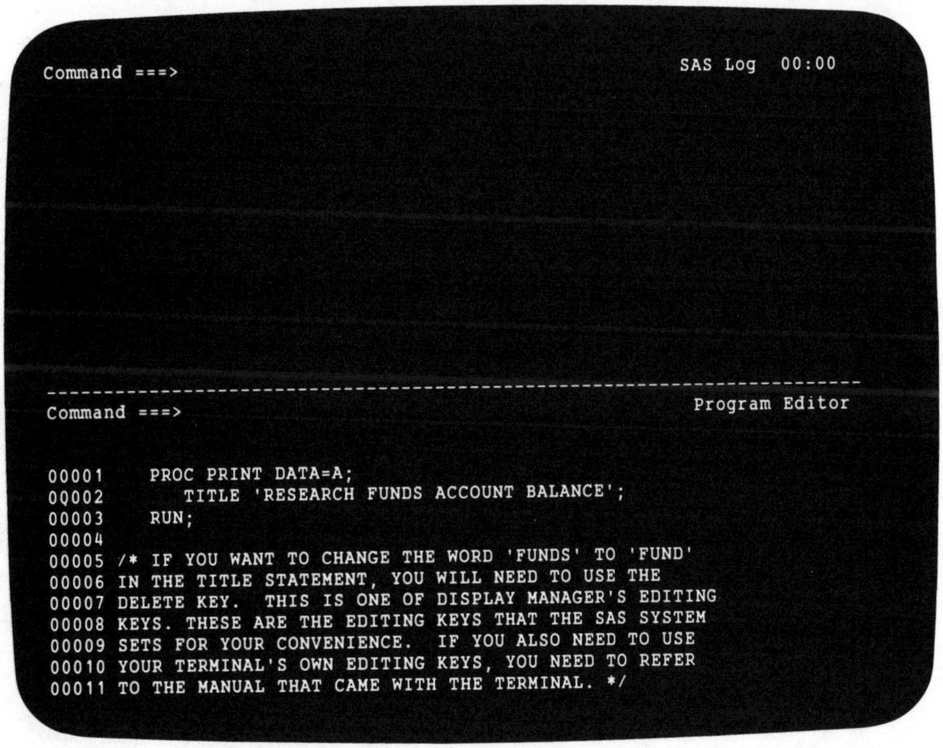

Screen A4.4 Deleting Characters with an Editing Key

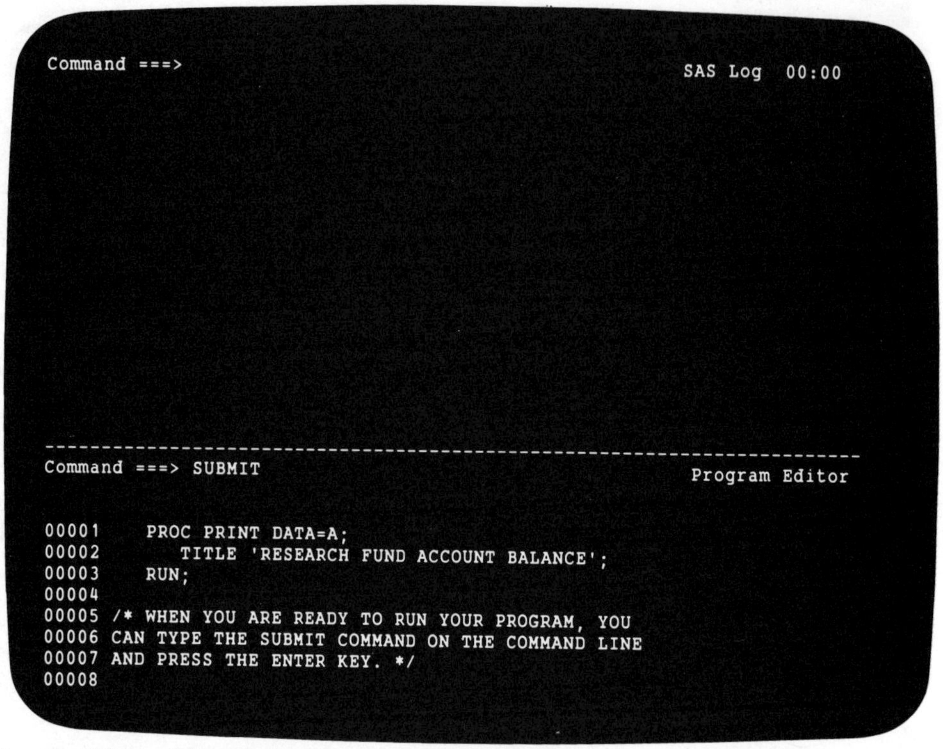

Screen A4.5 Submitting SAS Program Statements

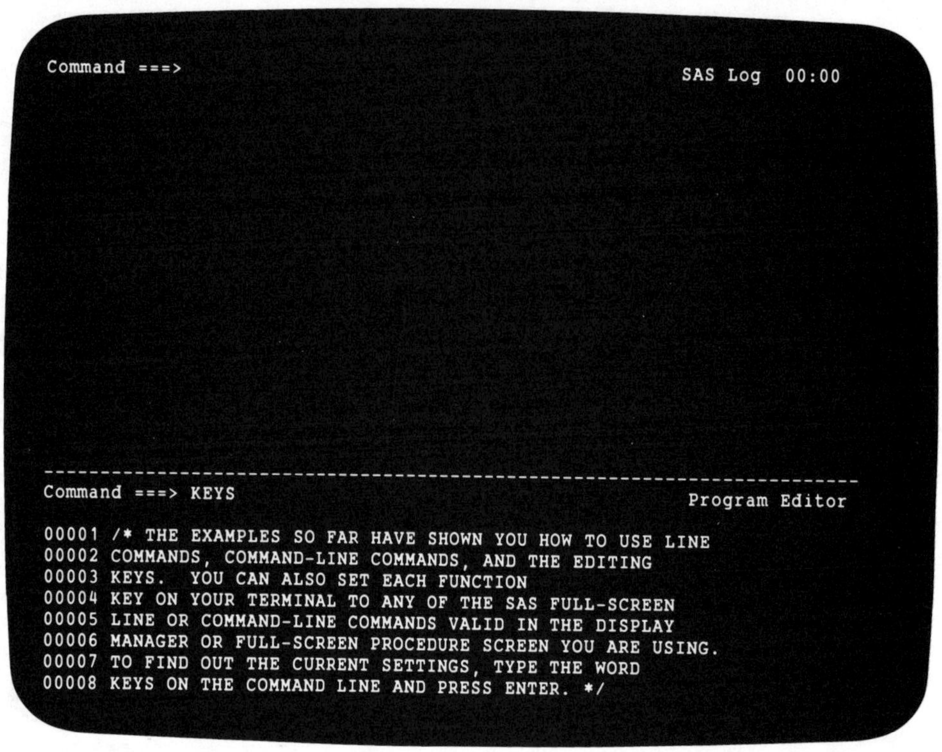

Screen A4.6 Function Key Settings

The result of the KEYS command is shown below. These are the default function key settings that SAS Institute provides to your site; yours may be different from those shown.

```
                FUNCTION KEY DEFINITIONS
Command ===>
KEY     COMMAND
01      help
02      split
03      submit
04      recall
05      rfind
06      rchange
07      backward
08      forward
09      output
10      left
11      right
12      cursor
13      help
14      split
15      submit
16      recall
17      rfind
18      rchange
19      backward
20      forward
21      output
22      left
23      right
24      cursor
```

Screen A4.7 Function Key Definition Screen

Notice that one of the function keys is set to execute the SUBMIT command. Instead of typing the word SUBMIT on the command line and pressing ENTER as you did above to submit your program statements, simply press the function key set to execute the SUBMIT command.

EDITING KEYS

The editing keys you can use with display manager and the procedures that allow full-screen editing are shown below. You can use these same keys when editing text on data lines and commands on command lines. In general, you use an editing key to make a change to one character or one line of an unprotected field on the screen and a function key to search or scroll an entire file. The editing keys you can use in full-screen editing are listed and defined in **Figure A4.1**.

Note: the words or symbols on the editing keys described in **Figure A4.1** may not be the same as those on the terminal you are using.[1]

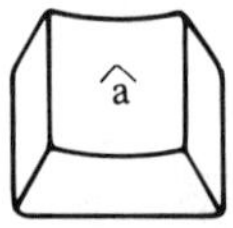

The INSERT key allows you to insert characters within a line. Press the key and position the cursor where you want to insert text. Characters are shifted to the right to make room for new text. *

The DELETE key erases the character either preceding the cursor position or in the current cursor position, depending on the terminal keyboard you are using.

The ERASE EOF (End-of-Field) key deletes or erases all the characters from the cursor position to the end of either a data entry line or, on some screens, the end of a field.

The HOME key moves the cursor to the first column of the first unprotected field on the screen, the entry area of the command line on most screens. **

The REFRESH key redisplays the contents of the screen line-by-line. It removes messages from the operating system and is especially useful for removing unwanted characters input since the last time you pressed ENTER or a function key. ***

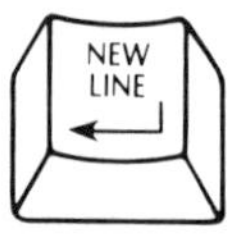

The NEW LINE key moves the cursor to the first unprotected field of the next line. Use the NEXT FIELD key to move the cursor from the line number to the data entry area.

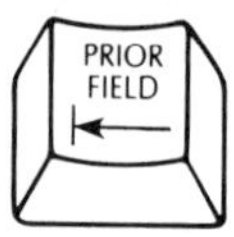

The PRIOR FIELD key moves the cursor to the previous unprotected field.

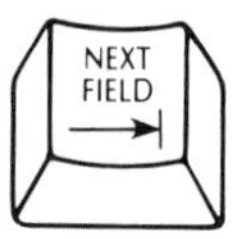

The NEXT FIELD key moves the cursor to the next unprotected field.

The ENTER key executes commands entered on a command line or on a line number.

Figure A4.1 Editing Keys

---

* **IBM users**: On a 3270 series terminal, press the RESET key to turn INSERT off.
Minicomputer users: Press the INSERT key again to discontinue the INSERT.

** **IBM users**: Press the ALT and Home keys.

*** **CMS, OS, and VM/PC**: Press ALT PA2.
VSE: Press ALT CLEAR.

COMMANDS

Command Conventions

SAS full-screen editing commands follow these conventions:

COMMAND OPTION | *option* [| **OPTION** | *option* | ...]

where

bold CAPS
indicates a **KEYWORD**; use exactly the same spelling and form as shown.

lowercase italic
indicates you supply the actual value.

vertical bar |
means *or;* use only one of the terms separated by vertical bars.

brackets [ ]
indicate optional information or keywords.

three periods (...)
mean that more than one of the terms preceding ... can be optionally specified.

For example, in the FIND command

FIND *characterstring* [**PREFIX** | **SUFFIX** | **WORD**]

FIND
is the command **KEYWORD**.

characterstring
is a user-defined option. You supply the value of the string of characters you want to locate. It is not in brackets so you know you are required to specify a character string.

[**PREFIX** | **SUFFIX** | **WORD**]
are three system-defined option **KEYWORDS** that appear in bold uppercase letters, enclosed by brackets [ ], separated by vertical bars |; the bold uppercase letters indicate that each is entered exactly as written; the brackets indicate that these options are allowed but not required; the vertical bars indicate that you can specify only one of the three.

Line Commands

You can use line commands to perform such tasks as moving, copying, inserting, and deleting lines or blocks of lines, and designating target locations for moved, copied, and inserted lines. As an example, a list of line commands that you can use for full-screen editing in the text editor in SAS software products follows. See the "SAS Display Manager" appendix for the line commands available in the display manager program editor.

SINGLE COMMANDS:

A,B	target position, A (after) or B (before), of an M, MM, C, CC, or COPY command.
C	copy a line to the location indicated either by an A (after) or B (before) line command. To copy more than one line, see the CC line command below.
D[*n*]	delete one or more lines.
I[*n* | A[*n*] | B[*n*]]	insert one or more lines immediately following or preceding an I command.
M	move a line to the location indicated either by an A or B line command. To move more than one line, see the MM line command below.
MASK	enter the mask to be used for newly inserted lines.
O	target position command that overlays the contents of one or more lines with moved or copied lines.
R[*n*]	repeat a line *n* times immediately following that line.
TF[*n*]	flow lines of text, deleting trailing blanks. You can follow TF with some number *n* to specify the right margin.
TS[*n*]	insert one or more blank lines within a line of text.

BLOCK COMMANDS:

CC	copy block of lines designated by CC on the first and last lines.
DD	delete block of lines designated by DD on the first and last lines.
MM	move block of lines designated by MM on the first and last lines.
RR	repeat block of lines designated by RR on the first and last lines.

SPECIAL SHIFT COMMANDS:

>*n*	shift data *n* columns to the right.
<*n*	shift data *n* columns to the left.
>>*n*	shift data on block of lines *n* columns to the right.
<<*n*	shift data on block of lines *n* columns to the left.

For text editor command definitions, see the **GLOSSARY OF TEXT EDITOR COMMANDS** at the end of this appendix.

Command-Line Commands

You can use command-line commands to perform many editing and file management tasks. As an example, the command-line commands that you can use in the SAS text editor are listed below by function:

Scrolling Commands

AUTOADD	LEFT
BACKWARD	*n*
FORWARD	RIGHT
TOP	HSCROLL
BOTTOM	VSCROLL

File Management Commands

COPY	END	INCLUDE

General Editing Commands

CHANGE	CAPS
RCHANGE	CPRO
DES	CUNPRO
FILL	CURSOR
FIND	NULLS OFF/ON
RFIND	NUMS OFF/ON
BOUNDS	PREVCMD
CANCEL	RESET

Help, Function Keys, and Host-level Commands

HELP	KEYS	X command

Many of these commands can also be used in other screens in SAS full-screen procedures, as well as in display manager. See "SAS Display Manager" for a list and glossary of display manager commands. A glossary of text editor commands appears at the end of this appendix.

USING COMMANDS: MORE EXAMPLES

Entering Commands Directly

Both command-line commands and line commands can be entered directly or executed with function keys. To execute a command with a function key, you need to know the function key settings. In some procedures you can alter function key settings and then permanently store the new settings. See the **FUNCTION KEYS** section for a discussion of executing commands with function keys.

Entering command-line commands directly To enter a command-line command directly, type the command on the command line and press the ENTER key. For example, to scroll backward the default vertical scroll amount, type

```
BAC
```

on the command line and press ENTER. The BAC command is an example of the most basic kind of command to enter; it requires only that you type a keyword and press ENTER. The examples below include commands that allow options and commands that require cursor placement.

Command-line commands with options The BAC command allows options to be specified. For example, to scroll backward the maximum amount, type

```
BAC MAX
```

on the command line and press ENTER.

Entering line commands directly To enter a line command directly, type the command over a line number and press the ENTER key. In the text editor screens of most full-screen procedures, unlike the program editor screen in display manager, the numbering facility is OFF by default. To number the data entry lines, use the NUMS ON command-line command. Type NUMS ON on the command line and press ENTER.

Examples below include single line commands, line commands with options, line commands requiring target commands and positioning of the cursor, and block commands. Note the underscore (_) marking the cursor position in several of the examples.

Single line command As an example, to insert a new line for entering text, type I, the insert line command, on any part of a line number

```
00I001 data line one
000002 data line two
000003 data line three
```

and press ENTER. One new line, the default, is inserted between the first and second lines.

```
000001 data line one
000002 _
000003 data line two
000004 data line three
```

Line command with option Some line commands, the I line command, for example, allow you to specify an option for which you supply the value, such as some number *n*. To specify how many lines to insert, follow the I line command with some number *n*, such as 3, and a blank space

```
I3 001 data line one
000002 data line two
000003 data line three
```

and press ENTER. Three new lines are inserted between the first and second lines.

```
000001 data line one
000002 _
000003
000004
000005 data line two
000006 data line three
```

Line command requiring cursor position The TS (text split) line command requires that you enter the command, then position the cursor before pressing ENTER. Enter the TS command on a line number, position the cursor,

```
TS0001 Split this line after the semicolon;_then add new copy
```

and then press ENTER. A new line is inserted:

```
000001 Split this line after the semicolon;_
000002
000003                                          then add new copy.
```

Line command requiring a target command The following example shows how to use the M (move) and A (after) line commands:

```
M00001 Move this line
A00002 after the second line
000003 with the M (move) and A (after) line commands.
```

The first line becomes the second line:

```
000001 after the second line
000002 Move this line
000003 with the M (move) and A (after) line commands.
```

Block line command You can also use line commands to affect blocks of lines. For example,

```
MM0001 Move the first two lines
MM0002 after the third line
A00003 with the M (move) and A (after) line commands.

000001 with the M (move) and A (after) line commands.
000002 Move the first two lines
000003 after the third line
```

See **Command Conventions** earlier in this appendix for a description of command conventions.

Executing line commands without line numbers If your data lines are not numbered, you can still execute line commands without having to use the NUMS ON command to display line numbers. Type the line command, preceded by a colon (:), on the command line, position the cursor on the line you want to be affected by the line command, and press ENTER. For example, to execute the TS (text split) line command from the command line, type :TS on the command line, position the cursor, and press ENTER.

You can also execute a line command with a function key even when line numbers are not displayed. Position the cursor where you want the command to take effect, and press a function key set to execute that line command. See **Altering Settings: the Function Key Definition Screen** for setting a function key to execute a line command.

Entering Multiple Commands

You can enter a series of commands on the command line by separating the commands with semicolons. For example, you can type the BACKWARD MAX scroll command and the FIND command on the command line, separate them with a semicolon,

```
BACKWARD MAX; FIND 'DATA ONE'
```

and execute both by pressing the ENTER key once.

FUNCTION KEYS

Executing Commands with Function Keys

Executing a command with a function key can be as simple as pressing the function key instead of typing a command on the command line and pressing ENTER. To use a function key to execute a command with an option, you can either assign that function key the command with the option, such as BACKWARD MAX, or you can type the option MAX on the command line and press the BACKWARD function key. You can execute a command that requires cursor placement, such as SPLIT, by positioning the cursor before pressing the SPLIT function key.

Function keys and multiple commands You can also combine the use of function keys and the submission of multiple commands. For example, if you set a function key to execute the command and option BACKWARD MAX followed by a semicolon,

```
BACKWARD MAX;
```

then you can enter

```
FIND 'DATA ONE'
```

on the command line and execute both by pressing the key you set to execute BACKWARD MAX; . The procedure executes the BACKWARD MAX command first and then the FIND command.

Altering Settings: the Function Key Definition Screen

You can alter the function key settings to execute any commands that are valid for the particular screen in the SAS full-screen software product that you are using. Use the KEYS command to display the function key definition screen for the screen you are currently using. Twenty-four function keys with settings are listed although some terminals may have only twelve function keys.

You can assign any valid command-line command or line command to any function key on your terminal. Precede line commands with a colon (:). You can use editing keys such as EOF and DELETE, or simply type over a function key setting to alter it. On the function key definition screen, you can use the following commands:

BACKWARD
CANCEL
FORWARD
END

You can use any of these commands by pressing a function key set to execute it or by typing it on the command line and pressing the ENTER key. You can scroll backward and forward to view the entire list of key settings; you can cancel any changes made; you can use the END command, or a key assigned to execute the END command, to save your altered settings and return to the screen on which you executed the KEYS command. Altered function key settings remain in effect until you exit from the procedure or until you alter the settings again. The next time you enter the procedure, the original default settings will be in effect again.

To keep your altered function key settings from one session to another, you must store them in your own user profile catalog. At the beginning of each SAS session, use the appropriate operating system commands to make your user profile catalog available. See the sections **User Profile** and **Access to Your PROFILE Catalog**.

SAS USER PROFILE

Installation Profile

Each installation of the SAS System receives a special SAS data library that contains information used by SAS software to control various aspects of your SAS session. For example, in base SAS software, a catalog in the installation profile library contains the default function key settings for the SAS Display Manager System and PROC DATASETS; similiar information for additional SAS software products is contained in other catalogs within that same library. In some cases, these default settings can be tailored to your site by your SAS Installation Representative.

Keep in mind that any changes made to the installation profile library are universal for your site. That is, the default settings stored in the catalogs in this library are for everyone using the SAS System at your installation. If these default settings are not suitable for your own applications, you can set up your own user profile. See **User Profile** below.

User Profile

A user profile catalog is available for customizing default function key settings to meet individual needs and preferences. When looking for current function key settings, for example, the SAS System searches the user profile for function key settings stored under the appropriate names before it looks in a catalog in the installation profile library.

Your own user profile information is stored in either a permanent catalog named SASUSER.PROFILE or a temporary catalog named WORK.PROFILE.[2] SASUSER is a reserved libref and PROFILE is a reserved SAS catalog name. The PROFILE catalog stores the function key settings for a particular screen or procedure each time you enter the function key definition screen and save the settings. You create a function key definition screen in your user profile catalog each time you use the KEYS command to display a function key definition screen and then save that screen by exiting it with the END command. By default, any function key definition screen that you create in this way is automatically stored under the appropriate name in the PROFILE catalog. For example, in base SAS software, you can have different function key settings for each display manager screen and PROC DATASETS because the system assigns a reserved name to each function key definition screen when it stores it in the user profile catalog. When you are using a particular display manager screen or full-screen procedure, the system looks for your function key setting information stored under a particular name for that screen or procedure only.

The user profile catalog is intended to be a personal catalog and cannot be accessed by more than one SAS user. Normally, an individual's profile is associated with an individual's user id.[3] It should not be stored in a SAS data library that is shared by a number of users.

Access to Your PROFILE Catalog

The individual user profile information is stored in a catalog named PROFILE in a SAS data library.[4] You should have access to your own user profile. In some cases, the reserved libref and catalog name SASUSER.PROFILE is used in a command procedure and automatically accessed when you invoke the SAS System at your site. In other cases, you may need to make the catalog SASUSER.PROFILE available to your session each time you execute the SAS System.

If you do not make the catalog SASUSER.PROFILE available to your session, WORK.PROFILE is opened, and any function key definition screens you create are stored there. As with SAS data sets placed in temporary storage, your function key definition screens placed in the catalog WORK.PROFILE are available only for that session.

The library referenced by SASUSER, unlike the library containing the profile information for the entire installation, does not exist until you create it. (You can, however, reference an existing SAS data library using the libref SASUSER.) You must use a host operating system command to create a file or data set to contain a SAS data library that is associated with the reserved libref SASUSER. The system creates a PROFILE catalog automatically the first time you make a library referenced by SASUSER available to your session. Note that you must have write access to this SAS data library.

GLOSSARY OF TEXT EDITOR COMMANDS

Line Command Definitions

Below are defined the line commands that you can use on the text editor screen in each SAS full-screen software product that gives you access to the text editor.

A,B A line command that marks the target position of a *source* line(s), a line or lines being moved or copied with a C, M, CC, MM, or COPY command. Indicate an A (after) on the line number of the line you want the source line(s) to follow. Use a B (before) to mark the line you want the source line(s) to precede. See also the O line command.

C A line command that copies a line to another location in the file, indicated by a target line command. Indicate C on the line number of the line to be copied. Then indicate an A on the number of the line you want the copied line to follow, a B on the number of the line you want it to precede, or an O on the line you want it to overlay.

CC A line command that copies a block of lines to another location in the file, indicated by a target line command. Indicate CC on the line numbers of the first and last lines of the block of lines to be copied.

D[*n*] A line command that deletes one or more lines. Indicate D on the line number of the line to be deleted. By default, one line is deleted. To delete more than one line, follow D with some number *n* and a blank space.

DD A line command that deletes a block of lines. Indicate DD on the line numbers of the first and last lines of the block of lines to be deleted.

I[*n*] This line command is used to insert one or more new lines. By default one line is inserted after the line on which you execute the I command. To insert more than one line, follow I with some number *n* and a blank space. See also the IA and IB commands below.

See the MASK command to insert lines with a defined content other than a blank line. See the TS (text split) command to insert space within a line of text.

IA[*n*] Use this line command to insert one or more new lines after the line on which you enter the IA (insert after) command. By default, one line is inserted. See also the I and IB commands.

IB[*n*] Use this line command to insert one or more new lines before the line on which you enter the IB (insert before) command. By default, one line is inserted. See also the I and IA commands.

M A line command that moves a line to another location in the file, indicated by a target line command. Indicate M on the line number of the line to be moved; then specify an A on the line number of the line you want the moved line to follow, a B on the line you want it to precede, or an O on the line you want the moved line to overlay.

MASK A line command that defines the initial contents of a new line. Type MASK on the line number of the line containing the contents of the MASK. That line then disappears from the screen. After you define a MASK, a line with the contents of the MASK line is inserted when you use the I (insert) line command.

The MASK remains in effect throughout the session. To redefine it, simply repeat the steps described above. To return to the default, a blank line, simply type MASK on the line number of a blank line.

MM A line command that moves a block of lines to another location in the file, indicated by a target line command. Indicate the block to be moved with an MM line command on line numbers of the first and last lines of the block.

>[*n*] This data shift line command shifts data one or more spaces to the right. Indicate > or > followed by some number *n* and a blank space on the line number of the line to be shifted. Note that a data shift command allows no loss of data. The default is one space.

<[*n*] This data shift line command shifts data one or more spaces to the left. Indicate < or < followed by some number *n* and a blank space on the line number of the line to be shifted. Note that a data shift command allows no loss of data. The default is one space.

>>[*n*] This data shift line command shifts a block of lines one or more spaces to the right. Indicate >> or >> followed by some number *n* and a blank space on the line number of the first line of the block to be shifted, another >> or >>*n* on the last line number of the block. Note that a data shift command allows no loss of data. The default is one space.

<<[*n*] This data shift line command shifts a block of lines one or more spaces to the left. Indicate << or << followed by some number *n* and a blank space on the line number of the first line of the block to be shifted, another << or <<*n* on the last line number of the

block. Note that a data shift command allows no loss of data. The default is one space.

O A line command that marks the target position of a C or M line command. Indicate the O (overlay) line command on the line number of the line you want the contents of the *source line*, the moved or copied line, to overlay. Characters from the source line overlay blank or null spaces on the *target line*, the line marked with the O line command.

If any characters occupy the same positions on the source and target lines, the characters on the target line remain and characters from the source line do not appear. If you are executing the M (move) command, you receive an error message, and the moved line remains in its original position.

R[*n*] A line command that repeats a line one or more times immediately following. Indicate R, on the line number of the line to be repeated. To repeat a line more than once, follow R with some number *n* and a blank space.

RR A line command that repeats a block of lines immediately following that block. Indicate RR on the line numbers of the first and last lines of the block of lines to be repeated.

TF[*n*] A line command that flows a paragraph by removing trailing blanks from each line. You can use the TF (text flow) line command to move text into wasted space left at ends of lines, especially after performing insertions and deletions. Either type TF on a line number, position the cursor where you want the text flowing to begin, and press ENTER, or position the cursor and press the :TF function key. You can follow the TF command with some number *n* and a blank space to specify the right boundary. This right boundary specification temporarily overrides the one set by the BOUNDS command. See also the BOUNDS command-line command.

TS[*n*] A line command that inserts one or more blank lines for insertion of new text. Either type TS (text split) on a line number, position the cursor where you want the text to split, and press ENTER, or position the cursor and press the :TS function key. Follow TS with some number *n* and a blank space to insert more than one blank line when the text is split. See the I (insert) command for inserting space between lines rather than within the text of a line.

Command-line Command Definitions

Below are defined the command-line commands that you can use on the text editor screen in each SAS full-screen product that gives you access to the text editor. Though display manager and full-screen procedures, such as PROC FSEDIT and PROC BUILD, have many command-line commands in common, some are specially tailored to the environment of a particular procedure or screen within a procedure. For a complete list of command-line command definitions, see the documentation on each full-screen procedure and on the SAS Display Manager System.

Note: in the text editor you can abbreviate the keyword of any command-line command to the shortest possible *unique* form. For example, RFIND (repeat find) can be executed as RF and RCHANGE (repeat change) as RC. In the command definition lists, commonly used abbreviations are mentioned.

AUTOADD ON | OFF

The AUTOADD ON command adds data entry lines to the bottom of your screen each time you scroll forward so that you do not have to use the INSERT command to insert new lines for data entry. If line numbers are on (NUMS ON), these lines are numbered each time you scroll forward. If you specify AUTOADD OFF, the editor does not add new lines for data entry each time you scroll forward. The default is AUTOADD ON.

BAC [*n* | **MAX**]

You can use the BACKWARD command to scroll toward the top of the screen. The amount of scroll is controlled by the VSCROLL command.

You can specify the number of lines to scroll backward by entering BAC *n* (*n* is the number of lines you want to scroll backward) or scroll the maximum amount by entering BAC MAX.

The scroll value specified with the BAC command is operative only for that scroll and temporarily overrides, but does not alter, the default scroll value or the one set by the VSCROLL command.

BOTTOM

Use the BOTTOM command to scroll the last line of your file to the bottom of the display screen.

BOUNDS *n1 n2*

Use the BOUNDS command to designate a section of the screen that you want to be affected by the TF (text flow) line command. For example, if you want the text flowed between horizontal spaces 10 and 60, inclusive, execute

```
BOUNDS 10 60
```

Each time you execute a TEXTFLOW command after executing this BOUNDS command, the text is flowed between spaces 10 and 60, inclusive, until you issue another BOUNDS command. See also the TF (text flow) line command.

CANCEL

Use the CANCEL command when you do not want to save alterations made to a screen or the contents of a new screen. The contents of an existing screen will remain as it was previously stored. If you cancel a new screen, it will not be stored and its name will not appear in the catalog.

CAPS OFF | ON

The CAPS ON command signals the editor to translate all unprotected characters entered after the command was executed into uppercase. CAPS OFF signals the editor to leave copy as entered.

The CAPS command is in effect until you exit from the screen you are building or until you change it. The default is CAPS OFF.

CHANGE *'string1' 'string2'* [**WORD | SUFFIX | PREFIX**] [**ALL**]

Use this command to change one or more occurrences of string1 to string2. Enclose each string in single quotes if it contains special characters or embedded blanks. For example the first command requires no quotes, the second does:

```
C your my
C 'your dog' 'my cat'
```

If you know that the string occurs in several different ways, but you only need to locate one, then you can restrict the amount of searching by specifying how the string occurs. For example, if you specify

```
C YOUR MY PREFIX
```

the only occurrences of YOUR that are located and changed to MY are those where YOUR is a prefix, not a separate word or a suffix. For example, YOURDATA is changed to MYDATA.

If you do not indicate WORD, SUFFIX, or PREFIX, the system changes string1 to string2 regardless of context. You must indicate ALL to change all occurrences of the string throughout the file; otherwise, the command changes only the first appearance of that string after the current cursor location. You can then use the REPEAT CHANGE key or RCHANGE command to change the next occurrence of the string.

If you set CAPS ON, any character string not in single quotes is translated into uppercase by the editor. Character-strings enclosed in single quotes are left as entered, even if CAPS ON is in effect. If CAPS OFF is in effect, all character-strings are left as entered.

Notice that the CAPS ON and CAPS OFF commands affect only characters entered after the command is executed. They do not alter characters on lines already entered unless you subsequently modify those lines.

COPY
COPY *name.type*
COPY *libref.catalog.name.type*
COPY *libref.catalog.*.**

Use the COPY command to copy the contents of another catalog entry. The copied contents are inserted at the bottom of the current screen or wherever you specify with the A or B line command.

COPY

You can copy the contents of an entry from the catalog in which you are working by simply entering COPY and pressing ENTER. The catalog directory screen of your current catalog is displayed and you can type an S (select) in the selection blank of the entry you want to copy.

COPY *name.type*

If you know the name and type of the entry, you can specify them in the COPY command and not use the catalog directory screen.

COPY *libref.catalog.name.type*

To copy an entry from another catalog, you must specify the libref of the SAS data library containing that catalog. The libref must have previously been assigned to that SAS data library.

COPY *libref.catalog.*.**

If you do not know the name and type of the entry you want to copy from another catalog, type asterisks in place of the name and type. The catalog directory screen of that catalog is displayed, and you can select the entry to be copied.

CPRO *color* [*highlight*]

Use the CPRO command to change the color or color and highlighting of some protected areas of the screen. In a protected area you are not allowed to enter text or make changes. The CPRO command changes only the color of the title.

Valid colors are		Valid highlights are	
r	red	h	high intensity
p	pink	l	low intensity
g	green	b	blinking
y	yellow	r	reverse video
b	blue	u	underline
c	cyan		
w	white		

Specify only the first letter of a color or highlighting attribute. The default color of the title line is cyan.

CUNPRO *color* [*highlight*]

Use the CUNPRO command to change the color or color and highlighting attributes of the unprotected areas of the screen. These are the areas of the screen where you enter text and make changes. The CUNPRO command affects only the data entry area and the line numbers, not the entry area of the command line.

Valid colors are		Valid highlights are	
r	red	h	high intensity
p	pink	l	low intensity
g	green	b	blinking
y	yellow	r	reverse video
b	blue	u	underline
c	cyan		
w	white		

Specify only the first letter of the color or highlighting attribute. The default is yellow.

CURSOR

The CURSOR command is designed to be executed with a function key. When you press the CURSOR key, the cursor returns to the entry area of the command line of whatever screen you are using.

DES *character string*

Use the DES command to change the description on the screen from that of the *name.type* to whatever character-string you choose, up to forty characters. The description you choose also appears on the catalog directory screen as the description of that screen.

END

Use the END command to save your current letter, form, or screen and to return to the screen from which you entered the text editor.

From the text editor, you return to a catalog directory screen, to a screen modification menu, or to SAS line-prompt mode or display manager, depending on which procedure you are using.

FILL [*fill-character*]

Use this command to fill a line from the cursor position with the default or specified fill-character. If no fill-character is specified, the line is filled with dashes. Type the command on the command line, then position the cursor where you want the fill to begin, and press ENTER.

FIND *character-string* [**PREFIX | SUFFIX | WORD**]

You can search for a specific string of characters in the text editor with the FIND command. Remember to enclose the string in single quotes if it contains embedded blanks or special characters.

In the FIND command, a delimiter is any symbol other than an uppercase letter, a lowercase letter, or a digit. A WORD is one or more symbols preceded and followed by a delimiter. For example

```
ABC123
```

is a word, but

```
ABC$123
```

is two WORDs separated by the delimiter $. A PREFIX or SUFFIX is treated just as its grammatical definition. In the first example, ABC123, you could specify ABC as a PREFIX and 123 as a SUFFIX. In the second example, ABC$123, ABC and 123 are WORDs, not a PREFIX and a SUFFIX.

To find the first occurrence of the prefix "your" after the current cursor position, use the command

```
F YOUR PREFIX
```

Press the FIND key or use the RFIND (repeat find) command and the ENTER key to locate the next occurrence of "your." By indicating "prefix," you ask the system to find each "yourdata" but not to include a phrase such as "your data set" in its search.

Remember to use single quotes to enclose character strings with special characters or embedded blanks. For example,

```
F YOUR
F 'YOUR DATA SET'
```

If you set CAPS ON, any character-string not in single quotes is translated into uppercase by the editor. Character-strings enclosed in single quotes are left as entered, even if CAPS ON is in effect. If CAPS OFF is in effect, all character-strings are left as entered.

FOR [*n* | **MAX**]

You can use the FORWARD command to scroll toward the bottom of the screen. The amount of scroll is controlled by the VSCROLL command.

You can specify a particular number of lines to scroll forward by entering FOR *n* (*n* is the number of lines you want to scroll forward) or scroll the maximum amount by entering FOR MAX.

The scroll value specified with the FOR command is operative only for that scroll and temporarily overrides, but does not alter, the default scroll value or the one set by the VSCROLL command.

HELP [*keyword*]

When you enter the HELP command, one of the following screens is displayed.

If you last	and you specify	then the panel displayed is
pressed the ENTER key	no command keyword	a primary menu
entered a valid command	no command keyword	a HELP screen on the last command
entered any command	any valid command keyword	a HELP screen on the command keyword specified

If you want access to the help information on the procedure itself, not just the command you have most recently entered, press the ENTER key again before issuing the HELP command.

HSCROLL HALF | PAGE | *n*

The HSCROLL command sets the horizontal scroll amount, the amount the screen scrolls when you press the LEFT or RIGHT function keys or when you enter the LEFT or RIGHT commands.

If you specify PAGE, the scroll amount is equal to the entire width of the display area. If you specify HALF, the scroll amount is one-half of the display area. If you specify some number *n*, the scroll amount is *n* columns. HALF is the default.

INCLUDE *fileref | fileref(membername)*

Use the INCLUDE command to copy the contents of an external file to the screen you are building. The fileref must have been previously assigned to a file or data set with a host operating system command.

VSE: You can place a /FILE statement, an ICCF control language statement, in the ICCF procedure that invokes the SAS System. You cannot use the X command or statement in the ICCF environment. If you are including a member of an ICCF library, the fileref must be ICCF.

KEYS

Use the KEYS command to get information on the current settings of the function keys of the current screen and to alter those settings. The single letter K is an accepted alias of the KEYS command.

LEFT [*n* | **MAX**]

Use the LEFT command to scroll the screen to the left. By default the screen scrolls half of its width. To override the scroll amount temporarily, type LEFT and some number *n* on the command line for the number of columns you want the screen to scroll, and press ENTER. Enter LEFT MAX to scroll the screen to the left boundary.

n

Type a line number on the command line and press ENTER to scroll that line to the top of your screen.

NULLS ON | OFF

When you specify NULLS ON, all data lines are padded with nulls instead of blanks. Note that both nulls and blanks have the same appearance on the screen. Turning NULLS ON allows you to use the INSERT editing key to insert characters between text already entered on a line.

If you specify NULLS OFF, the data lines are padded with blanks. To use the INSERT editing key, you must first use the EOF key to turn those blanks into nulls.

NULLS ON is the default.

NUMS OFF | ON

Use the NUMS ON command to create line numbers for data lines on your screen. If your screen already contains text, all data are shifted to the right and the line numbers appear on the left. Execute NUMS OFF to remove line numbers and shift text back to the left. NUMS OFF is the default.

If your data lines are numbered, you can type line commands directly over line numbers. If you set NUMS OFF, you can still execute line commands by entering them from the command line. Precede the line command with a colon when executing it on the command line rather than on a line number. For example, type :TS (text split) or :I (insert) on the command line, position the cursor, and then press ENTER.

PREVCMD

Use the PREVCMD command to recall to the command line as many as sixteen previously executed commands, one at a time.

RCHANGE

Use the RCHANGE command to repeat the execution of the most recently entered CHANGE command without having to reenter the string1 string2, identifying the character-string to be changed and its new form.

RESET

Use the RESET command on the text editor to clear any pending line commands. Note that this is a command-line command.

RFIND

Use the RFIND command to repeat the execution of the most recently entered FIND or CHANGE command without having to reenter the string, or in the case of the CHANGE command, to locate the string before pressing the RCHANGE function key to execute the change.

RIGHT [*n* | **MAX**]

Use the RIGHT command to scroll the screen to the right. By default the screen scrolls half of its width. To override the horizontal scroll amount temporarily, type on the command line RIGHT and some number *n* for the number of spaces you want the screen to scroll, and press ENTER. Enter RIGHT MAX to scroll the screen to the right boundary.

TOP

Use the TOP command to scroll the first line of your file to the top of the display screen.

VSCROLL HALF | PAGE | *n*

The VSCROLL command sets the vertical scroll amount, the amount the screen scrolls when you press the FORWARD or BACKWARD function key or when you enter the FOR or BAC command.

If you specify PAGE, the scroll amount is equal to the entire depth of the display area. If you specify HALF, the scroll amount is one-half of the display area. If you specify some number *n*, the scroll amount is *n* lines. HALF is the default.

X *'host-level command'* | *'host-level command string'*

You can use the X command to execute a host-level command or string of host-level commands. The screen clears after you enter an X command, and any output you request is then displayed.

CMS and VM/PC: When you execute a host-level command with an X command, the command must be typed in capital letters. With an X command, you specify only one CMS command at a time, not a string of commands.

VSE: The X command is not supported.

NOTES

1. If you are using one of the terminals listed below, use **Table A4.1** to determine the keys that have been assigned special editing functions in SAS full-screen procedures and display manager. See **Figure A4.1** for a description of the functions of these editing keys. If you are using a terminal other than one of those listed below that does not have keys matching the words or symbols shown in **Figure A4.1**, consult your SAS Representative. If you are using an IBM terminal in the 3270-series, you can disregard this section.

Full-Screen Editing Key	**PT45 Key**	**PST100 Key**	**PT25 Key**
â (INSERT)	ichar or shift/del	insert or backspace	shift/del
a̸ (DELETE)	dchar or backspace	delete or del	backspace
ERASE EOF	line feed	erase	shift/f8
HOME	home	home	home
REFRESH	control/ clear	pf10	control/erase
NEW LINE	return or enter	return or enter	new line or enter
NEXT FIELD	f13	f2	shift/f5
PRIOR FIELD	f14	f3	shift/f6
ENTER	f3 or f15	f1 or pf13	f3 or shift/f7
MOVE CURSOR UP	↑	↑	↑
MOVE CURSOR DOWN	↓	↓	(not available)
MOVE CURSOR LEFT	←	←	←
MOVE CURSOR RIGHT	→	→	→

Full-Screen Editing Key	TEK4105 Key	VT100 Key	DASHER Key
â (INSERT)	backspace	backspace	C1
a̸ (DELETE)	rub out	delete	DEL
ERASE EOF	line feed	line feed	erase EOL
HOME	– (minus sign on numeric keypad)	– (minus sign on numeric keypad)	home
REFRESH	, (on numeric keypad)	, (on numeric keypad)	erase page
NEW LINE	return	return	new line or enter
NEXT FIELD	. (on numeric keypad)	. (on numeric keypad)	C4
PRIOR FIELD	0 (on numeric keypad)	0 (on numeric keypad)	C3
ENTER	enter	enter	CR
MOVE CURSOR UP	F1	↑	↑
MOVE CURSOR DOWN	F2	↓	↓
MOVE CURSOR LEFT	F3	←	←
MOVE CURSOR RIGHT	F4	→	→

2. **CMS and VM/PC**: The SAS System automatically creates SASUSER.PROFILE for you on your A-disk the first time you enter display manager or a SAS full-screen procedure. The SASUSER.PROFILE catalog remains on your A-disk for use in different SAS sessions. Disregard all references to explicitly making SASUSER.PROFILE available to your session.

3. **CMS and VM/PC**: The SASUSER.PROFILE catalog is stored on your own A-disk. This catalog is created automatically by the SAS System. You need not issue any CMS commands to use it.

4. **CMS and VM/PC**: Skip the section **Access to Your PROFILE Catalog**.

Appendix 5
SAS® Display Manager

INTRODUCTION

The SAS Display Manager System is a full-screen facility that allows you to interact with all parts of your SAS job—program statements, log, and procedure output. It provides you with a full-screen editor for inputting and preparing your SAS statements and data, displays the SAS log created when you run a SAS job, and displays the output produced by your SAS program statements. Display manager has three primary screens:

- the program editor screen where you input, edit, and save SAS source files and submit SAS program statements
- the log screen where you can browse the SAS log
- the output screen where you can browse output from your SAS jobs.

You also have access to special screens, such as the function key definition screen, and to SAS HELP, an on-line help facility where you can browse information about the entire SAS System.

The display manager first shows you **Screen A5.1**. The bottom half is a program entry and edit area for your SAS statements; the top half of this split screen displays the SAS log.

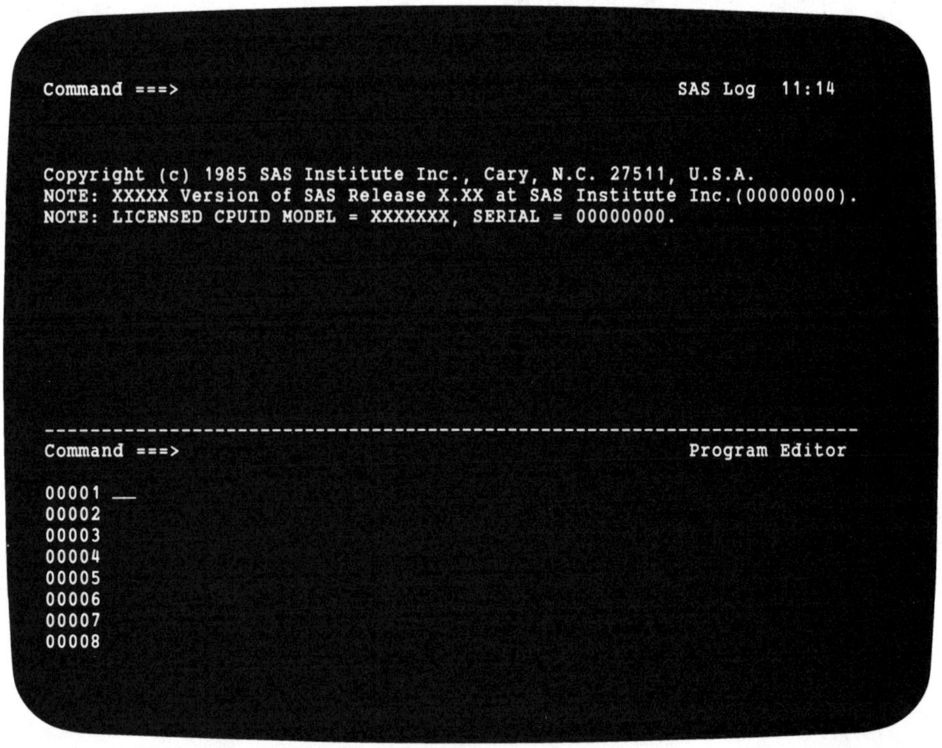

Screen A5.1 Program Editor/Log Screen

Program Editor Screen

You type SAS statements in the program editor, review, make changes, and submit the statements for execution. In a SAS line-prompt session your program statements are submitted to the SAS System each time you enter a line; in a display manager session, you can delete and insert lines, enter, edit, and re-edit your SAS program statements and then submit them to SAS all at one time.

Log Screen

The top half of **Screen A5.1** is the log screen. Statements submitted to the SAS System from the program editor produce the SAS log that, together with any notes or error messages, is displayed in the display manager log screen. Except for entering commands on the command line, you cannot alter any text displayed in the log screen. As statements and messages build up in the SAS log, lines scroll off the top of the screen. Scrolling commands, which can be executed from the command line as well as with function keys, are available for browsing text in the log screen.

Output Screen

When you submit SAS program statements containing a PROC step that produces printed output, you can view that output in the output screen. The display manager displays the first page of the output and then allows you to see the rest of the output, one page at a time, or to skip to the last page of output. After the last page of requested output has been displayed, you can choose to return to the program editor/log screen or to browse the output in page-browse or line-browse mode. You can use function keys to scroll in page-browse mode; you can use function keys and execute command-line commands in line-browse mode.

TERMINALS, KEYS, AND COMMANDS

Function Keys

The SAS Display Manager System defines function keys for you to use to prepare your SAS program statements, to scroll information displayed on each screen, and to move from one screen to another. Some keys on your terminal keyboard, therefore, take on new meanings when you enter display manager. The default function key settings for display manager that were provided to your SAS site are described in this chapter. To set your own function keys, see the appendix on "Full-Screen Editing" for a discussion of the user profile facility.

Function keys on each screen The set of function keys that is available to you depends on the display manager screen with which you are working. In addition to entering commands directly on the command line or on line numbers, you can use function keys to execute commands. See the appendix on "Full-Screen Editing" for a discussion of

- using function keys to execute commands
- viewing the default settings
- altering the settings
- storing your altered settings.

Editing Keys

You can continue using some of your terminal's own editing keys with display manager, such as enter, insert, delete, and cursor movement keys. Ask someone knowledgeable at your site if you need help getting started with these keys.

The editing keys you use with display manager are shown below. You can use these same keys when editing program statements in the program editor or when entering commands on the command line of the program editor, log, or output screens. You can use these keys in all **unprotected fields**. In general, you choose an editing key to make a change to one character or one line of an unprotected field on the screen, whereas you choose a function key to search or scroll an entire file.

Note: the words or symbols on the editing keys described in **Figure A5.1** may not be the same as those on the terminal you are using.[1]

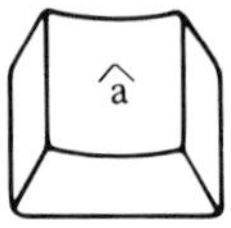

Press the INSERT key once to turn it on, and position the cursor where you want to insert a character. The next key you press inserts its character before the cursor position, shifting characters to the right to make room.*

The DELETE key erases the character either preceding the cursor position or in the current cursor position, depending on the terminal you are using.

The ERASE EOF (End-of-Field) key deletes or erases all the characters from the cursor position to the end of either a data entry line or, on some screens, the end of a field.

The HOME key moves the cursor to the first column of the first unprotected field on the screen, the entry area of the command line on most screens.**

The REFRESH key redisplays the contents of the screen line-by-line. It removes messages from the operating system and is especially useful for removing unwanted characters input since the last time you pressed ENTER or a function key.***

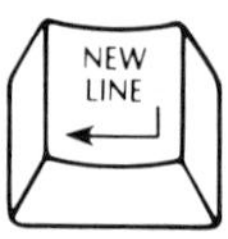

The NEW LINE key moves the cursor to the first unprotected field of the next line. Use the NEXT FIELD key to move the cursor from the line number to the data entry area.

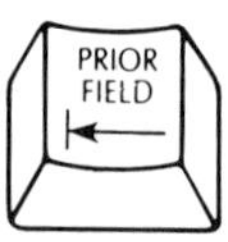

The PRIOR FIELD key moves the cursor to the previous unprotected field.

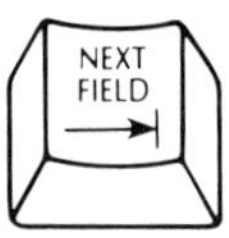

The NEXT FIELD key moves the cursor to the next unprotected field.

---

* **IBM users:** On a 3270 series terminal, press the RESET key to discontinue the INSERT.
Minicomputer users: Press the INSERT key again to discontinue the INSERT.

** **IBM users:** Press the ALT and Home keys.

*** **CMS, OS and VM/PC:** Press ALT PA2.
VSE: Press ALT CLEAR.

The ENTER key executes a command entered on a command line or on a line number. Do not confuse the ENTER key with the SUBMIT key. This key executes commands; the SUBMIT key submits SAS statements to the SAS System from the data lines of the program editor screen.

Figure A5.1 Editing Keys

Commands

Most of the commands you use with display manager are *command-line commands* entered on the command line of each screen. Notice in **Screen A5.1** that both screens in the program editor/log screen have a command line in the top left corner. You can also add a command line to the output screen.

Another type of command, called a *line command,* is used for editing SAS program statements and is available only in the program editor screen. See the appendix on "Full-Screen Editing" for a discussion of both kinds of commands, their execution, and command definitions. Commands you can use in display manager are listed according to screen in the sections that follow. Command definitions appear in the **COMMAND GLOSSARY** at the end of this chapter.

A COMPLETE EXAMPLE

This section uses an education example to go through a SAS display manager session step-by-step. This example illustrates a simple SAS program that you can use display manager to execute. You can enter your DATA and PROC statements in the program editor screen, use the log screen to view your SAS log, and use the output screen to view your output.

Suppose your company encourages employees to continue their education by taking night courses at a local college, weekend seminars, and so on. You have available for each person in your department:

- his or her name
- the number of credit hours he or she completed in the past year at the college
- the number of hours he or she spends in other educational activities
- the number of years he or she has been in your department.

You want to find out whether people who have been in your department for a short time participate more in continuing education than those with several years' seniority. You can:

1. create a data set, giving it a two-level name if you want to store it
2. identify your variables, the employee's name, the number of education hours spent in regular courses, the number of hours spent in special educational activities, the total number of education hours (the regular course hours multiplied by the number of weeks in the semester plus the hours spent in special educational activities), and the number of years employed
3. enter your data
4. print a chart showing employee names, educational activities, and the number of years employed
5. print a graph to examine the relationship between the hours spent in educational activities and the number of years employed.

To begin, log on to your system, and, after receiving the operating system prompt, invoke the SAS System by executing the command

```
SAS
```

Under some operating systems, you are required to identify the type of terminal you are using when you execute the SAS command.[2]

If the cursor is on the command line press the NEXT FIELD key twice to move the cursor to the data entry area. You are now ready to enter the SAS statements and data lines.[3]

Enter the statements and data lines for the DATA step. Remember that SAS statements can begin in any column and that you can split a statement between two lines or enter several statements on one line. You may find your programs easier to read if you follow our convention of beginning DATA, PROC, and global statements in column 1 and indenting other statements. **Screen A5.2** shows the program editor after you have filled in all the lines.

When you have filled in the last line on the program editor, press the FORWARD function key to scroll more lines into view. To control the forward and backward scroll amount, enter

```
VSCROLL n
```

(where *n* is the number of lines) on the command line of the program editor and press the ENTER key. You can also set the vertical scroll amount to HALF or PAGE for scrolling a half or a whole page at a time. HALF is the default vertical scroll amount.

Scroll forward each time you fill in the lines in the program editor screen until you have entered all statements and data lines (see **Screen A5.3**).

You can scroll back through the example to check for errors. When you are ready to run the DATA step, use the SUBMIT command or function key.

Screen A5.4 displays messages indicating completion of the DATA step in the log screen.[4] Move the cursor to the log screen with the UP or DOWN cursor key or the HOME key, and press the FORWARD or BACKWARD function key to scroll through the log. You can alter the vertical scroll amount by entering the command VSCROLL and the scroll amount on the command line of the log screen, just as you did in the program editor.

Notice that the program editor is now empty so you can enter more statements in **Screen A5.5**. To see the statements you entered before, browse the log. To rerun those statements, first return the cursor to the program screen and use the RECALL command or function key; the previously submitted lines are displayed in the program editor. Use the SUBMIT command or function key to submit these program statements to the SAS System for execution again.

Now enter the PROC PRINT and PROC PLOT steps in the program editor. Precede the PROC PRINT statement with the OPTIONS statement specifying the DATE and NUMBER options if you want the date and page number to appear at the top of your output.

```
Command ===>                                              SAS Log  11:14

Copyright (c) 1985 SAS Institute Inc., Cary, N.C. 27511, U.S.A.
NOTE: XXXXX Version of SAS Release X.XX at SAS Institute Inc.(00000000).
NOTE: LICENSED CPUID MODEL = XXXXXX, SERIAL = 00000000.










------------------------------------------------------------------------
Command ===>                                            Program Editor

data educatn;
   input name $ credhrs othered yrsexp;
   toted=(credhrs*16)+othered;
   cards;
aiken 0 16 3
barker 2 0 3
faulkner 3 8 2
house 3 16 2 _
```

Screen A5.2 Entering Your Program Statements

```
Command ===>                                              SAS Log  11:14

Copyright (c) 1985 SAS Institute Inc., Cary, N.C. 27511, U.S.A.
NOTE: XXXXX Version of SAS Release X.XX at SAS Institute Inc.(00000000).
NOTE: LICENSED CPUID MODEL = XXXXXX, SERIAL = 00000000.


------------------------------------------------------------------------
Command ===>                                            Program Editor

mailer 0 16 4
noble 0 0 5
parker 2 0 2
radner 3 4 1
restin 3 0 3
rusk 3 4 2
silver 0 8 5
smith 0 0 4
tate 3 8 2
tucker 0 0 4
volker 0 8 5
;
run;
```

Screen A5.3 Scrolling to Enter More Program Statements

```
Command ===>                                              SAS Log  11:14

NOTE: THE DATA SET WORK.EDUCATN HAS 15 OBSERVATIONS AND 5 VARIABLES.
   20 ;










-------------------------------------------------------------------------
Command ===>                                              Program Editor

00001 _
00002
00003
00004
00005
00006
00007
00008
```

Screen A5.4 Messages in the Log Screen

```
Command ===>                                              SAS Log  11:14

NOTE: THE DATA SET WORK.EDUCATN HAS 15 OBSERVATIONS AND 5 VARIABLES.
   20 ;










-------------------------------------------------------------------------
Command ===>                                              Program Editor

00001 options date number;
00002 proc print;
00003 run;
00004 proc plot;
00005    plot yrsexp*toted;
00006 run;
00007
00008
```

Screen A5.5 Entering More Program Statements

When you use the SUBMIT command or function key, the SAS System executes your program statements. Because these statements contain PROC steps that produce printed output, the program editor/log screen is removed, and the output screen appears, displaying the results of the PRINT procedure in **Output A5.1**.

Output A5.1 PRINT Procedure Output

```
                                    11:44 FRIDAY, JANUARY 18, 1985   1

OBS     NAME      CREDHRS    OTHERED    YRSEXP    TOTED

  1     AIKEN        0          16         3        16
  2     BARKER       2           0         3        32
  3     FAULKNER     3           8         2        56
  4     HOUSE        3          16         2        64
  5     MAILER       0          16         4        16
  6     NOBLE        0           0         5         0
  7     PARKER       2           0         2        32
  8     RADNER       3           4         1        52
  9     RESTIN       3           0         3        48
 10     RUSK         3           4         2        52
 11     SILVER       0           8         5         8
 12     SMITH        0           0         4         0
 13     TATE         3           8         2        56
 14     TUCKER       0           0         4         0
 15     VOLKER       0           8         5         8
```

When the PRINT procedure produces only one page of output, as in this example, you will hear a beep from the terminal when that one page has been displayed. Press the END function key to view the output of the PLOT procedure shown in **Output A5.2**. (By default, function keys number 3 and 15 on the output screen are set to execute the END command.)

Output A5.2 PLOT Procedure Output

```
                                     11:44 FRIDAY, JANUARY 18, 1985 2
          PLOT OF YRSEXP*TOTED  LEGEND: A = 1 OBS, B = 2 OBS, ETC.
RSEXP
  5 +A       B
    I
    I
  4 +B               A
    I
    I
  3 +                A               A               A
    I
    I
  2 +                                A                   A   B     A  A
    I
    I
  1 +                                                    A
    -+-------+-------+-------+-------+-------+-------+-------+-------+
     0       8      16      24      32      40      48      56      64
                                     TOTED
```

You will hear another beep from the terminal, signifying that all output produced by the PLOT procedure has been displayed. You can then browse the output in page-browse mode, enter line-browse mode, or return to the program editor/log screen. Press the COMMAND function key to enter line-browse mode. (By default, function keys number 2 and 14 are set to execute the COMMAND command.) A command line then appears at the top of the output screen. Use the END command or function key to return to the program editor/log screen.

When you return to the program editor/log screen, you see the most recent SAS statements and messages about your job (**Screen A5.6**). You can view the earlier statements by scrolling backward.

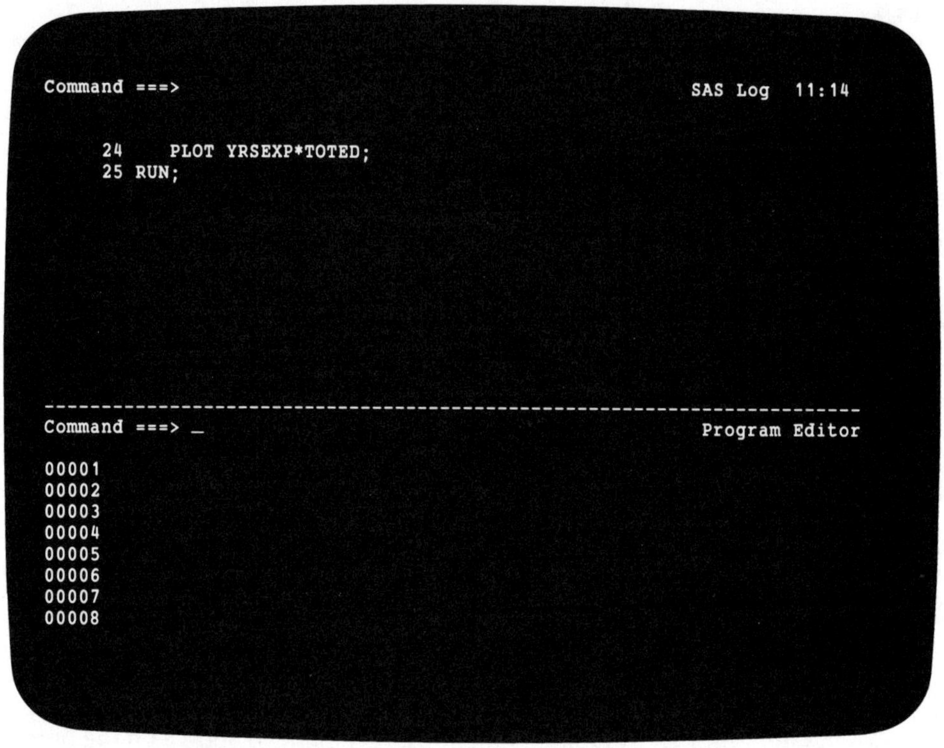

Screen A5.6 SAS Statements and Messages in the Log Screen

You can leave your SAS session in one of several ways. Enter /* in the first two columns of a data line and use the SUBMIT command or function key. Note that the /* must be the last two characters you submit from the program editor; otherwise, it is assumed to be the beginning of a comment. You can also enter

```
ENDSAS;
```

on a data line in the program editor and use the SUBMIT command or function key. On the command line of the program editor or log screen you can type the command

```
BYE
```

and press ENTER to end a SAS session.

NOTES ON USING DISPLAY MANAGER

Active Screen

On the program editor/log screen, only one screen is active at a time. The active screen is defined by display manager as the screen that the cursor is on. When you press ENTER or a function key, only the screen active at that time is affected.

Protected and Unprotected Areas

In display manager screens, protected areas are areas of the display that you are allowed to view but not alter in any way. Unprotected areas are those in which you are allowed to enter and alter text. For example, in the program editor screen, you can type commands in the entry area of the command line, line commands over the line numbers, and data in the data entry area that follows the line numbers; most of the program editor screen is unprotected. On the other hand, the log and output screens and the help facility are browsing screens. Most of the areas on these screens are protected; you are not allowed to enter or alter any text. The only area on these screens that is unprotected is the entry area of the command line. You can type and edit commands on the command lines of these screens.

The boxed areas in **Screen A5.7** mark the unprotected areas of the program editor/log screen:

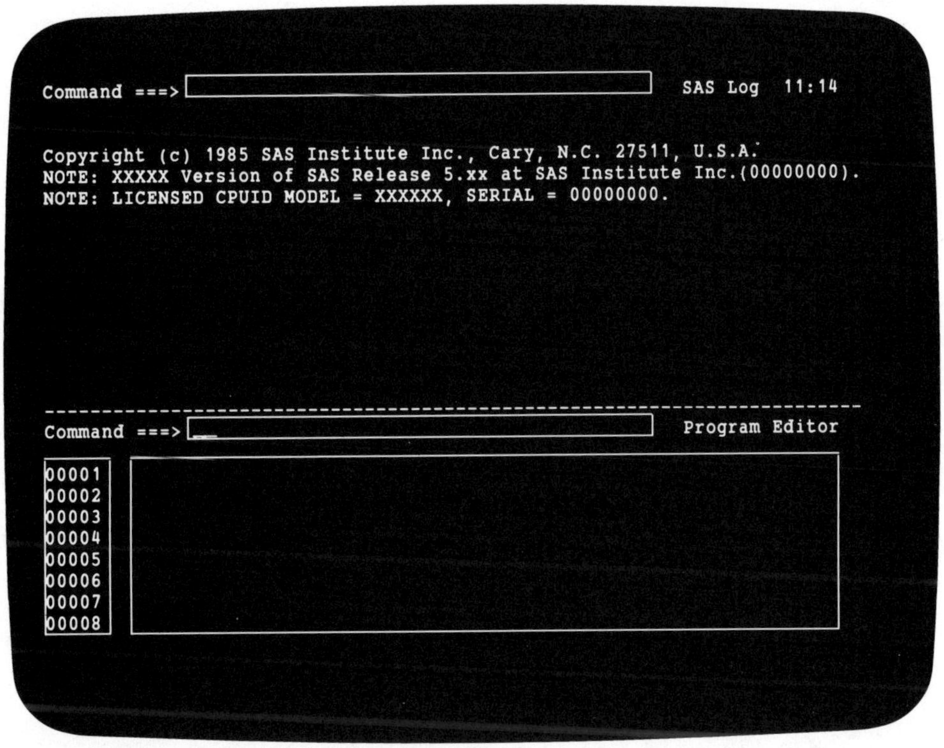

Screen A5.7 Unprotected Areas of the Program Editor/Log Screen

Color and Highlighting Attributes

If you are using a color terminal that has extended color and highlighting attributes in an environment that supports them, you can use the following display manager commands to set and change colors and highlighting:

CBANNER	to change the color or highlighting of the border, the line numbers, and screen description.
CPROT	to change the color or highlighting of all protected areas other than the banner. See CBANNER above.
CSOURCE	to change the color or highlighting of SAS source lines in the log screen.

CUNPROT to change the color or highlighting of unprotected areas.

The colors and highlighting you can use are determined by the features of your terminal. See the *SAS/GRAPH User's Guide* and the *SAS/GRAPH Guide to Hardware Interfaces* for the colors available for your terminal.

Color Use the following abbreviations to specify color attributes in display manager commands:

B blue
R red
P pink
G green
C cyan
Y yellow
W white

Highlighting Use the following abbreviations to specify highlighting attributes in display manager commands:

H highlight
U underline
R reverse video
B blinking

Setting both color and highlighting You can assign an appropriate highlighting attribute at the same time you set a color attribute. Follow the color code with a highlighting code. For example, to set the color attribute of unprotected fields to yellow and the highlighting attribute to underline, use the command

```
CUNPROT Y U
```

To turn off the highlighting attribute, reissue the same color command and specify only a color code. For example, execute

```
CUNPROT Y
```

to allow the color of the unprotected areas of the screen to remain yellow but to remove the underlining.

Function Key Definition Screen

You can display the function key definition screen for the screen you are currently using by executing the KEYS command. You can view the current function key settings, or you can alter a key setting by typing the name of another valid command over the current one. On the function key definition screen you can use the following commands or function keys set to execute these commands:

BACKWARD
CANCEL
END
FORWARD

You can scroll backward and forward to view the entire list of key settings; you can cancel any changes made; you can use the END command, or a function key assigned to execute the END command, to save your altered settings and return to the screen on which you executed the KEYS command.

Note that the function key settings displayed on the screen are those currently active. If you want to execute a command that a function key is not currently set to execute, you must enter the command on the command line. For example, on the program editor and log screens there is no END function key by default because there is no END command for these screens. Execute the END command from the command line to save your settings and exit the function key definition screens of the program editor and log screens.

Entering Multiple Commands

You can enter a series of commands on the command line by separating the commands with semicolons. For example, you can type the BACKWARD MAX scroll command and the FIND command on the command line, separating them with a semicolon, and execute them in order by pressing the ENTER key once.

```
BACKWARD MAX; FIND 'DATA ONE'
```

Function keys and multiple commands You can also combine the use of function keys and the submission of multiple commands. For example, if you set a function key to the command and option BACKWARD MAX followed by a semicolon,

```
BACKWARD MAX;
```

then you can enter

```
FIND 'DATA ONE'
```

on the command line and execute them in order by pressing the key you set to execute BACKWARD MAX; . The procedure executes the BACKWARD MAX command first and then the FIND command.

As a general rule, when you assign commands that do not allow any options to a function key, you may want to follow that command keyword with a semicolon. On the function key definition screen of the program editor screen, for example, you may want to place semicolons after the following commands:

```
BOTTOM;
RECALL;
SPLIT;
TOP;
```

Executing Display Manager Commands Stored in External Files

Executing command list at initialization time You can execute a list of display manager commands stored in an external file automatically at initialization time. When you enter display manager, the system looks for a file, a sequential data set, or a member of a partitioned data set assigned the reserved fileref SASEXEC. If you have assigned SASEXEC to an external file containing a list of display manager commands, those commands are automatically executed. If the system finds no such file, no action is taken, and all default settings are used when you enter display manager.

By executing a series of commands stored in an external file, you can save time and decrease the possibility of errors. Suppose there is a series of commands you want executed each time you enter display manager. You can:

- alter the default active screen
- alter the default colors of protected and unprotected areas of the screen
- execute host-level commands that make SAS data libraries, external files, or data sets available to your session

- copy and submit SAS statements that take you directly into a full-screen procedure.

Using the AUTOEXEC command You can execute a list of display manager commands stored in an external file at any time during your display manager session by executing the AUTOEXEC command. You can follow the AUTOEXEC command with any fileref assigned to a file or data set containing a list of display manager commands. If you do not specify a fileref, the system looks for a file assigned the fileref SASEXEC by default. Because you can specify a fileref other than SASEXEC, you can use the AUTOEXEC command to execute more than one file of display manager commands during your session. The syntax and definitions of the AUTOEXEC and AUTOSHOW commands are shown in the **COMMAND GLOSSARY** at the end of this chapter.

When you execute the AUTOEXEC command and specify the fileref of a file containing a list of display manager commands, the first command is then executed from the command line of the active screen, which is the screen from which you executed the AUTOEXEC command. You can send commands to all of the display manager screens, one at a time, by including commands that change the active screen. For example, if you issue the AUTOEXEC command from the program editor, the first command is sent to that command line to be executed. Use the LOG command to make the log screen active; all following commands are executed on the log screen. Similarly, you can use the OUTPUT command to make the output screen active and the PROGRAM command for the program editor.

An invalid command If an invalid command is encountered during the execution of your file of commands, an error message is displayed, and the AUTOEXEC processing stops.

Display of executing commands By default these commands are not displayed as they are executed. The command AUTOSHOW ON causes each command to be displayed on the appropriate command line just before execution. AUTOSHOW OFF turns off the display of the AUTOEXEC commands as they are being executed.

The AUTOEXEC and AUTOSHOW commands Enter the AUTOEXEC command to send a list of commands stored in an external file to one or more command lines in display manager. The list of commands is sent to the command line of the screen from which you enter the AUTOEXEC command.

You are not required to specify SASEXEC to execute commands stored in a file associated with the fileref SASEXEC; SASEXEC is the default. If you specify another fileref, the display manager commands stored in the file assigned that fileref are then executed.[5]

Use the AUTOSHOW command with the OFF or ON option to specify whether the commands are to be displayed on the command line as they are executed. AUTOSHOW OFF is the default.

Creating your file of display manager commands The commands you want to be executed from a display manager command line, whether at initialization time or with the AUTOEXEC command, must be stored in an external file, **not** a SAS data set. You can store them in a file, a sequential data set, or a member of a partitioned data set.

Here are some general rules to follow when entering a list of commands to be executed at initialization time or with the AUTOEXEC command:

1. Enter only one command on each line and follow each command with a semicolon. Note: when you are working in display manager and entering commands on the command line directly, one at a time, you do not need to end a command with a semicolon.
2. Do not type beyond the 80th column.[6]
3. You can send commands to each display manager screen one at a time. Use the commands PROGRAM, LOG, OUTPUT, and HELP to designate which screen you want to be active and, therefore, the one on which the following commands will be executed.[7]
4. After you designate the active screen, list only commands that are valid on that screen.
5. The file in which the list of commands is stored **must** be assigned the reserved fileref SASEXEC if you want it to be executed automatically when you enter display manager.[8]

A sample list of stored commands Below is a sample list of commands that you can store in an external file and execute with the AUTOEXEC command or at initialization time:

```
PROGRAM;
INCLUDE MYFILE;
SUBMIT;
CBA G;
LOG;
CURSOR 5;
SPLIT;
CSO G;
VSCROLL PAGE;
OUTPUT;
CPRO B;
PROGRAM;
OUTPUT OFF;
VSCROLL PAGE;
```

These commands are explained in detail below:

PROGRAM designates that the active screen is the program editor; therefore, all commands that follow this command are sent to the command line of the program editor screen to be executed **until** you specify that another screen is active. In a file executed at initialization time, you are not required to specify PROGRAM because the program editor is the active screen by default.

INCLUDE MYFILE brings the contents of the external file identified by the fileref MYFILE to the data lines of the program editor screen.[5] This file contains a series of SAS program statements that you want submitted from the program editor to the SAS System. It could, for example, make some SAS data sets available to your session by containing X statements that make fileref assignments through host-level commands; it may also be used to enter an OPTIONS statement.

SUBMIT submits the program statements that you brought into the data lines of the program editor with the INCLUDE command.

CBA G	sets the color of the banner on the program editor screen to green.
LOG	activates the log screen. All commands that follow the LOG command are sent to the command line of the log screen to be executed **until** you make another screen active.
CURSOR 5	positions the cursor five lines below its default position, the command line of the log screen. This command positions the cursor in preparation for the execution of the next command.
SPLIT	tells the screen to split at the cursor location. Because you just positioned the cursor five lines below the command line of the log screen, you have altered the default location of the split between the program editor and log screens.
CSO G	sets the color of the source lines on the log screen. CSO G sets the color of the source lines to green.
VSCROLL PAGE	alters the vertical scroll amount of the log screen and sets it to the full depth of the log screen. HALF is the default.
OUTPUT	activates the output screen in page-browse mode. All commands that follow are now sent to the output screen.
CPRO B	sets the color of the protected text in the output screen. CPRO B sets the color of the protected text to blue.
PROGRAM	activates the program editor screen. All commands that follow are now sent to the command line of the program editor screen.
OUTPUT OFF	indicates that you do not want output produced during your session automatically displayed in the output screen.
VSCROLL PAGE	alters the vertical scroll amount of the program editor screen and sets it to the full depth of the screen. The default is HALF.

This list is just a sample of the kind of commands you may want to store and execute from an external file.

PROGRAM EDITOR SCREEN

Notes on Using the Program Editor Screen

Submitting SAS source lines from the program editor You can think of the program editor as being entirely separate from the SAS System since SAS does not see the lines entered until you are ready to submit your job with the SUBMIT command or function key. After the job has executed, you can resume working in the program editor, entering commands, using editing keys and function keys, and entering and editing program statements or data.

Program editor screen line length When you submit SAS program statements for execution from the program editor screen, the data lines are broken into lengths of 80 columns. It is recommended that you not submit source lines longer than 80 columns. If you do submit longer source lines, do not continue a word from the 80th to the 81st column; it will be divided when submitted.[9]

Executing line commands without line numbers You can execute line commands even if you have set NUMS OFF. You can position the cursor where you want the line command to be executed and then press a function key set to execute a line command. For example, you can position the cursor where you want a line to split and then press a function key set to execute :TS (the text split line command preceded by a colon). You can also execute a line command from the command line by preceding it with a colon, just as you do when you set a function key. You can type :TS on the command line, position the cursor, and then press the ENTER key.

Line Commands

The line commands available in the program editor screen of display manager are listed below. You can use line commands to move, copy, repeat, insert, and delete lines or blocks of lines; and to designate target locations for moved, copied, and inserted lines. In display manager you can use line commands only on the program editor screen. The log screen, whether you are using it to view the SAS log or SAS HELP, and the output screen are browsing screens; therefore, you cannot use line commands to alter text. Below is a list of line commands. Complete definitions appear at the end of this chapter.

Single commands

A[*n*],B[*n*]
C[*n*]
COLS
D[*n*]
I[*n* | A[*n*] | B[*n*]]
M[*n*]
MASK
O[*n*]
P[*n*]
R[*n*]
TF
TS

Block commands

CC
DD
MM
OO
PP
RR[*n*]

Special shift commands

>[*n*]
<[*n*]
>>[*n*]
<<[*n*]
)[*n*]
([*n*]
))[*n*]
(([*n*]

Command-Line Commands

You can use the command-line commands listed below on the command line of the program editor screen. Definitions of all commands you can use with display manager appear at the end of this chapter.

ASSIGN*
AUTOADD*
AUTOEXEC
AUTOSHOW
BACKWARD
BOTTOM
BYE
CAPS
CBANNER
CHANGE
CPRO(T)
CUNPRO(T)
CURSOR
FIND
FORWARD
HELP
HSCROLL
INCLUDE
KEYS
LEFT
LINESIZE
LOC
LOG
NODMS*
NULLS
NUMBER
OUTPUT
PRINT
PROGRAM
RCHANGE
RECALL
RESET
RFIND
RIGHT
RULE*
SAVE
SCREEN*
SPLIT
SUBMIT
TOP
VSCROLL
X**

LOG SCREEN

Notes on Using the Log Screen

Line length The length of data lines on the log screen is sensitive to the value of certain line size options that you can specify with the OPTIONS statement.[10] You can scroll RIGHT to view data lines longer than the line length of your terminal screen.

---

* not in IBM versions.
** not available under VSE.

Command-Line Commands

You can use the command-line commands listed below on the command line of the log screen. Definitions of all commands you can use with display manager appear at the end of this chapter.

ASSIGN*	KEYS
AUTOEXEC	LEFT
AUTOSHOW	LOC
BACKWARD	OUTPUT
BOTTOM	PRINT
BYE	PROGRAM
CAPS	RFIND
CBANNER	RIGHT
CPROT	RULE*
CSOURCE	SAVE*
CUNPROT	SCREEN*
CURSOR	SPLIT
FIND	TOP
FORWARD	VSCROLL
HELP	X**
HSCROLL	

OUTPUT SCREEN

Notes on Using the Output Screen

When the output screen displays output resulting from any procedures you have executed, the procedure displays the first page of output and then waits for your prompt to go to the next page. To display each succeeding page of output, press the ENTER key or any function key **except** the END key.

If you have many pages of output and do not want to wait for the procedure to display them all, one by one, you can press the END key to cause the display manager to skip over all the intervening pages and display only the last page of output. All output is produced whether or not you choose to view each page. The terminal emits a beep when the last page of output is displayed.

When the last page of output is displayed and you receive the audible signal from the terminal, you are in page-browse mode. Now that you have entered page-browse mode, you have three choices; you can:

1. use the function keys operable in page-browse mode to browse the output
2. return to the program editor/log screen by pressing the END key
3. enter line-browse mode by pressing the COMMAND function key. A command line then appears at the top of the screen, and you can either use function keys or enter commands that are operable in line-browse mode.

Browsing more than one set of output If your submitted statements included more than one PROC step that produced output, you cannot return to the program editor/log screen from the last page of the first set of output by pressing the END key. You must reach the last page of the last set of output produced before you can exit the output screen.

---

* not in IBM versions.

** not available under VSE.

When you reach the last page of the first set of output, you can press the COMMAND function key to put a command line on the screen and to take you into line-browse mode for browsing that set of output; or you can proceed to the first page of the next set of output by pressing the END key. If you enter line-browse mode, pressing the END key also takes you to the first page of the next set of output. If you do not want to view all pages of a set of output, press the END key again to display the last page of that set of output. At this point, you have the same choices described above. You can browse the output in page-browse mode, browse it in line-browse mode by pressing the COMMAND key, or press the END key to return you to the program editor/log screen.

Using function keys in page-browse mode Because there is no command line available to you in page-browse mode of the output screen, you must use function keys to execute commands. The same function key settings apply to the output screen in both page-browse and line-browse mode. You cannot view the function key definition screen from page-browse mode unless you have a function key for the output screen defined to execute the KEYS command. Use the COMMAND function key to create a command line to take you into line-browse mode where you can execute the KEYS command to view the function key settings for the output screen. (By default function keys number 2 and 14 are set to execute the COMMAND command.) Use the END function key to take you to the next procedure's output or to exit the output screen. (By default function keys number 3 and 15 are set to execute the END command.)

You can also view the function key settings of the output screen by executing the following commands in sequence from the command line of the program editor or the log screen:

```
OUTPUT; KEYS
```

The OUTPUT command takes you to the OUTPUT screen; the KEYS command then displays the function key definition screen of the output screen.

Linesize on output screen The maximum line length depends on the operating system under which you are using the SAS System.[11]

Command-Line Commands in Line-Browse Mode

When viewing the output screen, you must enter line-browse mode to be able to enter commands directly. After hearing a beep from the terminal, which signifies that all of the output has been displayed and that you have entered page-browse mode, press the COMMAND function key to create a command line on the output screen and to enter line-browse mode. Then you can use the command-line commands listed below. Definitions of all commands you can use with display manager appear at the end of this chapter.

ASSIGN*	KEYS
AUTOEXEC	LEFT
AUTOSHOW	LOC
BACKWARD	LOG
BOTTOM	OUTPUT
BYE	PRINT
CAPS	PROGRAM
CBANNER	RFIND
COMMAND	RIGHT
CPROT	RULE*
CUNPROT	SAVE*
CURSOR	SCREEN*
END	SPLIT*
FIND	TOP
FORWARD	VSCROLL
HELP	X**
HSCROLL	

COMMAND GLOSSARY

Line Commands

A[*n*],**B**[*n*] A line command that marks the target position of a *source* line(s), a line or lines being moved or copied with a C, M, P, CC, MM, PP, or INCLUDE command. Indicate an A (after) on the line number of the line you want the source line(s) to follow. Use a B (before) to mark the line you want the source line(s) to precede. After the A or B, you can specify the number of times you want the source line or lines to be duplicated. Follow A or B with some number *n* and a blank space.

CMS, OS, VM/PC, and VSE: You cannot use the target commands with the INCLUDE command.

C[*n*] A line command that copies one or more lines to another location in the file, indicated by a target line command. Indicate C on the line number of the line to be copied. Then indicate an A on the number of the line you want the copied line to follow, a B on the number of the line you want it to precede, or an O or OO on the line or lines you want it to overlay. You can also specify *n* number of lines to be copied. Follow C with some number *n* and a blank space.

CC A line command that copies a block of lines to another location in the file, indicated by a target line command. Indicate CC on the line numbers of the first and last lines of the block of lines to be copied.

COLS A line command that creates a special line indicating the column numbers across your display screen. The column indicator line appears above the line on which you execute the COLS command. The COLS line is a

---

* not in IBM versions.

** not available under VSE.

special line that is not submitted when you submit program statements from the program editor. Use the RESET key or command or delete the line to remove the COLS line.

D[*n*] A line command that deletes one or more lines. Indicate D on the line number of the line to be deleted. By default, one line is deleted. To delete more than one line, follow D with some number *n* and a blank space.

DD A line command that deletes a block of lines. Indicate DD on the line numbers of the block of lines to be deleted.

I[*n*] This line command is used to insert one or more new lines. By default one line is inserted after the line on which you execute the I command. To insert more than one line, follow I with some number *n* and a blank space. See also the IA and IB commands below.

See the MASK command to insert lines with a defined content other than a blank line. See the TS (text split) command to insert space within a line of text.

IA[*n*] Use this line command to insert one or more lines after the line on which you enter the IA (insert after) command. By default only one line is inserted. See also the I and IB commands.

IB[*n*] Use this line command to insert one or more lines before the line on which you enter the IB (insert before) command. By default only one line is inserted. See also the I and IA commands.

M[*n*] A line command that moves one or more lines to another location in the file, indicated by a target line command. Indicate M on the line number of the line to be moved. If you move more than one line, follow M with some number *n* and a blank space. Then specify an A on the line number of the line you want the moved line to follow, a B on the line you want it to precede, or an O on the line you want the moved line or lines to overlay.

MASK A line command that defines the initial contents of a new line. Type MASK on any line number and press ENTER. Then type on that line whatever characters you want to be repeated and press ENTER again. After you define a MASK, a line with the contents of the MASK line is inserted when you use the I (insert) line command.

The MASK remains in effect throughout the session. To redefine it, simply repeat the steps described above. To return to the default, a blank line, use the same process and leave the line blank.

MM A line command that moves a block of lines to another location in the file, indicated by a target line command. Indicate the block to be moved with an MM line command on the first and last line numbers of the block.

`>[n]` A line command that shifts data one or more spaces to the right. Indicate `>` or `>` followed by some number *n* and a blank space on the line number of the line to be shifted. Note that a **data** shift command allows no loss of data. The default is one space.

`<[n]` A line command that shifts data one or more spaces to the left. Indicate `<` or `<` followed by some number *n* and a blank space on the line number of the line to be shifted. Note that a **data** shift command allows no loss of data. The default is one space.

`>>[n]` A line command that shifts a block of lines one or more spaces to the right. Indicate `>>` or `>>` followed by some number *n* and a blank space on the line number of the first line of the block to be shifted and another `>>` or `>>n` on the last line number of the block. Note that a **data** shift command allows no loss of data. The default is one space.

`<<[n]` A line command that shifts a block of lines one or more spaces to the left. Indicate `<<` or `<<` followed by some number *n* and a blank space on the line number of the first line of the block to be shifted and another `<<` or `<<n` on the last line number of the block. Note that a **data** shift command allows no loss of data. The default is one space.

`)[n]` A line command that shifts columns of data one or more columns to the right. Indicate) or) followed by some number *n* and a blank space on the line number of the line to be shifted. Note that a **column** shift command, unlike a **data** shift command, can cause loss of data. The default is one column.

`([n]` A line command that shifts columns of data one or more columns to the left. Indicate (or (followed by some number *n* and a blank space on the line number of the line to be shifted. Note that a **column** shift command, unlike a **data** shift command, can cause loss of data. The default is one column.

`))[n]` The column shift line command shifts a block of lines one or more columns to the right. Indicate)) or)) followed by some number *n* and a blank space on the line number of the first line of the block to be shifted and another)) or))*n* on the last line number of the block. Note that a **column** shift command, unlike a **data** shift command, can cause loss of data. The default is one column.

`(([n]` A line command that shifts a block of lines one or more columns to the left. Indicate ((or ((followed by some number *n* and a blank space on the line number of the first line of the block to be shifted and another ((or ((*n* on the last line number of the block. Note that a **column** shift command, unlike a **data** shift command, can cause loss of data. The default is one space.

O[*n*] A line command that marks the target position of a C, M, P, CC, MM, or PP line command. Indicate the O (overlay) line command on the line number of the line you want the contents of the *source line*, the moved or copied line, to overlay. Characters from the source line overlay blank or null spaces on the *target line*, the line marked with the O line command. After the O line command you can specify the number of target lines you want the source line or lines to overlay. Follow O with some number *n* and a blank space.

If any characters occupy the same positions on the source and target lines, the characters on the target line remain, and characters from the source line do not appear. If you are executing the M (move) command, you receive an error message, and the line intended to be moved remains in its original position.

OO A line command that marks a block of lines, identified by an OO on the line numbers of the first and last lines of the block, as the target position of source lines, lines marked with the C, M, P, CC, MM, or PP line commands. See the O line command.

P[*n*] A line command that copies or overlays one or more lines to another location in the file, indicated by a target line command. The P (pattern) line command is similiar to the C (copy) line command; the difference is that the system remembers the line marked with the P line command and copies it to the new location each time you enter a target line command until you remove the P line command. You can remove it with the RESET key or command or by using any of the editing keys you normally use to erase or remove characters, such as the EOF key, the character delete key, or the space bar. Indicate P on the line number of the source line, the line you want to copy. Then indicate an A on the number of the line you want the source line to follow, a B on the number of the line you want it to precede, or an O or OO on the line or lines you want it to overlay. You can also specify *n* number of lines to be copied. Follow P with some number *n* and a blank space.

PP A line command that copies a block of lines to another location in the file, indicated by a target line command. The PP (pattern block) command is similiar to the CC line command; the difference is that the system remembers the block of lines marked with the PP line command and copies it to the new location each time you enter a target line command until you remove the PP line command. You can remove it with the RESET key or command or by using any of the editing keys you normally use to erase or remove characters, such as the EOF key, the character delete key, or the space bar. Indicate PP on the first and last line numbers of the block of lines you want to designate as the source lines, the lines you want to copy. Then indicate an A on the number of the line you want the source lines to follow, a B on the number of the line you want them to precede, an O or OO on the first and last lines of the block you want the source lines to overlay.

R[*n*] A line command that repeats a line one or more times immediately following. Indicate R on the line number of the line to be repeated. To repeat a line more than once, follow R with some number *n* and a blank space.

RR[*n*] A line command that repeats a block of lines immediately following that block. Indicate RR on the line numbers of the first and last lines of the block of lines to be repeated. You can also specify how many times you want the block of lines repeated; follow RR with some number *n* and a blank space. You can specify *n* on the first or last RR command or on both.

TF A line command that flows a paragraph or an indicated block of text by removing trailing blanks from each line. You can use the TF (text flow) line command to move text into wasted space left at ends of lines, especially after performing insertions and deletions.

TS A line command that inserts a blank line for inserting new text. Either type TS (text split) on a line number, position the cursor where you want the text to split, and press ENTER, or position the cursor and press the :TS function key. See the I (insert) command for inserting space between lines rather than within the text of a line.

Command-Line Commands

Command-line commands that are available in display manager screens are defined below:

ASSIGN *filename fileref*

AOS/VS, PRIMOS and VMS only: Use the ASSIGN command to assign a fileref to an external file. You can specify a fully qualified file name, according to the requirements of the operating system you are using, or just an individual file name (and type under VMS) if it is in a directory to which you currently have access.

For example, to assign the fileref PROG1 to an AOS/VS, PRIMOS, or VMS fully-qualified file name, you can execute the ASSIGN command in the form

```
ASSIGN :UDD:youruserdir:PROG.SAS PROG1

ASSIGN [yourdir]PROG.SAS PROG1

ASSIGN <masterfiledirectory>userfiledirectory>PROG.SAS PROG1
```

See the INCLUDE and SAVE commands.

CMS, OS, and VM/PC: You can execute host-level commands before entering display manager or after entering display manager with the X command or statement.

VSE: You can place a /FILE statement, an ICCF control language statement, in the ICCF procedure that invokes the SAS System. You cannot use the X command or statement in the ICCF environment. See the INCLUDE and SAVE commands.

AUTOADD [**ON** | **OFF**]

AOS/VS, PRIMOS, and VMS only: The AUTOADD ON command adds data entry lines to the bottom of the screen each time you scroll forward so that you do not have to use an INSERT command to insert new lines for entering new data or text. If line numbers are on (NUMS ON), these lines are numbered each time you scroll foward. If you execute AUTOADD OFF, the editor does not add new lines for data entry each time you scroll foward.

AUTOEXEC [**SASEXEC** | *fileref*]

Enter the AUTOEXEC command to send a list of commands stored in an external file to one or more command lines in display manager. The first command in the list is sent to the command line of the screen from which you enter the AUTOEXEC command.

If you do not specify a fileref that you assigned to an external file through a host-level command, the procedure looks for a file assigned the fileref SASEXEC by default. If you specify another fileref, the display manager commands stored in the file associated with that fileref are then executed.

AUTOSHOW OFF | ON

Use the AUTOSHOW command with the OFF or ON option to specify whether commands being executed from an external file are to be displayed on the command line as they are executed. AUTOSHOW OFF is the default.

BACKWARD [*n* | **MAX**]

In addition to using a function key, you can scroll toward the top of the screen with the BAC command. The amount of scroll is controlled by the VSCROLL command.

You can specify a particular number of lines to scroll backward by entering BAC *n* (*n* being the number of lines you want to scroll backward). You can scroll the maximum amount by entering BAC MAX or BAC M. The scroll value specified with the BAC command, either *n* or MAX, is operative only for that scroll; it temporarily overrides but does not alter the default scroll value or the one set by the VSCROLL command.

BOTTOM

Use the BOTTOM or BOT command to scroll the last line of text to the bottom of the screen.

BYE

You can use the BYE command to end a SAS session. You can execute the BYE command from the command line of the log or program editor screen.

CAPS OFF | ON

When you execute CAPS ON, all text entered, as well as text on lines that have been modified, is translated into uppercase letters when you press ENTER or a function key. All text is left as entered when CAPS OFF is in effect. The CAPS command affects only the screen on which it is entered and is in effect for the remainder of the SAS session or until changed by another CAPS command. The default is CAPS ON in minicomputer versions and CAPS OFF in IBM versions.

CBANNER *color* [*highlight*]

The CBA command changes the color or color and highlighting attributes of the banner lines. These lines are the borders, line numbers if any, and command line. Specifying CBA affects only the screen on which the command is entered and is in effect for the remainder of the SAS session or until changed by another CBA command.

CHANGE *string1 string2* [**NEXT** | **FIRST** | **LAST** | **PREV** | **ALL**]
[**WORD** | **SUFFIX** | **PREFIX**]

Use the CHANGE command to change one or more occurrences of *string1* to *string2*. Follow the CHANGE command with the string of characters to be changed, a space, and then the new string, or type the strings on the command line and press the CHANGE function key.

You can specify on the CHANGE command that the system search for and alter the NEXT occurrence of the specified string after the current cursor location; the FIRST occurrence of the string in the file, regardless of your current cursor location; the LAST occurrence of the string in the file; or the PREVious occurrence. If you specify ALL, you receive a message that reports how many times the string occurs in the entire file, and each occurrence is changed. By default, the CHANGE command searches for and changes the NEXT occurrence of the specified string after the current cursor location.

You can also specify one of the following options: PREFIX, SUFFIX, or WORD. If you do not specify one of these, *string1* is changed to *string2*, regardless of context.

In the CHANGE command, as in the FIND command, a WORD is one or more symbols preceded and followed by a delimiter. A delimiter is any symbol other than an uppercase letter, a lowercase letter, a digit, or an underscore.

Remember to use single quotes to enclose strings with special characters or embedded blanks. Single word strings require no quotation marks. For example,

```
C YOUR MY
C 'YOUR DATA SET' 'MY DATA SET'
```

Also enclose your string in single quotes if CAPS are ON and you do not want lowercase letters in the string translated into uppercase letters.

If your string contains a single quotation mark, such as

```
C "Bob's" "Bill's"
```

enclose it in double quotation marks.

You can combine the use of the CHANGE command and RFIND function key (or command). For example, after you enter a CHANGE command, you can press the RFIND function key to locate the next occurrence of *string1* before pressing RCHANGE to change it to *string2*.

Also see the RCHANGE, FIND, and RFIND commands.

COMMAND

Use the CMD command, assigned to a function key, in page-browse mode of the procedure output screen to put a command line at the top of the screen, taking you into line-browse mode. Execute the command again to remove the command line and return you to page-browse mode.

CPROT *color* [*highlight*]

The CPROT command changes the color or color and highlighting attributes of protected fields on the log or output screen to those specified for the remainder of the SAS session or until changed by another CPROT command. This color or color and highlighting attributes become the default for the protected fields only for the screen on which you enter the command.

The CPROT command has no effect on the program editor screen since its protected areas are governed by the CBANNER command.

CSOURCE *color* [*highlight*]

The CSO command changes the color or color and highlighting attributes of SAS source lines on the log screen to those specified. The CSO command is in effect for the remainder of the SAS session or until changed by another CSO command.

CUNPROT *color* [*highlight*]

The CUN command changes the color or color and highlighting attributes of unprotected fields to those specified for the remainder of the SAS session or until changed by another CUN command. This color or color and highlighting attributes become the default for all unprotected fields that are not otherwise defined by color or highlighting attribute commands. Note: the CUNPROT command affects the unprotected fields only for the screen on which it is executed.

CURSOR [*rownumber*] | [*rownumber colnumber*]

The CURSOR command, without any options specified, is designed to be executed with a function key. Press the CURSOR key to return the cursor to the command line of whatever screen you are currently using.

Specifying options with the CURSOR command is especially useful when executing a list of commands stored in an external file. (See the AUTOEXEC command.) You can use the CURSOR command to position the cursor in preparation for the execution of a following command. For example, if you execute

```
CURSOR 10
```

on the command line of the log screen and then execute the SPLIT command, you can alter the location of the split between the program editor and the log screens. Note: do not move the cursor outside the boundaries of the screen from which you want the next command to be executed.

END

In line-browse mode of the procedure output screen, the END command either returns you to the program editor/log screen or takes you to the first page of the next procedure's output. In page-browse mode, it takes you to the next page of output or, if you are already viewing the last page, returns you to the program editor/log screen.

FIND *characterstring* [**NEXT** | **FIRST** | **LAST** | **PREV** | **ALL**]
[**PREFIX** | **SUFFIX** | **WORD**]

Use the FIND command to search for a specified string of characters. Remember to enclose the string in single quotes if it contains embedded blanks or special characters. You can execute the FIND command by entering it directly or by typing the character string on the command line and pressing the FIND function key.

You can specify in the FIND command that the system search for the NEXT occurrence of the specified string after the current cursor location; the FIRST occurrence of the string in the file, regardless of your current cursor location; the LAST occurrence of the string in the file; or the PREVious occurrence. If you specify ALL, you receive a message that reports how many times the string occurs in the entire file. By default, the FIND command searches for the NEXT occurrence of the specified string after the current cursor location.

You can also specify one of the following options: PREFIX, SUFFIX, or WORD. If you do not specify one of these options, the system searches for each occurrence of the string, regardless of context.

In the FIND command, a WORD is one or more symbols preceded and followed by a delimiter. A delimiter is any symbol other than an uppercase letter, a lowercase letter, a digit, or an underscore. For example,

```
ABC123
```

is a WORD, but

```
ABC$123
```

is two WORDs separated by the delimiter $. A PREFIX or SUFFIX is treated just as its grammatical definition. In the first example, ABC123, you could specify ABC as a PREFIX and 123 as a SUFFIX. In the second example, ABC$123, ABC and 123 are WORDs, not a PREFIX and a SUFFIX.

Remember to use single quotes to enclose strings with special characters or embedded blanks. For example,

```
F YOUR
F 'YOUR DATA SET'
```

Also enclose your string in single quotes if CAPS are ON and you do not want lowercase letters in the string translated into uppercase letters.

If your string contains a single quotation mark, such as

```
F "Bob's"
```

enclose it in double quotation marks.

See also the CHANGE, RCHANGE, and RFIND commands.

FORWARD [*n* | **MAX**]

In addition to using a function key, you can scroll toward the bottom of the screen with the FOR *n* command. The amount of scroll is controlled by the VSCROLL command.

You can specify a particular number of lines to scroll forward by entering FOR *n* (*n* being the number of lines you want to scroll foward). You can scroll the maximum amount by entering FOR MAX or FOR M. The scroll value specified with the FOR command, either *n* or MAX, is operative only for that scroll; it temporarily overrides but does not alter the default scroll value or the one set by the VSCROLL command.

HELP [*topic*]

When you enter the HELP command, SAS HELP, an on-line help facility, appears on your display screen. You can specify a topic at the same time that you execute the HELP command. If you do not specify a topic, a list of allowed topics is displayed.

CMS, OS, VM/PC, and VSE: You can execute HELP from any of the three display manager screens. SAS HELP is then displayed, occupying the entire display area. Use the END command or function key to return display manager to the screen.

AOS/VS, PRIMOS, and VMS: You can execute HELP from any of the three display manager command lines, but SAS HELP is always displayed in the upper portion of the program editor/log screen. You can browse help information by using the same commands and function keys that are available in the log screen. If you execute HELP from the output screen, you must return to the program editor/log screen to view the help information. After viewing the help information, you can return the SAS log to the log screen by entering the LOG command or submitting at least one statement from the program editor.

HSCROLL HALF | PAGE | *n*

The HSCROLL command sets the horizontal scroll amount, the amount the active screen scrolls when you press the LEFT or RIGHT scrolling keys. If you specify PAGE, the scroll amount is equal to the entire width of the display area. If you specify HALF, the scroll amount is one-half of the display area. HALF is the default.

INCLUDE *fileref | fileref(membername)*
INCLUDE *fileref | 'filename'*
INCLUDE *singlelinenumber | firstline lastline*

The INCLUDE command allows either an entire external file or lines from the log screen to be displayed in the program editor screen. When including lines from the log screen, you can specify particular lines. The included lines are inserted at the bottom of the list of SAS source statement lines or wherever you specify with the A, B, or O line command. When specifying lines on the log screen, you can optionally use a hyphen or a colon between your first and last line specifications.

CMS, OS, and VM/PC: If you are working with an external file, you should use a host-operating system command to assign it a fileref. You can execute it before invoking SAS or from display manager with an X command.

AOS/VS and VMS: You can bring an external file to the program editor screen with the INCLUDE command in one of four ways. The *filename* can be a fully qualified filename, according to the conventions of the operating system you are using, or the name (and type under VMS) of a file in a directory to which you currently have access.

1. Assign a fileref to a file name with a host-level command either before invoking SAS or from display manager with an X command.
2. Assign a fileref to a file name with the display manager ASSIGN command.

3. Specify an actual file name by enclosing it in single quote. In AOS/VS, the file name specified must be in your current working directory; in VMS, it must be specified in your home directory. Under VMS, you must include the file type.
4. Specify an unassigned fileref; the system then assigns that specified fileref to an existing file of the name *fileref*.SAS in your current working directory.

PRIMOS: See the note above for AOS/VS and VMS. You can use all but the first method listed.

VSE: You can place a /FILE statement, an ICCF control language statement, in the ICCF procedure that invokes the SAS System. You cannot use the X command or statement in the ICCF environment. If the file referred to is a sequential file, you must use a /FILE statement in the ICCF procedure. If it is a member of an ICCF library, you are not allowed to use a /FILE statement in the ICCF procedure. Instead, specify the actual ICCF member name.

KEYS

Use the KEYS command to display the function key definition screen. You can view the current settings or alter them and store your new ones. You can scroll forward and backward on the function key definition screen; use the END command or function key to return to the previous screen.

LEFT [*n* | **MAX**]

This command scrolls the screen *n* spaces to the left. By default the screen scrolls half of its width. To override the scroll amount temporarily, enter LEFT and the number of spaces you want the screen to scroll. Enter LEFT MAX to scroll the screen to the left boundary.

LINESIZE *n*

Use the LINESIZE command to alter the line length of data lines on the program editor screen; *n* can be any number between the width of your screen minus 1 and 256. The LINESIZE command allows you to use the INCLUDE command to display files of long data lines in the program editor for editing, for example, saved SAS output files. Note: if you specify a LINESIZE shorter than your current line length, your data lines will be truncated.

AOS/VS, PRIMOS, and VMS: The maximum line length of the program editor is 256 columns.

CMS, OS, VM/PC, and VSE: The maximum line length of the program editor is 80 columns.

LOC *n*

Use the LOC or LOCATE command, followed by some line number *n*, to scroll that line to the top of the display screen.

LOG

The LOG command moves the cursor to the command line of the log screen and makes it the active screen.

AOS/VS, PRIMOS, and VMS only: You can also use the LOG command to return the SAS log to the upper portion of the program editor/log screen, replacing the output screen or help information.

NODMS

AOS/VS, PRIMOS, and VMS only: The NODMS command takes you from display manager to line mode and turns off the SOURCE option. The screen is cleared, and you receive the SAS prompt. The SAS System is then ready to receive your next SAS statement. Leaving display manager does not close the file that is currently open or end your SAS session. When you leave display manager and enter line mode, all of your current WORK data sets are still available to you.

NULLS ON | OFF

When you execute NULLS ON, all data lines are padded with nulls instead of blanks. Turning NULLS ON allows you to use the INSERT editing key to insert characters between text already entered on a line.

If you execute NULLS OFF, the data lines are padded with blanks. To use the INSERT editing key, you must first use the EOF editing key to turn those blanks into nulls.

The effect of the NULLS command on how a file is saved with the SAVE command depends on the host operating system you are using.

AOS/VS, PRIMOS, and VMS: If NULLS are ON when you save the file, the file is saved with no trailing blanks. If NULLS are OFF, trailing blanks are saved.

CMS, OS, VM/PC, and VSE: If you are saving a file in a sequential or partitioned data set with a fixed block record format, the setting of the NULLS command has no effect. If you are saving to a data set with a variable block record format, NULLS ON causes no trailing blanks to be saved, and NULLS OFF causes the trailing blanks to be saved.

NUMBERS ON | OFF
NUMS ON | OFF

Use the NUMS ON command to create line numbers for data lines on your screen. If your screen already contains text, all data are shifted to the right, and the line numbers appear on the left. Execute NUMS OFF to remove line numbers and shift text back to the left. NUMS ON is the default on the display manager program editor screen.

If line numbers are displayed, you can type line commands directly over line numbers. If you set NUMS OFF, you can still execute line commands by entering them from the command line or by using a function key. Precede the line command with a colon when executing it on the command line rather that on a line number. For example, type :TS (text split) or :I (insert) on the command line, position the cursor, and then press ENTER. When using a function key, position the cursor, and then press the function key set to execute :TS.

OUTPUT
OUTPUT [**ON** | **OFF**]
OUTPUT [**TOP**]

The OUTPUT command, executed with no option specified, replaces the program editor/log screen with the output screen.

The OUTPUT command followed by ON or OFF specifies whether procedure output is displayed in the output screen immediately while the procedure is executing (ON) or held for later viewing

(OFF). If OUTPUT OFF is in effect, specify OUTPUT to view your output. The default is OUTPUT ON.

AOS/VS, PRIMOS, and VMS only: The OUTPUT TOP command replaces the log screen in the upper portion of the program editor/log screen with the output screen to allow you to view output while entering more SAS statements in the program editor.

PRINT [**PROGRAM** | **RECALL** | **LOG** | **OUTPUT**]
[*fileref* | *fileref(membername)*]

CMS, OS, VM/PC and **VSE only:** You can use the PRINT command to print the entire information stream of a display manager screen, not just what is currently displayed.

You can print the stream of information in the program editor by specifying the PROGRAM option; print all statements previously submitted from the program editor with the RECALL option; the stream of information in the log screen with the LOG option; and all procedure output with the OUTPUT option.

The contents of the log, program editor or output screen, or all previously submitted statements are sent to the default system printer.

You can also send the contents to an external file by specifying its previously assigned fileref or fileref followed by a member name.

PRINT [**ALL**]

AOS/VS, PRIMOS, and VMS only: With the PRINT command, you can print what is currently showing in the screen on the default system printer. By specifying ALL, you can print the entire contents of the current screen, not just what is visible at the time you enter the PRINT command.

PROGRAM
PGM

The PROGRAM command moves the cursor to the command line of the program editor screen and makes it the active screen.

RCHANGE

Use the RCHANGE or RC command to continue to FIND and CHANGE a string of characters previously specified in a FIND or CHANGE command.

See also the CHANGE, FIND, and RFIND commands.

RECALL

Use the RECALL command to bring back to the program editor screen any lines you have submitted to SAS since you entered display manager. The system adds the recalled lines to the top of the program editor screen in front of any other nonblank lines already entered. After you have used the RECALL command to recall the most recently submitted block of statements, you can enter it again to recall the next most recent block.

RESET

You can use the RESET command on the program editor screen to remove any pending line commands, any conflicting line commands, and the COLS and MASK lines.

RFIND

Use the RFIND or RF command to continue the search for a string of characters previously specified in a FIND or CHANGE command.

See also the FIND, CHANGE, and RCHANGE commands.

RIGHT [*n* | **MAX**]

This command scrolls the screen *n* spaces to the right. By default the screen scrolls half of its width. To override the scroll amount temporarily, enter RIGHT and the number of spaces you want the screen to scroll. Enter RIGHT MAX to scroll the screen to the right boundary.

RULE OFF | ON

AOS/VS, PRIMOS, and VMS only: You can use the RULE ON command to display a ruler on the message line beneath the command line. The ruler marks vertical columns and moves with the data lines as you scroll right and left.

The ruler is temporarily overridden by any message that SAS displays on the message line, but the ruler returns when the message is removed. The default is RULE OFF.

SAVE *fileref* | *fileref(membername)*

CMS, OS, and **VM/PC**: The SAVE command writes all program lines in the program editor screen into a file that you designate with a fileref (DDname).

See also the NULLS command.

VSE: The SAVE command writes all program lines in the program editor screen into a file that you designate with a fileref (DDNAME). If the file referred to is a sequential file, you must use a /FILE statement in the ICCF procedure. If it is a member of an ICCF library, you are not allowed to use a /FILE statement in the ICCF procedure. Instead, specify the actual ICCF member name.

See also the NULLS command.

SAVE *fileref* | *'filename'*

AOS/VS, PRIMOS, and VMS: The SAVE command writes the entire information stream of the display manager screen from which you execute the SAVE command into a file that you designate with a fileref or an actual file name. You can use a host operating system command to assign a fileref to a sequential file **before** you enter display manager (except under PRIMOS), or you can use the SAS display manager command ASSIGN once you have entered display manager. If you specify an unassigned fileref, the system writes the information stream into a file named *fileref*.SAS in your current working directory. If you specify an actual file name, enclose it in single quotes. The *filename* can be either a fully qualified file name, according to the conventions of the operating system you are using, or just the name (and type under VMS) of a file in a directory to which you currently have access.

See also the NULLS command.

SCREEN OFF | ON

AOS/VS, PRIMOS, and VMS only: You can use the SCREEN command to store the contents of the display manager screen in an external file, **not** a SAS data set or catalog. After you have entered the SCREEN ON command, a file is immediately created with the exact contents of what is displayed on the physical screen. Each time you press ENTER, SUBMIT, or any function key thereafter, another file is created. Each external file containing the contents of a screen is given a file name in the form

```
SCRNnnnn.SCR
```

The first file created is given the name SCRN0001, and each file is given the extension SCR. The screen file is stored in your current working directory.

Each time you begin a SAS session, the system begins numbering screen files with SCRN0001.SCR. If SCRN0001.SCR already exists, the newly created one is written over the existing one.

Enter the SCREEN OFF command when you no longer want the contents of the screen copied to external data files. The default is SCREEN OFF.

SPLIT

You can indicate where you want the screen to split between the log and program editor screens with the SPLIT command. Enter SPLIT on the command line, position the cursor where you want the split to occur, and press ENTER; or position the cursor and press the SPLIT function key. Note: you **must** position the cursor within the boundaries of the screen on which you entered the SPLIT command. Moving the cursor into the area of another screen activates the command line of that screen.

SUBMIT [*'SAS statement;'*]

Use the SUBMIT key or command with no option specified to submit SAS program statements from the data lines of the program editor screen

Optionally, you can submit a SAS program statement directly from the command line with the SUBMIT command. You can type the command, one or more SAS statements, each followed by a semicolon, on the command line and press ENTER, or you can type just the statements with semicolons on the command line and press the SUBMIT function key.

TOP

Use the TOP command to scroll the first line of text to the top of the screen.

VSCROLL HALF | PAGE | *n*

The VSCROLL command sets the vertical scroll amount, the amount the active screen scrolls when you press the FORWARD or BACKWARD scrolling function keys. If you specify PAGE, the scroll amount is the number of data lines currently displayed. If you specify HALF, the scroll amount is one-half of the display area. If you specify *n*, the scroll amount is *n* lines. HALF is the default.

X *hostcommand*
X *'hostcommand'*

You can issue many host commands by entering an X on the command line followed by one or more host commands. Note that in minicomputer environments, the host command or string of commands **must** be enclosed in single quotes if it contains special characters; in IBM environments you are not allowed to enclose the host command in single quotes.

See the documentation available for SAS under the operating system you are using for any restrictions on the execution of host operating system commands.

VSE: The X command is not currently supported.

NOTES

1. If you are using one of the terminals listed below in **Table A5.1**, use the following charts to determine the keys that have been assigned special editing functions in SAS full-screen procedures and display manager. See **Figure A5.1** for a description of the functions of these editing keys. If you are using a terminal other than one of those listed below that does not have keys matching the words or symbols shown in **Figure A5.1**, consult your SAS Software Consultant. If you are using an IBM terminal in the 3270-series, you can disregard this section.

Table A5.1 Full-Screen Editing Functions Assigned to Terminal Keys

Display Manager Editing Key	PT45 Key	PST100 Key	PT25 Key
â (INSERT)	ichar or shift/ del	insert or backspace	shift/del
✗ (DELETE)	dchar or backspace	delete or del	backspace
ERASE EOF	line feed	erase	shift/f8
HOME	home	home	home
REFRESH	control/ clear	pf10	control/erase
NEW LINE	return or enter	return or enter	new line or enter
NEXT FIELD	f13	f2	shift/f5
PRIOR FIELD	f14	f3	shift/f6
ENTER	f3 or f15	f1 or pf13	f3 or shift/f7
MOVE CURSOR UP	↑	↑	↑
MOVE CURSOR DOWN	↓	↓	(not available)
MOVE CURSOR LEFT	←	←	←
MOVE CURSOR RIGHT	→	→	→

(continued on next page)

Table A5.1 *(continued)*

Display Manager Editing Key	TEK4105 Key	VT100 Key	DASHER Key
â (INSERT)	backspace	backspace	C1
ǻ(DELETE)	rub out	delete	DEL
ERASE EOF	line feed	line feed	erase EOL
HOME	- (minus sign on numeric keypad)	- (minus sign on numeric keypad)	home
REFRESH	, (on numeric keypad)	, (on numeric keypad)	erase page
NEW LINE	return	return	new line or enter
NEXT FIELD	0 (on numeric keypad)	0 (on numeric keypad)	C4
PRIOR FIELD	. (on numeric keypad)	. (on numeric keypad)	C3
ENTER	enter	enter	CR
MOVE CURSOR UP	F1	↑	↑
MOVE CURSOR DOWN	F2	↓	↓
MOVE CURSOR LEFT	F3	←	←
MOVE CURSOR RIGHT	F4	→	→

2. If you are using one of the terminals listed in **Table A5.1**, you must identify it to the SAS System. If you have already invoked the SAS System, you can use the statement

```
OPTIONS DMS;
```

and then receive a prompt, asking you to identify the devicename. When invoking the SAS System, you can specify the devicename with the FSDEVICE= (FSD=) option. For example

AOS/VS	SAS/FSD=D1
PRIMOS	SAS -FSD=PT25
VMS	SAS/FSD=VT100

Table A5.2 Devices to Be Identified with the FSDEVICE= Option

TERMINALS:

Manufacturer	Model No.	Devicename
Data General	6052	DG6052 D1 (alias)
	6053	DG6053 D2 (alias)
	6093	DG6093 D3 (alias)
	D100	D100
	D200	D200
	D210	D210
	D211	D211
	D400	D400
	D410	D410
	D450	D450
	D460	D460
	D470C	D470C
	G300	G300
	G500	G500

Note: devicename DG605X is an alias for all Data General terminals.

Manufacturer	Model No.	Devicename
Digital Equipment	VT52	VT52
	VT100	VT100
	VT125	VT125
	VT131	VT131
	VT132	VT132
	VT220	VT220
	VT240	VT240
	VT241	VT241
Prime	PT25	PT25
Computer (PRIME)	PT45	PT45
	PST100	PST100
Tektronix	4105	TEK4105

3. **AOS/VS, PRIMOS, and VMS:** By default the program editor translates all characters into uppercase. If you want to prevent the translation, execute the CAPS OFF command on the program editor screen either from the command line or with a function key before entering program statements.

CMS, OS, VM/PC, and VSE: By default the program editor does not translate all characters into uppercase. Execute the CAPS ON command if you want text entered or lines altered after you execute the command to be translated into uppercase.

4. **AOS/VS, PRIMOS, and VMS:** A message indicating the use of computer resources is also displayed in the log screen unless you previously specified the NOSTIMER option.

5. **VSE:** If the file referred to is a sequential file, you must use a /FILE statement in the ICCF procedure. If it is a member of an ICCF library, you are not allowed to use a /FILE statement in the ICCF procedure. Instead, specify the actual ICCF member name.

6. **AOS/VS, PRIMOS, and VMS:** The display manager editor breaks information into 80-column lengths; a command that exceeds 80 columns is divided and may not be properly executed.

CMS, OS, VM/PC, and VSE: Any characters typed beyond the 80th column are truncated.

7. **CMS, OS, VM/PC, and VSE:** You can specify only PROGRAM, LOG, and OUTPUT to indicate an active screen.

8. **AOS/VS, PRIMOS, and VMS:** SASEXEC.SAS can be the actual file name and file type. As long as you have access to the directory in which SASEXEC.SAS is stored, you do not have to assign it a fileref. **Do not** give another file the name SASEXEC.

9. **CMS, OS, VM/PC, and VSE:** 80 columns is the maximum line length in the program editor.

AOS/VS, PRIMOS, and VMS: 256 columns is the maximum line length in the program editor.

10. **AOS/VS, PRIMOS, and VMS:** The length of the data line on the log screen is sensitive to the value of the LINESIZE= option in the OPTIONS statement. The maximum line length on the log screen is 256 columns.

CMS, OS, VM/PC, and VSE: The length of the data line on the log screen is sensitive to the value of the TLS= option in the OPTIONS statement. The maximum line length on the log screen is 132 columns.

11. **AOS/VS, PRIMOS, and VMS:** The maximum line length on the output screen is 256 columns.

CMS, OS, VM/PC, and VSE: The maximum line length on the output screen is 132 columns.

Index

Special Characters

A

B

C

D

E

F

M

N

O

P

SAS/AF® User's Guide, Version 5 Edition

Kathryn A. Council edited the *SAS/AF® User's Guide, Version 5 Edition*. **David D. Baggett** was copy editor. **Gigi Hassan** and **Frances A. Kienzle** provided editorial services. **Gail C. Freeman** and **Blanche Weatherspoon** performed data entry and coding.

Arlene B. Drezek provided composition and production. **Craig R. Sampson** and **Pamela A. Troutman** wrote the Text Composition Program. **Michael J. Pezzoni** provided the line illustrations.

Your Turn

If you have comments about SAS software or the *SAS/AF User's Guide, Version 5 Edition,* please let us know by writing your ideas in the space below. If you include your name and address, we will reply to you.

Please return this sheet to the Publications Division, SAS Institute Inc., SAS Circle, Box 8000, Cary, NC 27512-8000.